Nixon and Israel

SUNY series in Israeli Studies
Russell Stone, editor

Nixon and Israel

Forging a Conservative Partnership

Noam Kochavi

Published by
State University of New York Press, Albany

For information, contact State University of New York Press, Albany, NY
www.sunypress.edu

Production by Ryan Morris
Marketing by Michael Campochiaro

Library of Congress Cataloging-in-Publication Data

Kochavi, Noam, 1961–
  Nixon and Israel : forging a conservative partnership / Noam Kochavi.
     p. cm. — (SUNY series in Israeli studies)
  Includes bibliographical references and index.
  ISBN 978-1-4384-2781-2 (hardcover : alk. paper)
  ISBN 978-1-4384-2782-9 (pbk : alk. paper)
  1. United States—Foreign relations—Israel. 2. Israel—Foreign relations—
United States. 3. Nixon, Richard M. (Richard Milhous), 1913–1994.
  4. Jews—Soviet Union—Migrations—History—20th century. 5. Jews,
Soviet—Israel—History—20th century. I. Title.
  E183.8.I7K63 2009
  327.7305694—dc22
                                                                    2008051871

10 9 8 7 6 5 4 3 2 1

In loving memory of my father, Professor Moshe Kochavi,
who infected me with his love of history

CONTENTS

ACKNOWLEDGMENTS

In completing this book, I have incurred numerous personal debts I would like to acknowledge here. This book is the culmination of my shift in research focus from the history of American–East Asian relations to the history of détente and American–Middle Eastern relations. Many friends and colleagues facilitated this process, providing advice and reading portions of the manuscript. For their encouragement, generosity of time, and ideas, I am grateful to Raymond Cohen, Joseph Heller, and Pauline Peretz. I am particularly indebted to Arie Kacowitz for the original notion of devoting a book-length manuscript to the subject, and to Uri Bialer who stands out for unceasing support and countless hours of patient guidance through the maze of Israeli diplomatic history. I have been especially fortunate to enjoy the invaluable editorial assistance of Scott Streiner. I have also received thoughtful feedback from anonymous reviewers for the journals *Diplomatic History*, *Cold War History*, and *International History Review*. I am thankful for the corrections and insights of my colleagues, though any faults that remain in this book are mine alone.

Archivists and librarians at a number of institutions have made research for this book much less arduous. Special thanks go to Michal Saft at the Israeli State Archives, and to the devoted staff of the Nixon Presidential Project for their assistance in locating and facilitating access to crucial documentation.

Finally, this book is dedicated in loving memory to my father, Moshe Kochavi, who infected me with his passion for history, and to the anchors of my world, my wife, Leah Glicksman-Kochavi, and sons, Nadav and Omri.

Copyright Acknowledgments

An earlier version of chapter 1 appeared as "Joining the Conservative Brotherhood: Israel, President Nixon, and the Political Consolidation of the 'Special Relationship,' 1969–1973," *Cold War History* (November 2008) (http://www.informaworld.com). An earlier, much abbreviated version of chapter 2 appeared as "Idealpolitik in Disguise: Israel, Jewish Emigration from the Soviet Union, and the Nixon Administration, 1969–1974," *International History Review* 29:3 (September 2007): 550–572. And earlier versions of portions of chapter 4 appeared as "Insights Abandoned, Flexibility Lost: Kissinger, Soviet Jewish Emigration, and the Demise of Détente," *Diplomatic History* 29:3 (June 2005): 503–530.

INTRODUCTION

BEYOND GEOSTRATEGY

The first half of the 1970s was a critical juncture for U.S.-Israel relations. Marked by a significant consolidation followed by temporary cooling, it has shaped American-Israeli dynamics ever since and, by extension, American policy and fortunes in the Middle East and beyond.

Existing scholarship on the dynamics of the American-Israeli relationship has tended to understate the significance of the Nixon years, due both to limited access to key documentary evidence and to a tendency to rely excessively on geostrategic factors that, though important, are insufficient on their own to explain the developments of the period. This book addresses both lacunae, making extensive use of recently opened archives and adding texture and nuance to established interpretations by identifying elements, in addition to geostrategic calculations, that help explain both the strengthening of relations and subsequent frictions.

Analysts have traditionally contended that President Richard M. Nixon and National Security Adviser (and, from September 1973, also secretary of state) Henry A. Kissinger deepened American-Israeli relations between the Jordanian crisis of September 1970 and the Arab-Israeli war of October 1973. During that time, Nixon and Kissinger saw the Jewish state as a "strategic asset" in the Middle Eastern arena and, by extension, in the global struggle against the Soviet Union, acting, to a certain degree, in defiance of the spirit of détente and the letter of the American-Soviet General Principals agreement concluded at the 1972 summit.[1] Some scholars also point to a sense of shared values and skillful practice of interest-group politics by Israel and its American Jewish champions during this period.[2] Similarly, scholars typically argue that after the 1973 war, the president and secretary of state constrained relations with Israel because they began to see the close association as a more mixed strategic blessing, and because the war had undermined domestic support for détente in the United States as it confirmed the perception that the Soviets could not be trusted.

1

While there is much truth to this geostrategic reading of events, it misses the role of ideational and psychological factors and the emotional impact on Nixon and Kissinger of specific choices made by Israel *outside* the Middle Eastern context. At the beginning of the decade, and especially during the lead-up to the 1972 presidential election, Israeli Prime Minister Golda Meir and her ambassador to Washington, Yitzhak Rabin, led a "conservative turn" in Israeli policy that resonated deeply with the president and Kissinger. Coupled with a purposeful courtship of the evangelical movement, Israel's public support for the administration's approach in Vietnam and for Nixon's reelection campaign won appreciation and sympathy in the White House, and fostered a sense of common purpose that went well beyond a strict strategic calculus. By the same token, in 1974, Israel's discreet backing for the Jackson-Vanik amendment linking U.S.-Soviet relations to the Jewish emigration issue—backing itself motivated more by the self-image and emotional commitments of Israeli leaders than strategic considerations—undermined Nixon's and Kissinger's perception of Israel as a trusted, like-minded ally, since they both strongly opposed the amendment and placed great stock in the unswerving loyalty of friends. Ironically, Israel's position in favor of Jackson-Vanik and, implicitly, against détente, was in many respects a natural extension of the "conservative turn" that the administration had encouraged and welcomed just a few years earlier. The friction of 1974, then, was to a considerable degree the child of the honeymoon of 1971–1973.

Ultimately, U.S.-Israeli tensions during the latter part of the Nixon-Kissinger era did not reverse the consolidation of the relationship during the earlier phase, but did leaven it with a modicum of caution. Thus, the basic "DNA" of the American-Israeli relationship in the last few decades—characterized as it has been by abiding connections punctuated by episodes of friction—was laid down during the Nixon years. Moreover, the "conservative turn" initiated by Meir and Rabin cemented the foundations for an alliance between elements in the Israeli leadership and conservative and neoconservative forces in the United States, which has had substantial longer-term implications and which continues to this day. True, the alliance sprang in large measure from developments on the global and American scenes beyond Israel's control, and from an atavistic distrust of the Soviet Union the Israeli leadership shared with American neoconservatives; and yet, the active role Israel played was important, and complex. Part expediency, Israeli leaders simply sought to curry favor with the Republican president. Part ideology, and somewhat paradoxically, they also chose to covertly foster Jackson-Vanik, a neoconservative cause which Nixon opposed.

The book also seeks to serve a general theoretical purpose. By closely examining the evolution of U.S.-Israel relations during the first half of the

1970s, we can not only obtain better insights into the period itself and the enduring ways that it shaped the bilateral relationship, but also gain a greater appreciation of how, more generally, emotional attachments, self-perceptions, and subjective feelings of appreciation and disappointment interact with dispassionate geostrategic assessments to produce international relations outcomes.

The Evidence

Until recently, conditions were inauspicious for a balanced assessment of the evolution of American-Israeli relations in the early 1970s. The potent mix of the controversial figure of Nixon, the sensitive Jewish dimension, and the perennial Arab-Israeli conflict lent an overly polemical cast to much of the extant literature.[3] The veils of official secrecy were compounded by the acute sensitivity of issues like Israel's nuclear capability, as well as by Nixon's policy-making style. Secretive by nature, suspicious (sometimes rightfully so) of leaks, and desirous to retain presidential deniability in a policy area he deemed domestically explosive, Nixon played his Israeli policy cards very close to his chest. As National Security Council (NSC) staffer William Quandt testifies, few ever knew what the president was thinking,[4] and sometimes, at crucial junctures, no one did.[5] The result is that Nixon's early Israeli record has remained under-addressed in the literature.

During the last few years, a much more promising research climate has emerged. The passage of time allows for a more detached perspective and, though the record remains incomplete, recently declassified Israeli and American documentation affords an excellent basis for better understanding how Nixon's Middle East policy evolved and how Jerusalem endeavored to affect it. To date, however, studies have employed this historiographic opportunity to reconsider specific dimensions of Nixon's record rather than the comprehensive picture.[6]

The book will address this gap, drawing upon a substantial range of American, Israeli, and translated Soviet documentation. American archival collections include, for instance, Kissinger's telephone conversations and the Nixon tapes, which offer particularly telling insight into the flavor and content of the policy-making deliberations that took place between Nixon and Kissinger, as well as between Nixon, Kissinger, and third parties (such as Ambassador Rabin, Reverend Billy Graham, or Attorney General John Mitchell). The papers of the American Jewish organizations, as well as the Oral History collections at the New York Public Library, have not been sufficiently tapped by international history scholars and provide invaluable insight into intracommunity deliberations and the complex triangular interrelationships between Jerusalem, Washington, and the American Jewish community.

As for Israeli documentation, although most of the Israeli government's deliberations are still under lock and key, the recently declassified documentation from the Prime Minister's Office combine with the papers of Meir-aide-turned-ambassador Simcha Dinitz to provide critical access to the most sensitive channel of communications between the Prime Minister's Office and the White House.

These materials are supplemented by compilations of recently declassified Soviet documents (in translation) and several interviews conducted with the former chairperson of the National Conference on Soviet Jewry, as well as veterans of the clandestine Israeli organization in charge of Soviet Jewish affairs, Nativ. In aggregate, this documentary base opens new vistas on the most crucial research questions at hand.

Chapter Overview

This book has four substantive chapters, bound together by the illustrations each of them provides for the book's central theoretical thesis: psychological and ideological factors figured importantly in the shaping of American-Israeli relations during the Nixon years.

The first chapter, "Joining the Conservative Brotherhood," examines the forging of the American-Israeli "special relationship," focusing mainly on the evolution of Nixon's role vis-à-vis Israeli principals and American Jews. At the beginning of his presidency, Nixon leaned toward the State Department's view that regional instability benefited the Soviets, Israel's intransigence was the root cause of Soviet gains in the region, and the administration could not simply sit idly by.[7] He valued the goal of "honorable extrication" from Vietnam so much that, as files from Nixon Presidential Materials Project reveal, he contemplated the idea of offering Moscow concessions in the Middle East (presumably in Israeli currency) in exchange for Soviet assistance in Vietnam.[8] The idea never materialized into policy directives, partly because of his obsession with Jewish political clout.[9] The new archival disclosures of Nixon's early ambiguous commitment to Israel reveal just how profound his shift was when, in December 1971, he dramatically raised the scale of his administration's commitment to Israel in all the crucial dimensions: financial aid, diplomatic backing, and military supplies.[10]

While the prevailing, geostrategic analysis identifies "Black September" 1970 as the turning point in American-Israeli relations, recent archival revelations show that Nixon's shift toward Israel was completed more than a year later and in part for different reasons; namely, Israel's manifest support of Nixon in the contexts he valued most: Vietnam and success against political opposition at home.[11] These elements in the Israeli conservative turn were well attuned to Nixon's obsession with loyalty and assuaged his hitherto lingering suspicion that Israel was under the sway of his perceived domestic enemies.[12]

The next two chapters explore another foundation of the partnership between Israel and conservative American forces: the struggle for Soviet Jewry.

The second chapter, "Israel, Soviet Jewish Emigration, and Ideal politik," offers the first detailed, archival-based analysis of Israel's Soviet Jewish emigration policy during the Nixon years, with a particular emphasis on Israel's Jackson-Vanik record.[13] There has been a debate in the literature around the questions, did the Israeli government, as contemporaneous right-wing critics charged and some scholars continue to argue, genuinely endorse a low-key stance on the Soviet Jewish emigration issue in order to avert a confrontation with Nixon,[14] or would it be more accurate to assign Israel major "behind-the-scenes" responsibility for the galvanization of Jackson-Vanik forces?[15] On balance, the evidentiary record supports the latter view, showing that Meir herself established a policy of official neutrality in the skirmish between the White House and Congress combined with discreet backing for Jackson-Vanik.[16] Ideology played a crucial role in Israel's Soviet Jewish emigration policy, leading Jerusalem to drag its feet in response to the administration's demands that it disavow the amendment and in so doing, to put at risk a carefully cultivated relationship. Israel's leaders ran a secret and effective campaign in support of Jackson-Vanik because the amendment addressed some of their most fundamental emotional dispositions and ideological goals, which in this instance trumped the dictates of Realpolitik.

The third substantive chapter, "Kissinger, Soviet Jewish Emigration, and the Demise of Détente," shifts to the Soviet Jewish movement on the American scene. By focusing on Kissinger's failure to block Jackson-Vanik, The chapter again argues the salience of ideological and psychological factors. Kissinger failed in large part because he was not in sync with the basic ideological undercurrents of his policy environment. He was too wedded to a realist outlook and to the strategic design of detente to fully grasp the deep ideological attraction Jackson-Vanik had for Americans: it enabled America to regain the moral high ground it had lost in Vietnam[17] and it appealed to two pillars of the American self-image: a "nation of immigrants" and a "redeemer nation." The contribution of Kissinger's own psychological makeup to his failure in this policy sphere is related also to another key finding emerging from the documentary record: the policy Kissinger pursued in practice was inconsistent with the perceptive guidelines for sound statecraft he had devised as a historian. He overcommitted the administration to a single course and, in so doing, inflicted more damage to Kissinger's détente policy than was necessary.

Why did Kissinger fail to follow his theoretical insights through to their logical, real-world conclusions? He was thwarted in part by overextension and by the complications reality always presents to those seeking to implement preconceived designs. But at least as salient were more personal factors: his limited ability to adjust to unexpected and challenging decision-making environments, his difficulty listening to the views of domestic advisers and adversaries, and his growing hubris after years of power and what he perceived as foreign policy successes.[18]

The chapter also reconsiders, on the basis of new evidence, why Jackson-Vanik struck a responsive chord with both American Jews and the American public at large, and why the administration failed to legitimize détente with those audiences and with Israel. The evidence shows that the struggle for Soviet Jewry became, both by happenstance and design, a common rallying point for both Israel and the more conservative and neoconservative segments of American society—segments that would soon become the backbone of Reagan's domestic support—solidifying their relations in the post-October war period.[19] Despite the fact that Brezhnev had warned Nixon and Kissinger about the probability of war well before it erupted and stood his ground firmly against opposition to détente within the politburo once it started,[20] many Americans quite naturally saw more confrontational Soviet actions—such as the massive airlift during the war and the support for the Arab oil embargo and radical Arab regimes in its aftermath[21]—as proof that Moscow could not be trusted. Conservative and neoconservative leaders and commentators—quite a few of them Jews for whom the war had given existential pause and rekindled group identity[22]—argued that the conflict revealed the illusory nature of détente.[23] Meanwhile, Kissinger's shuttle diplomacy in the aftermath of war, however considerable an accomplishment, both reignited tensions with Israel[24] and undermined détente because of the manifest exclusion of Moscow.[25] Ultimately, Nixon, Kissinger, and other proponents of détente found themselves unable to prevail in the battle to preserve the domestic legitimacy of détente, their failure symbolized by the passage of Jackson-Vanik.

The concluding chapter, "Nixon's Final Months, the Legacy of the Period, and the Lessons of the Case," begins by tracing the development of American-Israeli relations in the final months of Nixon's presidency and the enduring impact of the changes that had occurred in the bilateral relationship during the early 1970s. It then elaborates at length on rich insights the case offers for students in four fields: American history, Israeli history, American-Israeli relations, and foreign policy-making and international affairs.

1

JOINING THE
CONSERVATIVE BROTHERHOOD

"It is time for Israel (and I don't think it will do any good to suggest this the American Jewish community [sic]) to face up to the fact that their only reliable friends are the hawks in this country . . . we are going to stand up in Vietnam and in NATO and in the MidEast, but it is a question of all or none. . . . We are going to be in power for the next three years and this is going to be the policy of this country. Unless they understand it and act as if they understood it beginning now they are down the tubes."

—Nixon to Kissinger, 17 March 1970*

President Nixon's Middle Eastern policy shifted considerably in the direction of Israel during his first five years in office. Nixon's early disposition troubled a good many Israeli observers. In December 1968, the president-elect's special emissary to the Middle East, former governor of Pennsylvania William Scranton, recommended the adoption of a more "evenhanded" American policy.[1] In a press conference on January 27, just a week after his inauguration, the new president called the Middle East a very explosive "powder keg" that "needs to be defused."[2] It was not long before Nixon authorized the launching of parallel exploratory discussions—with the Soviets (the two-power talks) and with the Soviets, French, and British (the four-power talks)—declaring that Moscow might be disposed to assume a "peacemaking role" in the Middle East to avert superpower confrontation.[3] Nixon's denials notwithstanding,[4] this flurry of diplomatic initiatives evoked the specter of an imposed solution to the Arab-Israeli conflict. Jerusalem would have been even more anxious had its leaders been privy to Nixon's instructions behind closed doors. The president's overriding desire to honorably disentangle the United States from the Vietnam imbroglio led him to consider a quid pro quo with Moscow under which American concessions in the Middle East—almost certainly at Israel's expense—would

7

be traded for Soviet assistance in Southeast Asia.[5] Worse still from the Israeli perspective, Nixon was not beholden to American Jewry, having received barely 17 percent of the Jewish vote in 1968. So eager was he to demonstrate indifference to Jewish pressure that he explicitly instructed his top aides to leave domestic political considerations out of Middle Eastern policy deliberations.[6] Nixon and Israel seemed destined to collide, and, during the heyday of American-Soviet détente between late 1971 and late 1973, matters could well have come to a head; after all, we now know that in order to break the ice with the People's Republic of China, Nixon was perfectly willing to compromise in advance the most vital interests of another small ally endowed with a potent (albeit, in this case, declining) lobby in the United States—the Republic of China or Taiwan.[7]

Instead of this scenario, just the reverse took place. Nixon's turning point occurred in late 1971, when the Moscow summit was already in sight, and by the eve of the 1973 October war, the administration had come around to essentially accepting Israel's adherence to the status quo in the Middle East. American financial assistance to Israel had nearly quadrupled, and the sale of sophisticated American military equipment had been institutionalized. The very partial documentation at hand suggests further that Nixon played a pivotal role in striking a new "don't ask, don't tell" deal between Israel and the United States that allowed Israel to cross the nuclear threshold without confronting much international criticism.[8] During the initial and critical stages of the 1973 war, it was Nixon, again, who made the crucial decision to send a massive airlift to replenish Israel's depleted military arsenal. No wonder, then, that at least until early 1974 the Israeli leadership regarded Nixon favorably, as a president who had dramatically increased the scale of American strategic commitment to Israel.[9]

To understand the reasons for this fascinating and fateful evolution of the American-Israeli relationship during the Nixon years, it is necessary to carefully retrace the historical record. We will begin with a review of Nixon's Israel policy until the autumn of 1970, followed by an examination of the debate in Israel over how best to respond. We will then carry the story forward to the autumn of 1971, exploring reasons for Nixon's shift toward Israel. Finally, we will look at how and why the American-Israeli relationship cemented further between late 1971 and the 1973 war and what this tells us about the broader debate regarding the nature and roots of the American-Israeli "special relationship."

Nixon's Early Record

Through the autumn of 1970, American-Israeli relations were fraught with discord. Tensions surfaced frequently. On 9 December 1969, Secretary of State William Rogers launched the Rogers Plan, as it came to be known, which stipulated that in the context of peace and agreements on security, Israel would be required to withdraw to the pre-1967 international border between Israel and Egypt. Nine days later, U.S. Ambassador to the UN Charles Yost presented an essentially parallel plan for an Israeli-Jordanian settlement. Jerusalem rejected the plan vigorously, explicitly dubbing it an appeasement of the Arabs at Israel's expense.[10] Three months later, on 23 March 1970, Secretary Rogers announced that the president had decided to hold Israel's request for one hundred A-4 Skyhawk and twenty-five F-4 Phantom jets in abeyance, pending further developments in the area.[11] Relations reached a new low point in early August, in the wake of Israeli Prime Minister Golda Meir's grudging endorsement of an Egyptian-Israeli ceasefire proposed by the State Department, at the cost of a dissolved National Unity government and shrinking plurality in the Knesset. A virtual "dialogue of the deaf" across the Atlantic ensued about the details of Israel's commitments under the agreement, with Kissinger sarcastically commenting on Israeli procrastination and Meir accusing the State Department of forging the Israeli signature.[12]

These tensions largely reflected the web of interrelated policy dilemmas that would have severely tested the resourcefulness of any newcomer to the White House in 1969: globally, how to curb Soviet influence in the Middle East without eliciting Soviet retribution in Vietnam, let alone triggering direct superpower confrontation; regionally, how to woo Arab radicals from the Soviet orbit and strengthen Arab moderates without alarming Israel; and domestically, how to maintain support for a major commitment in distant lands in a country torn by the trauma of Vietnam. As historian Ephraim Karsh observes, juggling so many balls would have been challenging even in the most benign of circumstances, and the highly charged atmosphere of a spiraling Israeli-Egyptian War of Attrition, when the perceptions of enemies were light years apart, was anything but benign.[13]

Yet, the flashpoints also bear Nixon's distinctive fingerprints. Two features stand out. First, inevitably perhaps, but nevertheless unfortunately, Vietnam sapped Nixon's attention and constantly shaped his policy decisions. Second, Nixon's dysfunctional obsession with American Jewish political clout fueled his proclivity to detect conspiracies, lending a capricious and haphazard quality to American Middle East policy and generally making a difficult policy-making environment worse.

At the outset, Nixon's principal concern was that the Soviet Union seemed poised to make further inroads into the Arab world through the exploitation of Arab frustration over the post-1967 impasse.[14] Moscow, Nixon believed, correctly calculated that the American people would not have the stomach to open a second military front and stand up to the challenge.[15]

Quite at a loss himself on how to tackle the problem,[16] Nixon at this
stage leaned toward the State Department's view that regional instability
benefited the Soviets, Israel's intransigence was the root cause of Soviet
gains in the region, and the administration could not simply sit idly by.[17]
Not trusting Kissinger, his Jewish national security adviser, to act impar-
tially in this policy area, he thus consigned the Middle East portfolio to an
enthusiastic State Department, keeping in the department's hands both the
four-power talks (Yost) and the more substantial two-power talks (Joseph
Sisco, the new assistant secretary of state for Near Eastern / South Asian
Affairs). For several months, the discussions Sisco conducted with Soviet
Ambassador Anatoly Dobrynin represented a genuine effort on Nixon's
part to seek out a solution: he allowed the State Department to present a
demanding "general principles" paper to visiting Israeli foreign minister
Abba Eban, generating a sour Israeli response[18] and, more than he would
ever do later, kept abreast of the minute details of the discussions.[19]

It was not long, however, before Sisco's disappointing round of meetings in Moscow led Nixon to conclude that "the goddam Russians don't
seem to want a settlement,"[20] closing the door on the most concerted attempt during his tenure to reach an understanding with the Soviet Union
on the Middle East. This quick turnaround on Nixon's part suggests he
had always doubted the Soviets would prove responsive;[21] it also corroborates Kissinger's observation that Nixon's delegation of a major policy
role to the State Department sprang largely from his wish to keep a dis-
tance from a policy area in which, to him, success seemed unlikely and the
risks of adverse domestic reaction were high.[22]

This pursuit of leeway for the president—the office and the person—is
defensible enough, but not so when the quest acquires Machiavellian char-
acteristics, as was the case in Nixon's deliberate undermining of the Rogers
Plan. True, as an instrument of launching an era of negotiations in the Middle East, the plan was doomed to fail; Rogers himself conceded that irre-
spective of the Israeli position, the inflexibility of both the Soviets and the
Egyptians almost certainly precluded a major breakthrough.[23] Still, Rogers
pleaded with Nixon to go ahead with the plan, emphasizing two sets of objectives. First, on the eve of the Arab summit in Rabat, it was crucial to bol-
ster moderate voices in the Arab world and stem the momentum of
radicalism manifested in civil turmoil in Lebanon, the toppling of Libya's
King Idris, and Arab threats to withdraw acceptance of UN Resolution 242
as the legal framework for resolving the conflict. Second, a more evenhanded
American policy would not only point the way to a just solution, but would
also gain the administration points with its important European allies.[24]

Nixon did not dispute the logic of Rogers's argument. He too dreaded
a "domino-type" advance of radicalism across the Middle East[25] and he sec-
onded the idea of a symbolic gesture as one means to stem the tide, know-

ing that the delivery of the first American F-4 Phantom aircraft to Israel in September had caused the Arab world to erupt in furious protest.[26] He found the plan objectionable, however, on domestic political grounds. To his mind, it was bound to trigger a wave of protest orchestrated by the American Jewish community, at precisely the delicate moment when he was preparing a response to the largest and most dramatic anti-Vietnam War action ever, the moratorium.[27] Nixon was determined to shield himself from the expected wrath of the Jewish community in response to the Rogers Plan. And with his habitual distrust of the State Department reinforced by a leak from his confidential discussions with Golda Meir in late September,[28] Nixon wanted to be certain the fire would be diverted to the State Department.

In Nixon's own words, he contrived with Kissinger to stage a "charade."[29] In October, at the same time that he gave Rogers the green light to disseminate his plan among the parties, he had aides put out the word to American Jewish community leaders suggesting that he was disassociating himself from the proposal that the State Department was drawing up.[30] The surreptitious gambit was repeated in December: Nixon approved the Rogers Plan announcement for an Israeli-Jordanian settlement, but then rushed confidential instructions to Leonard Garment, his liaison with the Jewish community. Garment later explained that Nixon's game of "creative duplicity" involved "ask[ing] a foreign head of state [Meir] to undercut the U.S. secretary of state at the instruction of the president of the United States."[31] Meir and American Jewish leaders readily obliged.[32]

Although favorable in December, Nixon's fixation with putative Jewish power boded ill for Israel the next March. Israel's request to purchase twenty-five F-4E Phantom and one hundred A-4 Skyhawk combat planes had been at the forefront of the bilateral agenda ever since Israel secured a pledge along these lines from outgoing president Lyndon Johnson. During his first meeting with Golda Meir in late September, Nixon did not shy away from linking arms with a sensible Israeli position on the contours of a future peace;[33] however, on balance, he was more amenable to Israel's requests than his secretaries of defense and state. He appeared to accept Kissinger's argument that the imperatives of deterring the Arabs and reassuring the Israelis actually required that the United States keep the balance of military power tipped in Israel's favor. For example, in July 1969, Nixon torpedoed the suggestion of the Department of Defense to use the sale of F-4 jets as leverage to roll back Israel's nuclear ambitions,[34] and in September, he approved the dispatch of the first batch of Phantoms, again overruling Secretary of Defense Melvin Laird (and expecting to garner some gratitude from American Jews).[35]

Why, then, did Nixon change direction in March (sending Rogers—again!—to announce the bad news to Israel)?[36] By all eyewitness accounts, Nixon made the decision in a fit of rage at American Jewry for the stormy protests that embarrassed visiting French president Georges Pompidou.[37]

The occasion brought Nixon's instinctive distrust of Jews into the open: as Kissinger was laboring to minimize what he termed a near "major disaster" in Nixon's attitude toward Israel, the president was complaining to his closest aide about Kissinger's meddling.[38] This was the state of mind in which Nixon scribbled his warning cited in the epigraph of this chapter: instead of taking its cue from the *New York Times*, Israel must adjust to the fact that its best friends were not to be found among the "weak reeds" of the liberal center and the New Left, but among their opponents, the hawkish conservatives who "stand up" in Vietnam.

The record is too obscure to allow a determination of whether Nixon was also driven by another motive, one far more legitimate because it was integral to the Middle East policy scene: inducing Israel to halt its aerial bombings of the Egyptian Nile Valley heartland. Israel opened this new chapter in the War of Attrition in early January, with a threefold purpose in mind: to force Egyptian president Gamal Abdel Nasser to terminate the war; if possible, to unseat Nasser; and to forestall the imposition of a solution akin to the Rogers Plan.[39] Except for a low-key démarche by American ambassador to Israel Wohlworth Barbour, the administration initially looked the other way;[40] like Jerusalem, Washington failed to anticipate that the Israeli escalation would beget escalation, triggering, or at least providing a convenient pretext for, the largest direct involvement of Soviet combat forces outside the Warsaw Pact during the Cold War until Afghanistan.[41] Whether Nixon was, by March, signaling a red light or a green light to Israel had become a point of controversy between practitioners at the time and researchers ever since, who continue to haggle over a particularly spotty and vexing body of evidence.[42] To illustrate, in a conversation on March 10 with Kissinger, Nixon explains his Phantom decision as a lever to stem the escalation in the Middle East;[43] a week later, in contrast, Kissinger's notes record Nixon as intimating to a flabbergasted Rabin his hope that Israel would "knock out" the SA-3 antiaircraft batteries the Soviets had installed in Egypt.[44] The contradictory evidence may well reflect the difficulty Nixon's interlocutors faced in deciphering his intentions; after all, the president could not be too explicit about a suggestion to a small ally to persist in an operation that ran the risk of confronting the Soviet Union directly. But the confusion seems also to suggest genuine ambivalence on Nixon's part: as in Vietnam, Nixon may have been torn between his instinct for brinkmanship and his awareness that the climate of opinion at home placed limits on military adventurism.[45]

Whatever his intentions in March, by the summer of 1970 Nixon was growing eager to promote an Egyptian-Israeli ceasefire. The spring had seen Nixon grappling with his most serious political crisis since being elected president. The abortive invasion of Cambodia and the killings of student protesters at Kent State University incurred widespread hostility, forcing him to tread cautiously in the Middle East.[46] Meanwhile, the danger of superpower confrontation loomed larger in the region itself, as Soviet Red Army artillery shelled Israeli positions and Soviet pilots engaged Israeli jet fighters.[47] From Nixon's perspective, a negotiated ceasefire was not only the most politically viable solution, but also an outcome that could, to some extent, release him from a double domestic and international bind.

At that juncture, Nixon's diagnosis of the problem was for once actually shared by all the branches of government: Kissinger, Nixon, and even Rogers agreed that the spiraling war in the Middle East was mainly due to Soviet machinations.[48] They also shared a realization that the specter of superpower collision had rendered the military option untenable. Israel concurred with the assessment that the escalating situation was attributable to Soviet actions and, to at least some degree, subscribed to the view that a diplomatic solution was essential. This helps explain the Israeli decision to shelve its deep penetration strategy in the aftermath of the air battle with Soviet pilots.[49] When Rogers introduced a simple and modest "stop shooting, start talking" formula for the ceasefire in June, these basic points of consensus should have facilitated a quick and smooth progression to an agreement between Washington and Jerusalem on the terms of the ceasefire, but that was not to be.

While Jerusalem was partly to blame for the tumultuous and nearly abortive dialogue that in fact transpired, the complications were, to a considerable extent, of Nixon's doing. As we have seen, since his assumption of power, Nixon had fostered an Israeli policy sphere marked by intrigue and bureaucratic schizophrenia. By the summer of 1970, these habits had become too entrenched to change. As Nixon and Kissinger anticipated, Rogers's very association with the ceasefire proposal made it suspect for Golda Meir, who was hardly on speaking terms with the secretary of state.[50] In Washington, meanwhile, Rogers and Kissinger resumed a pattern of virulent bickering, flinging accusations of deceit and disloyalty.[51]

It took a series of inducements from Nixon to persuade Israel to accede to the ceasefire agreement. Obviously impressed by a letter signed by seventy-two senators protesting the March Phantom decision, Nixon in late May overruled the State Department and approved the delivery of the remaining planes from the December 1968 arms deal, but he made no promise to sell additional aircraft.[52] In an interview on television on July 1, he stated that Israel must withdraw to "borders that are defensible"—a most welcome improvement, from Israel's standpoint, on the Rogers Plan's endorsement of the 1967 borders.[53] In a personal letter to Meir on July 24, the president added a formulation that would later serve as the foundation of Israel's position: "[N]o Israeli solider should be withdrawn from the present lines until a binding contractual peace agreement satisfactory to you has been achieved." Israel responded positively to these inducements and—after one last confused effort to obtain a different phrasing of the ceasefire document floundered on a rare united front of Nixon aides[54]—Jerusalem accepted a three-month ceasefire, which went into effect on August 7.

Only two days later, Israel reported that the Egyptians had violated the agreement by moving antiaircraft missiles into the demilitarized stand-still zone. Apparently seeing some conspiracy in the Israeli reports, Rogers refused to credit them even after American photo intelligence produced incontrovertible confirming evidence. Only after Meir made her case to Nixon and Kissinger did the State Department issue a public comment on Egyptian violations.[55] The first phase in Nixon's Israeli policy—a phase marked by uncertain positions, suspicion, and inconsistencies—thus ended on an appropriately discordant note.

Israel's Search for a Response

The administration's outburst of initiatives in early 1969 put Israel's policy-makers on the defensive. Israel's America-watchers struggled to gauge Nixon's intentions and formulate a response. A number of ranking Israeli Foreign Service officers viewed Nixon's ascendancy with trepidation. Comparing Nixon unfavorably with his predecessor, they contended that the new president's disposition to apply pressure on Israel was well in-grained and could be traced back to his tenure as Eisenhower's vice president. The president, they judged, was too influenced by the domestic neo-isolationist sentiment and, if the opportunity arose, might well strike a deal with the Soviets and, in the words of foreign ministry secretary General Gideon Rafael, "sell Israel down the river."[56] Based on Nixon's statements, the exacting major policy paper the administration presented to Eban in March, and Joseph Sisco's reluctance to debrief Israel about the details of the two-power talks in a timely manner,[57] this assessment was also reinforced by the American Jewish community's suspicion of Nixon, as well as by some personal friendships formed between key Israeli embassy officials and President Johnson and his aides.[58]

Rather than drawing policy recommendations from this grim projection, most members of this group adopted a wait-and-see approach. An exception to this rule was Nixon's sharpest critic among the Israelis, Ambassador Rabin's second-in-command, Shlomo Argov. He considered the situation so severe as to warrant an all-out public campaign that would explicitly target Nixon. Only this extreme measure, he cabled Jerusalem, might display enough Israeli resolve to deter the president from sacrificing vital Israeli interests.[59]

But public denunciation of Nixon was anathema to his superior.[60] Rabin approached the Nixon issue from a different vantage point. Upon his release from the army, this celebrated chief of staff of the 1967 war had surprised Prime Minister Levi Eshkol by his unorthodox request to serve as Israel's ambassador to the United States. Once installed, Rabin did not cooperate closely with the Johnson administration or with the leaders of the American Jewish establishment and lobby; by July 1968, for instance, he held Johnson personally responsible for attempts to break the ice with Moscow and Cairo, and for holding off the decision to sell Phantoms to Israel.[61] He also proved impatient with what he perceived as the Foreign Service's cumbersome procedures, breeding of mediocre thinking, and propensity to leak sensitive information (American as well as Israeli), going as far as sharing his impatience with the press. These dispositions provided instant and lasting common ground between Rabin and the incoming administration. Moreover, Rabin had met both Nixon and Kissinger several times prior to 1969, finding common language with their Realpolitik outlook on world affairs and their underlining of the Soviet threat. The social setting of some of these meetings fostered mutual amity: Rabin had participated in a Kissinger seminar in 1964 and, as chief of staff, had played host to a grateful out-of-politics Nixon in 1966.[62] Accordingly, early 1969 saw Rabin seeking to keep the antagonism with the White House to a minimum. Within the embassy, he ameliorated the language of the embassy's widely circulated bulletins when they described American positions that Israel opposed and wanted to modify.[63] And in his communications with Jerusalem, he advised the government to stoically weather the diplomatic storm. A perceptive observer of the American domestic scene, Rabin explained that the burgeoning neo-isolationist current left Nixon no choice but to launch discussions with Moscow on the Middle East. Although less confident of Nixon's reliability as Israel's advocate than he would later claim in his memoirs, Rabin correctly predicted that the whole diplomatic exercise would come to naught because of Soviet rigidity.[64]

Eliciting a rare endorsement from Foreign Minister Eban, Rabin's recommendation that Israel maintain a low profile was accepted.[65] His victory was precarious, however, since Rabin's patron and new prime minister, Golda Meir, tended to tilt toward confrontation. Powerful memories fed Meir's alarm about the two- and four-power talks. Meir chose to open her memoirs with a palpable recollection of herself as a young girl hiding out from a pending Russian pogrom.[66] The evidence at hand suggests that sixty years later, the prime minister still retained an instinctive, atavistic distrust of Russian authorities of whatever stripe, deeming Soviet leaders irrevocably anti-Semitic and holding out no hope for a genuine change of heart in the Kremlin with regard to Israel.[67] Moreover, diplomatic initiatives by an administration led by Eisenhower's vice president rekindled in former foreign minister Meir painful recollections of

Israel's American-coerced withdrawal in the aftermath of the Suez War.[68] No wonder, then, that when Ambassador Barbour explained to Meir that the administration was seeking a "meeting of the minds" with the Soviet Union, the plain-speaking prime minister shot back, "[T]hat is precisely what troubles us."[69]

During a visit to Jerusalem in the spring, Rabin managed to bring Meir a little closer to his more measured judgment of Nixon.[70] But the first real milestone in the erratic course of relations between the Prime Minister's Office and the White House occurred during Meir's visit in September.

Although much of the record of that visit is already in the public domain, the details of the most important piece of evidence, the ultra-sensitive tête-à-tête at the Oval Office on September 26, may never be disclosed: if a record of the meeting exists at all, it has not yet surfaced.[71] For the purposes at hand, it suffices to evaluate the impact of this first encounter between Nixon and Meir on the basis of subsequent developments—in particular, the curious dualism revealed through Meir's references to Nixon following the visit.

On the one hand, "Israel has a friend in the White House" became her token praise of the president, a common refrain in both private communications and public speeches.[72] Meir was not one to merely parrot a figure of speech between allies; the term genuinely denoted her profound appreciation of Nixon's double contribution to the improvement of relations. First, Nixon placed American policy toward Israel's nuclear program on a new footing, as described earlier, and removed this irritant from the bilateral agenda, to Israel's satisfaction. For Meir, in all likelihood, this measure in itself attested to Nixon's commitment to Israel's survival. Second, the principals agreed to reserve their most important communications to a direct back channel between their offices.[73] This arrangement effectively sidelined Eban and his foreign ministry on the Israeli side,[74] and contributed (for 1969–1971) to the cacophony of voices on the American side previously discussed. The procedure was based on an explicit quid pro quo: Rabin would be given direct access to the White House and Israel, as Kissinger repeatedly reminded Rabin, would refrain from directly attacking the president.[75]

On the other hand, Meir remained worried about some crucial dimensions of the administration's Middle Eastern policy, including the use of arms deliveries as leverage to exact Israeli concessions vis-à-vis the Egyptians and the Jordanians,[76] and harbored lingering suspicions that Nixon would at some point strive to coerce Israel into accepting an American-Soviet solution.[77] By late June, the time of Rogers's second "stop shooting, start talking" initiative, anxiety threatened to overtake friendship: Meir was on the verge of rejecting the initiative finally and unambiguously, and a troubled Rabin managed only to tone down her messages to the

White House.[78] Utterly distrustful of Rogers, constrained by right-wing ideologues in her National Unity government, fearing a competition for premiership from charismatic Defense Minister Moshe Dayan, and absolutely convinced that Nasser was bent on destroying Israel, Meir wavered for weeks on end. Nixon's aforementioned string of inducements finally convinced her to accede to the initiative,[79] but the language attached to the acceptance, blistering even for Meir, betokens a crisis of confidence: "[T]he conduct of the U.S. is an insult to Israel, its government, and its people . . . this attitude bears the mark of dictation, not consultation."[80]

Nixon's Transition, September 1970–November 1971: Standard Explanations

The clouds on the horizon of American-Israeli relations dispersed rather quickly. By March 1971, Rabin was able to happily tell Kissinger he saw "no problems" brewing in the near future.[81] A number of developments had prompted this change. The maintenance of the ceasefire on the Suez Canal and the death of Nasser had served to reduce the danger of U.S.-Soviet confrontation[82] and the situation in the region appeared more manageable to American policy-makers. A relieved Nixon immersed himself in the November midterm elections and Southeast Asia[83]—to the point, his aides complained, of losing his grip on Middle East developments.[84]

Nixon was also influenced by another episode that, according to the prevalent view, marks a watershed in his Israeli policy—the dramatic crisis in Jordan. In mid-September 1970, civil war broke out between King Hussein's army and Palestinian organizations, the latter backed by invading Syrian forces. Overestimating Soviet involvement, Nixon and Kissinger perceived the Syrian intervention as a Soviet attempt to shift the regional balance of power in Moscow's favor. As political scientist Bar-Siman-Tov writes, limits in American regional capabilities convinced Nixon to accept Kissinger's advice and coordinate a military "division of labor" with the Israelis: Jerusalem would deter Syria, and the United States would deter Moscow from intervening against Israel. As hoped by Washington and Jerusalem, this coordination helped tip the military balance in Hussein's favor. Probably oversimplifying the situation, Nixon came to believe that it was the threat of Israeli military might—demonstrated through Israeli overflights of Syrian armored columns—that had caused Damascus to withdraw and secured victory for Hussein and thereby boosted the administration's morale and credibility on the eve of congressional elections, when such a boost was sorely needed. Moreover, in light of Jerusalem's deference to American guidance, Nixon came to perceive Israel as a responsible partner, a "strategic asset" for the United States in the Middle

East. According to a wide range of veteran practitioners, historians and political scientists, this was the moment that Nixon shifted his policy toward Israel.[85] To illustrate the long-term significance of this episode, they cite Kissinger's communication to Meir on Nixon's behalf: "[T]he President will never forget Israel's role in preventing the deterioration in Jordan and blocking the attempt to overturn the regime there. He said that the United States is fortunate in having an ally like Israel in the Middle East. These events will be taken into account in future developments."[86]

Recent archival revelations partially corroborate this analysis,[87] but also show that although Nixon's shift toward Israel may have begun with "Black September" 1970,[88] it was completed more than a year later and, to a certain degree, for different reasons.

The emerging picture for most of 1971 is of an ambivalent, slightly perplexed president straddling the Arab-Israeli issue and showing his typical Janus face to Kissinger and Rogers. During the winter, he was content with doing little, pleasing his national security adviser and the Israeli government.[89] Following Rogers's May 1971 visit to Egypt, however, Nixon changed tack. Historian Claire Diagle only slightly overstates his case when he argues that for several months at least, the president endorsed evenhandedness.[90] Convinced by Rogers that Sadat was mellowing in his attitude toward Israel and that the expulsion of Soviet military advisers from Egypt could be had in exchange for Israeli carrots, he authorized the secretary to press the Israelis into an interim agreement on the Suez Canal, providing this explanation: "[I]t is essential that no more aid programs for Israel be approved until they agree to some kind of interim action on the Suez or some other issue . . . the interests of the United States will be served . . . by tilting the policy . . . on the side of 100 million Arabs rather than on the side of two million Israelis."[91]

In June, Nixon coupled word with deed and suspended the delivery of Phantoms, telling his chief of staff and confidante H. R. Haldeman that he would not "play the Jewish game" of "strin[ging] us along until the elections . . . when they hope to replace us."[92] He reversed course somewhat toward the late summer, partly because of concern lest a diplomatic offensive in the Middle East overshadow and undermine the dramatic China policy initiative, and partly because of disappointment over Sadat's decision to sign a treaty of friendship with the Soviet Union.[93] This reversal did not suffice to alleviate the apprehensions of Meir and other top Israeli officials about the conditions placed on the flow of arms, Washington's failure to fully brief Israel about American contacts with Sadat, and the president's inability or unwillingness to rein in the state and defense departments.[94]

It was only at a meeting with Meir in early December 1971 that Nixon's shift toward Israel was truly completed. Only then did he raise the scale of his administration's commitment to Israel in all crucial areas. First, instead of urging Meir to substantially moderate Israel's negotiating stance on the interim agreement, he merely emphasized the importance of keeping up the appearance of negotiating in good faith, underlining two objectives: to avoid jeopardizing the 1972 American-Soviet summit, and to place the American delegation to the summit in a reasonably comfortable bargaining position.[95] In doing so, Nixon shunned British impressions that Sadat signed his treaty of friendship with the Soviet Union not out of affinity with Moscow but in order to secure his domestic political survival, and that Sadat was disposed to exit the Soviet orbit if Israel accepted the principle of returning to the 1967 border lines.[96] Second, Nixon signed a long-term supply agreement with Meir that ended the ad hoc nature of arms supply and the linking of it to Israeli policy.[97] Third, heeding Meir's complaints about State Department intrusions and probably spurred on by the proven utility of back channels in other policy contexts, Nixon and Meir found means to intensify and institutionalize the practice of communicating through Rabin and Kissinger while keeping the State Department and the Israeli foreign ministry in the dark. Subsequently, both principals would meticulously adhere to this procedure.[98]

Having established the partiality of the "strategic asset" argument, let us canvass the field of alternative explanations pertinent to the *timing* and *endurance* of Nixon's shift, in the ascending order corresponding to the importance of the Israeli role in bringing the factor to bear on Nixon.

First, Israel had obviously very little to do with one key determinant: the unflinching Soviet rigidity regarding the Arab-Israeli conflict between 1969 and 1971. Several historians have suggested that during high détente, Nixon and Kissinger's Cold War–driven refusal to cooperate with the Soviets hindered diplomatic management of the conflict.[99] To some degree, one may level the same criticism against the Kremlin for the years 1969–1971. Unable or unwilling to bear upon their Arab clients, Moscow continuously missed diplomatic opportunities to drive a wedge between Israel and Nixon, or even to embarrass Jerusalem. The Soviet policy-makers responded unimaginatively to Sisco's suggestions at the two-power talks. They dismissed the Rogers initiative of 1969 out of hand, saving Israel from being blamed for its failure.[100] And in 1971, they played to Israel's script by signing the treaty of friendship with Sadat.

Second, since Nixon tended to personalize his dealings with foreign countries, the opinion he formed of Rabin and Meir must be taken into account. Although the impact of his rapport with the ambassador can hardly be overstated, this is not the case in his dealings with the prime minister: impressed by her patriotism and toughness, Nixon was uncomfortable with what struck him as Meir's typically Jewish emotionalism.[101] More generally, Nixon was not significantly driven by a value-based commitment to a small, fellow democratic state vis-à-vis an alien Arab world. He did occasionally make this argument, but largely in the Realpolitik terms of preserving American Cold War credibility with friends (and the deterrence of foes) or with a clear instrumental goal in mind.[102]

Third, Kissinger's growing bureaucratic clout certainly helped Israel secure the president's ear. Kissinger was hardly always at one with the Meir government, but the convictions informing his recommendations (at least from late 1969 onward) generally accorded with the Israeli perspective. He deemed a comprehensive Arab-Israeli settlement unattainable at that time and tried to persuade Nixon that America's troubles in the Arab world were due less to the Arab-Israeli conflict and more to Soviet encroachment and Arab radicalism.[103] Since Nixon initially confined Kissinger to the limited role of diverting domestic criticism away from the White House, these assessments began to shape American policy only in the wake of the September 1970 Jordanian crisis.[104] Even afterward, the national security adviser became Nixon's point person on the Middle East only in fits and starts,[105] in part simply because Rogers and Sisco enjoyed the advantage of focusing their attention on the region, while Kissinger spread himself thin by insisting on personally masterminding a multitude of crucial back channels in other key policy spheres.

Kissinger played the bureaucratic game skillfully. He managed to keep a partial watch on the State Department through close contact with Sisco.[106] He intimated his plans only to a few Nixon confidantes well disposed toward Israel, like Attorney General John Mitchell.[107] Most importantly, he treaded carefully with Nixon. First, he overplayed Israel's trust in Nixon, taking advantage of the president's need for constant praise.[108] Second, the Jewish intellectual endeavored to be perceived by Nixon as an advocate of neither Israel nor the American Jewish community, sensing Nixon's anti-Semitic streak and knowing that any hint of pro-Jewish policy on his part would be exploited by his bureaucratic rivals. He thus downplayed his points of agreement with Jerusalem. For instance, the Nixon tapes show that during a preparatory discussion with Nixon on the eve of Meir's seminal December 1971 visit to the White House, he suggested that Nixon link the supply of arms to Israeli flexibility about the interim agreement with Egypt—and was relieved when Nixon proceeded to do just the reverse.[109]

The Israeli side cooperated seamlessly with Kissinger's measures. The pattern of a back channel that bypassed and sidelined the Israeli foreign ministry (and the State Department) was consistent with both the tradition of policy-making in Israel[110] and the personal preferences of Meir and Rabin.[111] The partnership between Kissinger and Rabin was also enhanced by their shared lack of respect for Eban and Rogers;[112] For example, Rabin went as far as bluntly chastising his superior for "failing to understand that deeds rather than words ultimately determine foreign policy outcomes," while the foreign ministry reciprocated by wryly reminding Rabin and his staff that "statecraft consists of assessing, exploiting and shaping uncertainty."[113] Hence, Rabin reminded the more suspicious Meir that Israel's interests would best be served by acknowledging Kissinger's need not to be vulnerable to accusations of double loyalty. Rabin was probably an influence, also, in a message welcome to Nixon in substance and tone: Meir's communication, at the December 1971 meeting, of her willingness to consider a minor withdrawal from the Suez Canal provided the negotiations would be conducted exclusively through the good offices of the White House.[114]

Kissinger's clinching of lasting policy dominance on the Middle East certainly coincided with Nixon's turn toward Israel at the December 1971 meeting: in late September, Nixon advised Soviet foreign minister Gromyko to negotiate with Kissinger rather than Rogers,[115] and in January 1972 he instructed Rogers to slow down the State Department's diplomatic activity in the area.[116] Despite Kissinger's substantial influence, however, it would be misleading to assign him sole or even primary responsibility for the timing and the endurance of Nixon's shift, as it is clear that the national security adviser's standing with the increasingly envious Nixon grew quite precarious following the string of spectacular summitry successes of 1972.[117] The specific timing of the change had much to do with, first, Nixon's wish to counter India's victory over Pakistan by manifesting America's backing of client state Israel,[118] and second, Nixon's belief, especially in light of Sadat's unpredictability, that a turn toward Israel made sense during an election year.[119] The endurance of the shift, in turn, resulted in large part from Nixon's new confidence in Israel as his firm supporter and member of the conservative camp.

Israel's Conservative Turn and Nixon's Shift

Rewarding loyalty and punishing disloyalty is a staple of the human condition and of political life, one that American presidents have been known to practice with passion and venom. But Nixon's extremes in valuing loyalty places him on his own among American presidents, as Watergate all too clearly illustrates. He infused the administration with his vindictive "Us vs. Them" mentality to a pathological degree.[120] The Israeli government made several policy choices, largely overlooked in the literature, that were well attuned to Nixon's obsession with loyalty and had a palpable impact on his image of, and policy toward, Israel.[121]

The first choice concerned the Soviet Union. Israeli representatives kept their American counterparts immediately and fully informed of several Soviet feelers designed to open a direct channel of discussion with Jerusalem. Interestingly, on one such early occasion Rabin told Kissinger, in strict confidence and "for White House knowledge only," that Israel had indicated its willingness to participate provided the designated Israeli representative would be able to talk to the two top Soviet leaders directly. Probably in accordance with Israeli expectations, this precondition was never met.[122]

The second choice concerned Vietnam. Previous Israeli governments had given Washington only very guarded support in this matter (and had neither diplomatic nor military relations with South Vietnam itself).[123] The Eshkol government refused to comply with President Johnson's public insistence that "anyone who gave so much to Israel . . . was entitled to a little consideration on . . . Vietnam."[124] The official Israeli explanation conveniently shifted the blame to the prime minister's need to keep a *modus vivendi* with a Socialist party that was part of his coalition, but the actual overriding reason was the need to avoid further antagonizing watchful Kremlin leaders who held sway over two and a half million Jews.[125]

Golda Meir broke away from this pattern of ambiguity and reticence. On 7 November 1969 she sent Nixon a private and secret letter that praised his keynote "silent majority" speech as providing reassurance to small nations fighting for their survival. She then surprised even Ambassador Barbour by letting the letter make headline news in the United States and aligning Israel publicly with Nixon on the floor of the Knesset.[126]

There is no reason to doubt the sincerity of the message. Meir spoke for her cabinet members, including the more dovish Eban, and the great majority of the Jewish members of Knesset.[127] Most Israelis feared that a swift American withdrawal from Vietnam would deal a heavy blow to American prestige, signal a general American retreat from world affairs, and embolden the Soviets and Arabs to take the offensive against a more vulnerable Israel.[128] The message was also expressive of Meir's mood of active defiance of the Soviet Union, soon to reveal itself in such other spheres as Israel's Soviet Jewish emigration policy.

Yet, the message was indisputably calculated primarily to curry favor with Nixon. In writing this letter, Meir was heeding the advice of her ambassador,[129] who had developed sharp instincts for Nixon's personality and outlook on the domestic scene.[130] Following the unfolding of the Vietnam drama closely, he realized the deep antagonism between Nixon and the antiwar movement and proposed to bring the point of Israel's common concern about a neo-isolationist surge home to Nixon. Moreover, Nixon actually signaled to Israel, through Garment, that public support would be rewarded,[131] and the Israeli principals in turn regarded the publication of the letter as an investment in Nixon, a move that would secure, as Argov put it, Nixon's support in the campaign to "block the State Department and the Russians."[132]

The letter set the direction for Israeli policy throughout the Nixon years. Receding to the background, probably because of the objection of

American Jewish liberals, Meir and Rabin responded to White House requests and continued to spread the word among Jews and gentiles about Israel's support of Nixon's Vietnam stand.[133] They even took pains to apologize for the insignificant, few, and far-between anti–Vietnam War protests of anti-Zionist Jewish leftist groups in Israel.[134] The effort bore fruit. Nixon appreciated Meir's public rush to second his "silent majority" speech, since the speech to his mind was pivotal in holding the line against unpatriotic radicals who represented a threat to national security.[135] By the beginning of 1972, he spoke favorably about Israel's Vietnam record, not merely in his communications to close aides and Israeli officials, but even in the midst of his periodic anti-Semitic diatribes.[136]

The third choice concerned the evangelical movement in the United States. As Melanie McAlister has pointed out, Israel's victory in the 1967 War generated a flood of evangelical support for Israel, since the movement interpreted the victory as evidence of the quickening pace of God's action in human history. The importance of this development did not escape the attention of Meir's government. The relationship had first emerged after Israeli officials watched the film *His Land* by the Reverand Billy Graham, Nixon's confidante and the nation's most influential evangelist. The officials were impressed by the potential base of support they might find among evangelicals. Recognizing the value of evangelicals as an important political bloc, Meir's government made a strategic decision to return the evangelicals' interest. The most conspicuous manifestation of this new Israeli policy of courtship came in 1971, when Israel provided the venue for "the Jerusalem conference on Biblical Prophecy." Drawing fifteen hundred delegates from thirty-two countries, the gathering was greeted by no less than former Prime Minister David Ben-Gurion. [137]

Students of the period are familiar with the most conspicuous example of the fourth Israeli choice: intervention on Nixon's behalf in the 1972 presidential race. In an interview with Israeli radio in June 1972, Rabin made news with this reply: "[W]hile we appreciate support in the form of words we are getting from one camp, we must prefer support in the form of deeds we are getting from the other camp."[138] Recently declassified archival evidence shows just how purposeful this diplomatic faux pas was. Although his action was sparked in part by a suggestion by Nixon aide Ken Clawson,[139] it was taken happily, as Rabin deemed a McGovern victory as spelling American retreat from world affairs, and hence inimical to Israeli interests.[140] His government felt the same way.[141] Indeed, behind closed doors Rabin went to great lengths to promote a Nixon victory, advising the foreign ministry to play down a McGovern stopover in Israel, and even giving advice, through Kissinger, to the Committee to Reelect the President on how to take advantage of mistakes Rabin believed the Democrats had been committing regarding American Jewry and Israel.[142]

Of course, Nixon could not have factored in this manifest 1972 support when he committed himself fully to Israel in late 1971. Yet, late 1971 already saw Meir and Rabin both actively lobbying for Nixon in American Jewish circles[143] and extending repeated feelers to Billy Graham.[144] Word filtered back to Nixon and he certainly took notice, distinguishing much more starkly than before between the "radical and left wing" American Jews and "the best Jews," the Israelis.[145] This new image of Israel was integral to his late 1971 decision.

December 1971–October 1973: Honeymoon and Complacency amid High Détente

During the next two years, the partnership between the White House and the Prime Minister's Office grew uncommonly intimate. Kissinger not only treated Rabin to unflattering portraits of State Department officials, but also hinted at his uneasiness about the president's tendency to err in Vietnam and then shift the blame to his subordinates.[146] That Rabin's role in shaping Nixon's view of Israel by far exceeded that of the standard ambassador had become obvious by the time he left office in early 1973. Remarking to Kissinger that Rabin "has been a great friend and by God, we're going to reward our friends," Nixon made time to part with the ambassador in a long private discussion.[147]

Jerusalem furthered this process by continuing to offer discrete political services after Rabin's departure. The Israeli embassy lobbied on Kissinger's behalf during the confirmation proceedings leading to his appointment as secretary of state, and even tried its best to neutralize the criticism Kissinger faced on account of wiretapping his staff. Kissinger reciprocated by cultivating the new ambassador, Simcha Dinitz (who succeeded Rabin in April 1973), as much as he did Rabin.[148] A rare exception to this pattern of intimacy was Meir's disinclination to send Nixon a letter of encouragement regarding Watergate. She cited as her reason, however, not moral scruples, but the embarrassing repercussions should the letter surface.[149]

Meir and Rabin also astutely looked for ways to keep Israel in Nixon's good graces by minimizing the matters in dispute. For instance, realizing that the die had been cast, Meir led her government into acquiescing to a major American arms supply deal to Saudi Arabia and Kuwait.[150] Meir also took every precaution to mitigate the only source of friction with Nixon during this period: Soviet Jewish emigration policy. Seeking to preserve détente, Nixon and Kissinger demanded that Israel expressly disavow the Jackson-Vanik Amendment. Rabin was inclined to comply,[151] but Meir was torn, since the amendment spoke directly to some of her most profound principles and commitments. Finally, she settled on a two-pronged policy of projecting strict neutrality while at the same time running a carefully guarded covert campaign in support of Jackson-Vanik, an approach that will be described in greater detail in the next chapter.[152] The strategy was well executed and largely kept Nixon and Kissinger's anger over Jackson-Vanik from spilling over to other dimensions of their Israeli policy.

These Israeli efforts to fix Nixon's Israeli policy in place reflected the feeling that Israel had "never had it so good," as Meir told Nixon during their amicable meeting on 1 March 1973.[153] Meir was not alone. The sense of satisfaction engulfed the Israeli foreign ministry and filtered down to the Israeli public, who ranked the amused Nixon third in a popularity poll.[154]

The confidence in Nixon of Israeli policy-makers was enhanced by the role they believed he played at the first and second U.S.-Soviet summits. Receiving mixed signals from Kissinger prior to the 1972 summit, Meir had been, characteristically, quite apprehensive about an American-Soviet deal behind Israel's back.[155] After the summit, her alarm faded. True, she remained opposed to some major points of agreement reached between the superpowers before and during the summit, including the references to the abortive round of negotiations previously conducted by UN envoy Gunnar Jarring, the refugee problem, and the safeguarding of a future settlement by means of UN forces and international guarantees.[156] This was offset by the encouragement she drew from the relative marginality of the Middle East at the summit, as well as from Nixon's evident firmness, the Soviet reluctance to confront Nixon on Sadat's behalf, and Sadat's utter disappointment with Moscow.[157] Rabin, and Israel's principal source of strategic assessments, the analysis branch of military intelligence, went further and developed a positive appraisal of détente on the basis of two arguments. First, the Arab-Israeli conflict had been fueled by unmitigated superpower rivalry. Détente was bound to bring more stability to the area. Second, although détente represented the greatest shift in American strategy since 1945, it still aimed at containment, though via a different track: the notion of transforming the Soviet Union into a status quo power with a stake in preserving the international order. In short, far from partaking in imposing a solution on the parties, Washington could be expected, in the context of détente, to continue to strive to restrain Soviet adventurism in the Middle East.[158]

By the second U.S.-Soviet summit in the summer of 1973, a triumphalist, complacent tone crept into Israeli assessments. Oblivious to Brezhnev's warning about the imminence of war unless progress was made, Israeli observers deduced that Moscow was so concerned about the Chinese threat and so in need of American economic assistance that it would lose its poise vis-à-vis the United States, and hence its credibility in the

Arab world.[159] Even Meir grew quite confident that Nixon would not cut an undesirable deal with the Soviets.[160]

Finally, Israel's trust in Nixon went hand in hand with the convergence of the American and Israeli perspectives on the Arab-Israeli conflict. A few dissident voices in both capitals favored the immediate initiation of substantive negotiations with the Egyptians. On the Israeli side, Deputy Prime Minister Yigal Allon reasoned that territorial compromise was the sine qua non of any settlement of the conflict, but time was of the essence because obtaining such compromise would only become progressively more difficult with the growing attachment of Israelis to the occupied territories.[161] Gideon Rafael, on his part, sensed the possibility that in the absence of progress Sadat might be driven to such desperate moves as launching a war.[162] On the American side, Rogers made a last stab on Middle East policy by suggesting secret Egyptian-Israeli peace talks, while the ever-active Sisco apparently came to share Rafael's premonition and was attentive to indications that the Arab Gulf states were on the verge of wielding the oil weapon. He was anxious enough to take the unorthodox step of presenting the case for prompt action directly to the Israeli public, over the head of the Meir government.[163]

These officials did not call the shots in either Washington or Jerusalem; Rogers and Sisco, the Israelis quickly learned, had the support of neither Nixon nor even many in the State Department.[164] The prevalent American line accepted Israel's adherence to the status quo. This was partly by default and partly by design. Nixon and Kissinger paid comparatively little attention to the Middle East, as they were preoccupied by Vietnam and the triangular détente game.[165] At least equally as important was a purposeful strategy based on the conviction that the standstill in the Middle East was working to America's advantage.

To understand this strategy, let us refocus briefly on Kissinger, its principal formulator and, as the summer of 1973 wore on and Nixon's authority was undercut by Watergate, increasingly the dominant figure in the conduct of foreign policy.[166] Kissinger aimed at a complete frustration of the Arabs, a policy he later admitted was shortsighted.[167] By maintaining Israel's military edge and a slow diplomatic pace, Kissinger believed the United States could impress upon the Arab side the futility of relying on Moscow to secure the recovery of the territories lost in the 1967 war. The less radical Arabs would then turn to the United States at the expense of the Soviets, a result Kissinger wholeheartedly pursued, détente notwithstanding.[168] Kissinger agreed with the Israelis that Sadat's expulsion of Soviet advisers in July 1972 vindicated this strategy.[169] He did take the measure of Israeli and Egyptian positions through diplomatic contacts in the first half of 1973.[170] He turned a cold shoulder, however, to the far-reaching outline of a settlement Egypt tabled during those contacts.[171] By the late summer,

Kissinger concluded that the moment was inauspicious for a diplomatic initiative, for several reasons. The Egyptians insisted on the demand that Israel would first withdraw from the Sinai and only then negotiate with the Palestinians.[172] Meir was engaged in an election campaign scheduled for late October and could not be expected to be conciliatory.[173] Perhaps most importantly, as Kissinger explained to the president's Foreign Intelligence Advisory Board, "Israel is so much stronger that the dilemma is on the Arabs."[174]

To be sure, Nixon's public speeches at the time suggest he was actually beginning to veer away from this standstill mentality as a result of public Saudi threats to link oil production to American policy toward the conflict.[175] But Kissinger was in no hurry. During the first few days of October, he advised Israeli and Arab ambassadors to expect the launching of a new American initiative, probably in January 1974.[176] These plans were overtaken by a cataclysmic event unforeseen by Washington and Jerusalem. On October 6, Yom Kippur, Egypt and Syria launched a surprise combined military offensive against Israeli forces in Sinai and the Golan Heights. Kissinger's (and Nixon's) policy lay in ruins; Israel—its society, government, and prime minister—experienced an earthquake that proved nothing short of a national trauma.

The Final Months: Picking Up the Pieces

Nixon's Israeli policy ended on a sour and deeply ironic note. The October War eroded popular support for détente in the United States. Brezhnev had actually alerted Nixon and Kissinger in advance about the likelihood of war, and fought attempts within the politburo to roll back détente after it started;[177] nonetheless, Soviet actions prior to, during, and following the conflict confirmed the suspicions of some Americans, and convinced others, that Moscow could not be trusted. Conservative and neoconservative political leaders and commentators argued that the war unmasked Soviet intentions and the risks of détente.[178] Quite a few of these figures were Jews, for whom the 1973 war gave existential pause and revived a sense of attachment to their Jewish identity.[179] They mounted a campaign to discard détente on the grounds that it had helped the Kremlin leaders to conceal their expansionist and offensive intentions. Nixon, Kissinger, and other proponents of détente found themselves fighting a rearguard and ultimately unsuccessful battle.

Having directly suffered the ordeal of the war, Israel shared the conclusions conservatives and neoconservatives drew from it and, as we will see in the next chapter, aligned itself quite openly with the campaign against détente.[180] Nixon was furious, grumbling about Israeli ingrati-

tude and betrayal and reverting to his older image of Israel as indistin-
guishable from untrustworthy American Jews.[181] As will be demonstrated
in the concluding chapter, this sentiment underlay his dealings with
Jerusalem from late 1973 through his August 1974 resignation from the
presidency, including his visit to Jerusalem in June 1974.[182] But had Nixon
reflected back on his entreaties to Israel in March 1970, he might have realized that he was the one who most aggressively pressed Israel to join
the conservative brotherhood—and that Israel had answered his call, only
too well. As in so many domains, Nixon was, in the end, a victim of his
own plans gone awry.

2

ISRAEL, SOVIET JEWISH
EMIGRATION, AND IDEALPOLITIK

The next two chapters trace the emergence of the "conservative partnership" around the struggle for Soviet Jewry, beginning with Israel and proceeding to the United States. Let us begin by placing Israel's Soviet Jewish emigration policy within the context of the basic dilemmas that Jewish immigration to Israel has presented to Zionist leaders.

The immigration of Jews to Israel is a central element of the Zionist ethos. The term *aliya* itself—meaning "ascent"—demonstrates the profound moral significance attached to this act by Israel's Zionist leaders. Zionism was conceived from its earliest days as a movement to provide Jews with a refuge from persecution and a center for a rejuvenated national life. Both these dimensions are inextricably linked to Jewish immigration. The Israeli leadership's deep commitment to Jewish immigration was reflected in the country's 1948 Declaration of Independence and, even more clearly, in the 1950 Law of Return, a quasi-constitutional statute that deems Jewish immigration to Israel as an inalienable right and enjoys support from across the political spectrum of Zionist parties in Israel.[1]

In practice, however, the ideological commitment to Jewish immigration has been tested by the exigencies of reality at critical junctures. This tension has expressed itself in both domestic and foreign policies. In the domestic context, Zionist leaders have had to balance the ideological imperative of promoting mass Jewish immigration and the practical need to restrict immigration according to the ability of the country to integrate newcomers. For example, the country's founding father and first prime minister, David Ben-Gurion, shifted away from an unequivocal embrace of Jewish immigration toward a more selective approach in late 1951, in the wake of the massive immigration wave that stretched the young state's infrastructure to the limit.[2]

Soviet and East European Jews were largely unaffected by such periodic tightening of attitudes toward immigration for domestic reasons. The Israeli elite, which was itself mostly of East European descent, tended to see immigration from the USSR and Eastern Europe as a "rescue mission," felt an affinity toward these Jewish communities, and saw them as sophisticated and modern—and therefore, as a crucial reservoir for building the country. But Ben-Gurion and his aides still had to reconcile themselves to a near-absence of immigration from the USSR during Israel's first fifteen years for nondomestic reasons; namely, the Soviet Union's strength, dominance over Eastern Europe, and growing hostility toward Israel, which compelled the Israeli leadership to abandon any notion of securing approval from the Kremlin for mass immigration. This resignation, as Uri Bialer writes, "stemmed from the sober assessment that Russia would never permit its Jewish citizens to emigrate, on the one hand, and that the stubborn pursuit would probably turn into a stumbling-block for immigration from the rest of Eastern Europe, on the other."[3]

Realpolitik considerations continued to govern Israeli policy toward the Soviet Jewish issue during the mid and late 1960s, after Ben-Gurion had left the political scene. Key figures, including Prime Minister Eshkol, refrained from any semblance of Israeli pressure on the Kremlin because they deemed mass exodus unattainable and because they believed any efforts in this direction would trigger Kremlin reprisals against Soviet Jewry and further fuel Moscow's support of the Arabs.[4]

But as the decade drew to a close, a subtle but important shift began to take place. Now at the helm in Israel was prime minister Golda Meir, who as ambassador to Moscow in the late 1940s had experienced firsthand the frustrations surrounding Israeli restraint on the immigration issue. Moreover, Soviet Jews themselves were increasingly less willing to wait for a chance to emigrate and were agitating for action. Meir therefore faced a new, aggravated version of the dilemma that had vexed her predecessors: how to reconcile the pragmatic considerations of avoiding an escalation with Moscow and nurturing the relationship with the White House—which strongly opposed a campaign on behalf of Soviet Jews, fearing they could heat up Cold War tensions—and the ideological imperative of supporting the Jewish emigration struggle. In this chapter, we will explore the solution devised by Meir and some of her closest advisors.

During the heyday of détente, in October 1972, American and Soviet negotiators completed a major trade agreement that called for the extension of Most Favored Nation (MFN) status to the Soviet Union. The ensuing congressional debate over legislation to implement the agreement, revolving principally around Soviet Jewish emigration policy, resulted in the previously mentioned Jackson-Vanik Amendment to the Trade Act of 1974, which barred the extension of MFN status to Communist countries that restricted the emigration of their citizens. The administration tenaciously fought to win Israeli support and overcome Congress, but to no avail. The amendment passed, and the administration's failure to block it hurt its credibility with the Kremlin. The amendment thus both reflected and contributed to the decline of détente.[5]

The triangular Soviet Jewish policy game between Jerusalem, Washington, and American Jewry during the Nixon years is a complex story that, until recently, has been difficult to recount dispassionately, not only because of the evidentiary challenges discussed in the introduction to this volume, but also because of the strong emotions it has engendered. As historian Benjamin Pinkus explains, the first wave of Jewish emigration in the early 1970s had numerous *accoucheurs*, with Soviet Jewish dissidents, American Jews, Israeli operatives, and even Kissinger vying for primary credit.[6] During the next decade, quarrels in the West about the wisdom of Jackson-Vanik reached their zenith, against the backdrop of perplexing swings in Moscow's emigration policy.[7] Throughout both periods, the issue of Jerusalem's role grew so sensitive within Israel as to provoke bitter political polemics characterized by some as veritable 'wars of the Jews.'[8]

During the last few years, as Soviet Jewish emigration has become more an event of the historical past than the political present, the winds of controversy have largely subsided.[9] This, together with the declassification of important Israeli, American, and Soviet documentation, allows for unprecedented insights into Israel's Soviet Jewish emigration policy.[10] Charting new ground as we take advantage of this opportune historiographic moment,[11] we will trace the evolution of Israeli conduct and examine a key question in the literature: just how important was Israel in the promotion of Jackson-Vanik? Did Israel maintain a low profile to avoid spoiling its relations with the White House, as some Soviet Jewish activists and right-wing politicians charged, or did it play a crucial if quiet role in mobilizing backing for Jackson-Vanik? After showing that the evidence largely supports the latter interpretation, we will explore the factors that shaped this strategy—which risked alienating an administration whose friendship Jerusalem had worked so hard to nurture—finding that the most salient was ideology. Israel's leaders covertly supported Jackson-Vanik because it resonated deeply with their strongest emotional dispositions and their sense of ideological purpose.

Prologue: Israel and Soviet Jewish Emigration Before Jackson-Vanik

When it comes to the Soviet Jewish emigration issue, the first Nixon administration, before the introduction of the Jackson-Vanik amendment, may be seen in retrospect as a valuable apprenticeship period for the Israeli government. Golda Meir and her aides were not yet forced to face the dilemma between ideological convictions and Realpolitik calculations, giving them an opportunity to gain experience walking the tightrope between right-wing opponents at home and capricious Kremlin leaders, and to develop vehicles for monitoring the evolving movement of agitated American Jewry to aid Soviet Jews without incurring the wrath of an irritable White House.

Israel maintained a low-key Soviet Jewish policy posture through November 1969 partly because some senior Israeli officials regarded mass exodus as unlikely, and partly for fear of triggering a backlash in Moscow.[12] Moreover, quiet diplomacy was compatible with key elements of the Soviet Jewry campaign strategy devised in the early 1960s by Binyamin Eliav, the foremost thinker of Nativ, a clandestine organization founded in 1952 and reporting directly to the prime minister whose goal was to make possible higher rates of Soviet Jewish emigration.[13] The strategy centered on prodding the Soviet Union to let the Jews leave by mobilizing world opinion and placing the issue on the agenda of East-West relations. But Eliav's sophisticated scheme stipulated prudent means to achieve this end, means designed to avert Arab pressure on the Soviet Union to keep the gates locked and to attract the support of Western public opinion. The idea was to keep the Soviet Jewish problem distinct from Cold War confrontations, steer clear of the struggles of other Soviet minorities, disclose no data about the numbers of Soviet Jewish émigrés making their way to Israel, and oversee the material distributed in the West to ensure that there could be no accusations of falsification, unreliability, or propaganda. Israel's emissaries in the United States (and the West at large) were instructed to operate indirectly through scholars and Jewish establishment institutions, and, while cultivating discrete contacts with legislators and Executive Branch staffers, observe absolute secrecy on the connection between Israel and the activists working on behalf of Soviet Jewry.[14]

An important turning point in official Israeli policy on public activity came late in 1969, when Meir told her country in an address to the Knesset about a petition from eighteen Georgian Jewish families to the Human Rights Commission of the United Nations. The statement was followed by a public submission of the petition by Joseph Tekoah, Israel's ambassador to the UN.[15] A number of factors led to this turning point, but their relative weight cannot be determined on the basis of available evidence. Then Jewish Agency chairman Louis Pincus identifies two principal considerations: a "tactical retreat" on the part of policy-makers who sought to retain control in the face of pressure from recent Soviet Jewish immigrants to Israel, who stirred domestic agitation and told Nativ that unless there was an immediate change in policy they would start independent action; and a genuine feeling that quiet diplomacy had not produced the hoped for results, not even the fulfillment of earlier Soviet promises to permit emigration under a family reunification program.[16] Some Nativ veterans, on the other hand, argue that the changes at the helm made a decisive difference. According to Yoram Dinstein, the Israeli consul to New York between 1966 and 1970, the Georgian petition merely provided a pretext for the recently appointed Meir to assume a more activist position. Others point to the influence of Nehemia Levanon, Meir's choice as the new Nativ director.[17]

Whatever the precise array of underlying causes, the process that produced the shift to a more public posture was marked not by consensus, but rather by hesitation and controversy, at least within Nativ.[18] Indeed, Israel's Soviet Jewish hands immediately discovered just how fragile and divisive the intricate new policy line might become if mishandled. At the turn of 1969, two Soviet Jewish activists went on a lecture tour of the United States, most probably in coordination with prominent right-wing Knesset MPs and certainly without the blessing of Israeli government bodies. One of these activists, Dov Sperling, intimated to the *New York Times* that a Jewish underground had been gathering force in the Soviet Union. His partner, Yasha Kazakov, soon staged a hunger strike at the United Nations' New York headquarters. Concerned that the tour would provoke a vindictive mood in the Kremlin, Nativ's head of operations in the West instructed his field operatives to advise American Jews against cooperation with Sperling and Kazakov. Consequently, the Israeli government found itself caught in a blaze of criticism. Prominent columnists and right-wing MPs accused the government of stifling the Soviet Jewish struggle. Rank-and-file American Jews found the government's behavior baffling. The rising tension took its toll on Nativ as well: Meir Rosenne, one of the organization's most seasoned professionals, resigned in protest.[19]

The Israeli government responded by creating a vehicle for regaining a measure of control over the issue within Israel: the nonpartisan yet semiofficial Public Council for Soviet Jewry. This initiative partially succeeded in marginalizing the most militant groupings of Soviet Jewish émigrés in Israel.[20] It took a Soviet miscalculation, however, to jump-start the government's complementary quest for an invigorated international movement, orchestrated behind the scenes by Israel. A group of Jews schemed to hijack a plane to Israel, despite Israel's opposition.[21] The Soviet authorities apprehended the group in June 1970 and sentenced two of the convicts to death at the highly publicized Leningrad trials. The death sentence aroused international public opinion. World condemnation reverberated, spanning the spectrum from the evangelist Reverend Billy Graham, to American New Left notables and West European leftist intellectuals and communist leaders.[22] Israel's principals saw this outburst of criticism bearing instant fruits. Midlevel State Department staffers established channels of consultation with Israel and championed a firm line with the Soviet Union regarding the Jewish question, a position quite prevalent within the department until the launching of détente in late 1971.[23] Moreover, the Kremlin commuted the death sentences—partly due to the efforts behind the scenes of Nixon, Rogers, and Kissinger.[24]

Galvanizing both Israeli and American Jews, the Leningrad drama also stimulated Israel's pressure on American Jewish leaders to restructure the American Jewish struggle for Soviet Jewry.[25] From Israel's perspective, the American Jewish Conference on Soviet Jewry (AJCSJ), the coordinating body Jerusalem had helped establish in 1964, was becoming ineffective and bogged down in squabbles with the principal representative organization of American Jewry, the Conference of Presidents of Major American Jewish Organizations.[26] There was a risk that another organization, the World Jewish Congress, would fill in the vacuum;[27] its chairman, Nahum Goldmann, had made himself a persona non grata in Israel's power circles by vocally criticizing the Israeli government's Middle Eastern policy, and by advocating a submissive line toward the Kremlin, placing a premium on the preservation of Jewish life within the Soviet Union rather than immigration to Israel, and contending that Israel's hawkish stance vis-à-vis the Arabs was the critical factor hindering Soviet Jewish emigration from the Soviet Union.[28] Prevailing over the foreign ministry, Nativ ruled out the possibility of the Conference of Presidents' taking over the activities and function of the AJCSJ, as it was too closely associated with Israel. Instead, Nativ employed the nongovernmental Jewish Agency to facilitate the creation of a new coordinating umbrella organization with its own staff and an independent budget, the National Conference for Soviet Jewry (NCSJ), which came into being in June 1971.[29] Through the mid-1970s, Israel succeeded in exerting effective yet inconspicuous influence over the new organization's policy.

By 1972, then, Israel learned the lessons of its earlier fumbles and developed a modus operandi for playing a significant role in the United States on the Soviet Jewish emigration issue while managing, for the most part, to conceal its activity.[30] The imperative of finely calibrating resolve and prudence only grew as the year progressed. On the one hand, as the May 1972 superpower summit approached, Jerusalem naturally hoped that Nixon would use his good offices in Moscow to improve the lot of Soviet Jews, and, during the summer that followed, wished the issue to stay in the public eye so as to secure a measure of commitment from both presidential candidates. On the other hand, caution dictated that Israel should not stand accused of hindering détente or injecting the Soviet Jewish issue into the election campaign in the United States.[31] Thus, Israeli officials did approach the White House—both directly and through the NCSJ and the Conference of Presidents[32]—with the request that the issue be broached at the summit, but otherwise toned down Israel's involvement by shunning maverick American Jewish grassroots organizations, refraining from participation in rallies, and broadening the base of the movement in the United States to engage non-Jewish organizations.[33]

This delicate balancing act produced mixed results. While the rich documentation available indicates that the American delegation to the summit chose to keep silent about the contentious Soviet Jewish issue, Nixon's inherent distrust of the Jewish voter did not detract from his positive image of the Meir government, despite the pressure cooker of the summit and the election season.[34] That this was the case had also much to do, however, with factors unrelated to Israel's Soviet Jewish conduct; namely, Nixon's preoccupation with Vietnam, the elections, and "triangular diplomacy" and his consequent lack of engagement with the Soviet Jewish problem and Israel's role in it.

Act I: The Amendment Is Introduced

This general inattention still prevailed when the democratic senator from Washington, Henry M. Jackson, first introduced his amendment on 4 October 1972. During the ensuing half-year, the Israeli foreign policy apparatus was free from any need to choose between the Nixon administration and the Jackson camp, or even formulate a coherent strategy, simply because Nixon and Kissinger all but ignored the amendment.

The events leading to Jackson's action were set in motion by another misstep typical of Moscow's blunders in the Soviet Jewish policy area: levying a prohibitively expensive education tax on would-be immigrants. It is not yet entirely clear why the Kremlin imposed the prohibitively expensive head tax. It may have been aimed at soothing Arab feelings at a time when the Soviet position in the Middle East was deteriorating. It also may have been another attempt to deter Soviet Jewish scientists and technicians from emigrating. Or, as Brezhnev himself reportedly stated, it may have been a "bureaucratic bungle."[35] Recently declassified Soviet documents actually suggest that Brezhnev's more conservative rivals stood behind the motion.[36] Whatever the explanation, the tax drew fire in the Senate and encouraged Jackson to introduce his famous amendment to the trade bill, although Jackson had been angling beforehand for a legislative opportunity to promote the Soviet Jewish cause.[37]

The majority view in Israel advocated a vigorous effort to get the tax repealed, partly in response to the sentiment of most Soviet Jewish activists,[38] partly out of genuine anger and conviction, and partly because of the instrumental opportunity to step up a global campaign on behalf of Soviet Jewry.[39] Multiple initiatives were undertaken. Meir sent a direct secret plea for assistance to Nixon,[40] and her deputy, Yigal Allon, broached the issue with Rogers.[41] Foreign Minister Eban employed the podium of *Face the Nation* to urge the international community to apply pressure with "a persistent tenacity and a growing intensity." The polished diplomat did not forgo the opportunity to profess Israel's endorsement of détente and present the tax as "a wanton and superfluous obstacle to international coexistence."[42] On the American domestic scene, the Israeli Embassy in Washington and Nativ worked in uncommon harmony to covertly encourage American Jewish lobbying against the tax.[43] The primary vehicle for this prodding was the NCSJ.[44]

Probably sensitized to the issue by previous contacts with Nativ emissaries,[45] midlevel staffers at both the White House and the State Department noticed the agitation in American Jewish and Israeli circles and sought to alert their superiors.[46] "Few issues," stressed a State Department briefing paper to Nixon, "have a deeper emotional meaning for Israelis than that of Jewish emigration from the Soviet Union."[47] The perceptive warning fell on deaf ears. Nixon and Kissinger's attempts to alert the Soviets to the adverse domestic ramifications of the education tax were short-lived, lasting only through the November 1972 elections. Thereafter, Nixon and Kissinger's interest dwindled noticeably, as they mistakenly believed the matter would fade away with the passing of the election season.[48] Understandably, their neglect was partly due to preoccupation with the concurrent Vietnam Paris peace talks. Less understandably, they remained sanguine about the Jackson challenge for a number of reasons, including the exhilarating success of summitry diplomacy, their innate disdain of Congress, and their mistaken calculation that Soviet Jewish emigration was a marginal issue that could not possibly develop into a major impediment to such a grand design as détente.[48]

Act II: Israel's Dual Strategy

Act II in Israel's Jackson-Vanik dilemma began in earnest in the spring of 1973. By that time, the administration could no longer be accused of ignoring the Jackson amendment. Nixon sent Congress the Trade Reform Act, which included provisions that would have paved the way for MFN status for the Soviet Union and specifically excluded linkages to the emigration issue; Jackson and seventy-six other senators reciprocated by reintroducing the Jackson amendment as an amendment to the act. Nixon and Kissinger reacted by launching a determined campaign to block the amendment.[50] Their opening gambit consisted of direct presidential lectures to Golda Meir (in March 1973) and a delegation of Jewish Leaders (in April) about the merit of quiet diplomacy.[51] Persuasion quickly gave way to blunt pressure. Only a few days elapsed before Kissinger told Ambassador Rabin that even a postponement of airplane deliveries was possible.[52] Other ringing messages about the unacceptability of Israeli evasion and the possibility of grave White House reprisals were sent to the Israeli government through such credible channels as journalists Rowland Evans and Robert Novak and Nixon's liaison to the Jewish community, Leonard Garment.[53] By the end of September, Kissinger minced no words, telling Ambassador Simcha Dinitz, who succeeded Rabin in April, that if Israel did not shift to Nixon's side in the Jackson-Vanik imbroglio, Israel would "lose the president."[54]

Israel endeavored to extricate itself from the administration's pressure by declaring neutrality. In public, official statements underlined Jerusalem's wish to stay out of the skirmish between the Executive and Congress, taking meticulous care to credit Nixon rather than Jackson by name for achievements on the Soviet Jewish emigration front.[55] This was paralleled by insistence to administration officials that legal and moral imperatives ruled out the possibility of Israeli meddling in American internal affairs. Meir capped the only tense exchange in her otherwise amicable March 1973 meeting with Nixon by retorting, "I can't talk to American Jews about Russian Jews"[56]—a commitment the prime minister personally carefully observed, avoiding even the semblance of providing guidance to American Jews.[57] Israeli domestic constraints rounded out the Israeli argument. As Dinitz emphasized to Garment, Meir was facing a tough re-election fight (scheduled for October 1973) of her own, and public debate about Soviet Jewish policy was escalating, with the Knesset floor and opinion climate dominated by right-wing (and some Soviet Jewish newcomers') accusations of government timidity and demands that Israel stand squarely behind Jackson.[58] This carefully constructed posture of straddling the issue was aimed at maintaining a balance between conflicting international and domestic pressures.

Nehemia Levanon, head of Nativ at the time, hints in his memoirs that after some soul-searching, Meir sanctioned a complementary secret effort to secure the passage of the Jackson amendment.[59] For several reasons, it is exceedingly difficult to confirm this claim. First, the records of Israeli cabinet (and intra-Nativ) deliberations on the issue are still under lock and key. Second, while most Nativ emissaries to the United States have spoken out about their past experiences, some important Americans who worked closely with them have chosen to remain silent.[60] And third, the historian can hardly expect a hidden-hand policy, if successful, to leave conspicuous fingerprints in the historical record. Yet, the few clues available corroborate Levanon's version: while support for Jackson-Vanik was unanimous neither in the cabinet nor inside Nativ,[61] and Golda Meir hoped for a compromise between Nixon and Jackson more than Levanon is willing to concede,[62] Israel did ultimately launch a covert and successful campaign on its behalf.

An Israeli foreign ministry report that slipped through cracks in the walls of secrecy provides evidence for this interpretation. Indeed, at first glance, it appears to leave no room for doubt: at a meeting some two weeks after Meir's March 1973 refusal to commit Israel either way in the White House, Meir, Levanon, Dinitz, and the director-general of the prime minister's office, Mordechai Gazit, affirmed Israel's covert backing of Jackson-Vanik. Cognizant of adamant White House opposition and deeming overt involvement detrimental to the amendment's passage and efficacy, they decided to take every precaution to keep the operation hidden from public view, even in the face of charges by opposition circles in Israel that the government was seeking refuge in indecision. Upon closer examination, however, this document seems less conclusive: the reporter, a foreign ministry official, was not present at the top-secret meeting, and his source, Levanon, was not an impartial observer but rather a champion of Jackson-Vanik who naturally sought to promote his agenda.[63]

Nevertheless, a string of strong circumstantial evidence from the spring and summer of 1973 suggests the reliability of the report. First, Meir privately yet explicitly consented to the public endorsement of the amendment by the establishment-oriented Public Council for Soviet Jewry.[64] Second, Israeli representatives tactfully sent American Jewish leaders signals that Jerusalem favored the amendment.[65] Less restrained by diplomatic norms and official status, nongovernmental notables like Jewish Agency chairman Pincus relayed the message more forcefully.[66] Third, the Israeli government constantly assured Jackson that Jerusalem's official impartiality reflected the dictates of Realpolitik and nothing more.[67] Fourth, the American Jewish organizations most intimately associated with Israel took the lead in bolstering Jackson's ranks when other American Jewish leaders seemed to be wavering under the administration's pressure. Both the Greater New York Conference on Soviet Jewry and its parent NCSJ organization were instrumental in bringing the grassroot Jewish sentiment in favor of Jackson-Vanik to bear on key Jewish establishment leaders.[68] Fifth, when the visiting Brezhnev sought to convert Congress to approving MFN unconditionally, Nativ and the NCSJ countered by highlighting both Brezhnev's poor performance in Congress and the harassment of Soviet Jews.[69] Finally, perhaps the best illustration of the Meir government's pro-Jackson leaning in the summer of 1973 comes from one of Meir's most trusted aides, Simcha Dinitz. The Israeli ambassador generally refrained from confronting Kissinger. But by the end of September, he faced down Kissinger's aforementioned threats on Jackson-Vanik by faulting the newly appointed secretary of state (and still national security adviser) for casting the issue as an internal Soviet problem. He said that Kissinger should have known better, since such language was bound to prompt analogies with the Holocaust and trigger a deeply emotional Jewish and Israeli reaction; against the backdrop of waves of repression in the Soviet Union, Kissinger's blunder accentuated the Soviet Jewish problem's moral and human rights dimension, rendering it inherently less manageable.[70]

Kissinger actually acknowledged some responsibility; it seems to have been Dinitz's rebuke, along with prodding from Nixon, which prompted him to launch long-overdue negotiations with Jackson.[71] His overture, however, was nipped in the bud by the unexpected intrusion of a cataclysmic event that would destabilize the policy–making environment and dominate Israeli-American relations for the rest of Kissinger's tenure: the October 1973 War.

Act III: The War and Its Aftermath

The duration and immediate aftermath of the war represents the third act in Israel's Soviet Jewish drama during the Nixon years. During this phase, Israel again ended up helping to nudge Jackson-Vanik forward, but this time more out of a breakdown in the chain of command and less out of a deliberate decision-making process controlled by the center.

During the first days of the war, when Kissinger still shared with most American (and some Israeli) officials a certain complacency regarding Israel's dire straits, he rushed to establish a trade-off: in exchange for American resupply efforts, Israel and the American Jewish community would withdraw their support for Jackson-Vanik. The secretary explicitly spelled out the proposed deal to the Soviet ambassador, Anatoly Dobrynin, and officials from the Conference of Presidents of Major American Jewish Organizations, securing the reluctant acquiescence of the latter.[72] In the aftermath of war, Kissinger resumed the attempt, painting a bleak picture for his Jewish and Israeli audiences: Israel now confronted a resurgent Arab world equipped with an effective oil weapon; a shift in the climate of American opinion (and even within the administration) against Israel might well be in the cards; and only with a quiescent Soviet Union could Israel hope to reap any regional dividends from the bitter war. Jerusalem's cooperation was thus cast as imperative, and disavowing Jackson-Vanik as a low price to pay for the advancement of vital Israeli interests.[73]

How Israel's principals handled the Jackson-Vanik dilemma during those difficult days is still largely a matter of speculation. The Israeli cabinet was traumatized by the conflict, and had little attention or energy to spare for other issues.[74] According to Nativ's New York station chief, Yitzhak Rager, the cabinet instructed Israeli representatives to stay clear of the executive-congressional duel over Jackson-Vanik. Cabinet members were too shell-shocked, however, to maintain communication and coordination between the relevant Israeli organs, both vertically and horizontally, and effectively lost control over the implementation of its instruction.[75]

As is often the case in acute crises, when headquarters—in this case, Jerusalem—was overwhelmed by the dire circumstances it faced, the locus of decision-making on other matters shifted to the field—in this instance, Israel's various representatives and allied organizations in the United States. Israel's embassy had long been struggling for policy and bureaucratic advantage with Nativ's two station chiefs, one operating out of Israel's New York General Consulate and the other from the embassy itself. Foreign Minister Eban, former ambassador Rabin, and Ambassador Dinitz were all not only relatively unenthusiastic about the Jackson amendment, but also strove to rein in the station chiefs' autonomy; the latter retaliated by complaining that some foreign service officers were insufficiently committed to the Soviet Jewish struggle.[76] The crisis atmosphere of the fall of 1973 brought the simmering tension to a boil. Anguished and burdened by the desperate war at home[77] and challenged by a secretary of state who exposed Israel's Jackson-Vanik dilemma in all its brutal clarity, Israel's representatives felt compelled to take a stand and circumvent the government's instructions to steer clear of the Jackson-Vanik struggle. Different actors, however, chose different stands. Dinitz tilted toward Kissinger's position and sent signals to this effect through the Conference of Major Jewish Organizations,[78] while Rager, backed by Levanon, found ingenious ways to circulate the word that Israel would not abandon the amendment.[79]

American Jewish leaders interpreted this Israeli cacophony as conclusive proof that even in times of extreme duress Israel would refrain from taking the lead in opposing the amendment. Since they balked at assuming that role themselves, this realization played a part in the tone of equivocation that the NCSJ set for the community, and ultimately contributed to the retreat of American Jewish leaders from the deal with Kissinger.[80] The most salient factors shaping the American Jewish position, however, had little to do with Israel's confused signals: the perception of many American Jewish influentials that Kissinger's October War record discredited him as a guardian of Jewish interests; the growing sentiment within the Jewish community that because the October War had revealed the illusory nature of détente, Jackson-Vanik was indispensable as a means to coerce the Kremlin to open the gates;[81] and, quite simply, Jackson's adamant refusal to back down.[82]

Genuinely concerned about a potentially fatal erosion of Israel's standing in the United States,[83] Kissinger kept prodding Israel through early 1974, only to find an evasive Dinitz—even Dinitz—retreating from his support for the secretary's reasoning during the October War and arguing that Israel's position "wouldn't make a difference" in the Jackson-Vanik battle.[84] In the end, Kissinger was forced to embark on a round of shuttle diplomacy between Jackson and the Soviets that lasted through the summer and fall of 1974.

Act IV: The Amendment Is Passed

Striving to manage the intricacies of near-simultaneous Middle Eastern and Soviet Jewish shuttles, Kissinger juggled carrots and sticks to press Israel toward greater flexibility. On the one hand, he no longer directly urged American Jewish leaders to support him against Jackson.[85] He divulged, as a token of confidence, intimate details about the negotiations with Moscow to Israeli principals, typically seeking to ingratiate himself further with the Israelis by disparaging the Kremlin's duplicity and mediocrity.[86] On the other hand, at sensitive moments in his dealings with Jackson, the overburdened secretary fumed to his Israeli interlocutors over American Jewish criticism of détente (and himself personally) and warned that negotiations with Jackson could break down. More ominously (and dramatically), he observed that relations between the two countries were eroding and suggested that he might completely wash his hands of Israel's problems.[87]

Neither the inducements nor the threats swayed Jerusalem. In fact, quite the reverse took place: in their protracted discussions with Kissinger, Israel's leaders came closer than ever to revealing their true, pro-Jackson colors. They embraced Jackson's insistence on extricating a specific annual figure of Soviet Jewish emigration from the Kremlin.[88] Deputy prime minister Yigal Allon sounded much like Jackson—and spoke to the paramount importance of ideology in Israeli Soviet Jewish policy—when he explained to the secretary that Soviet Jewry was the "litmus paper" (*sic*) of détente for the Jewish state.[89]

Israel's leaders reacted calmly to Kissinger's maneuvers because they perceived a shift for the better in the parameters of the Jackson-Vanik game. They realized that Watergate and a general reputation for deviousness had weakened the administration's hand. They sensed that both the October War and the wave of repression in the Soviet Union had fomented anti-Soviet sentiment in American public opinion. In short, they knew that American public opinion was turning against both détente and the Nixon-Kissinger team, bolstering Congress and throwing the administration on the defensive.[90] This assessment was reinforced by Nixon's August resignation in the face of congressional impeachment hearings. Israel's cogent survey of the American scene, combined with some less astute calculations discussed later, made for renewed Israeli self-assurance: reaching a rare near-consensus, the Israeli figures and organs dealing with Soviet Jewish matters fully expected the tripartite negotiation effort between Kissinger, Jackson, and the Soviets to bear fruit and secure a steady stream of Soviet Jewish emigration under the auspices of Jackson-Vanik. The only major exception to this consensus was Dinitz, but with Meir also leaving office in the summer, the ambassador's clout with his superiors was waning.[91] So confident was Israel that Nehemia Levanon quite openly lobbied for the amendment in the United States on the eve of its passage.[92] No wonder, then, that the breakdown of American-Soviet negotiations and Moscow's repudiation of the trade agreement at the end of 1974, shortly before President Ford signed Jackson-Vanik into law, sent shockwaves through the relevant Israeli bodies.[93]

Conclusion: The Impacts of Israel's Choices

Events in the year 1975 cast doubts on the wisdom of Israel's backing of Jackson-Vanik. The plummeting of Soviet Jewish emigration to less than half of the 1974 figure (from 29,000 to 13,000) provided easy ammunition for the amendment's opponents.[94] Moreover, the ebbing of American-Israeli relations, illustrated by the Ford administration's decision to declare a reappraisal of its Israel policy, stemmed in part from ill will in the wake of the Jackson-Vanik imbroglio.[95] And finally, even the alliance Israel forged with American Jewry in the struggle for Soviet Jewry fell apart. Long-standing resentments—rooted in American Jews' feeling that Israeli representatives were haughty and Israelis' impression of their American cousins as spineless[96]—came out into the open because of the wish of a growing percentage of Soviet Jewish émigrés to resettle in the United States rather than Israel. Soon enough, a bitter dispute erupted over what Israelis called "the dropout phenomenon" and American Jews, "Freedom of Choice."[97]

With the benefit of more than three decades of hindsight, however, Israel's Jackson-Vanik strategy appears in more favorable light. The wide fluctuations in Soviet Jewish emigration in the second half of the 1970s alone suggest that Soviet policy in this subject area stemmed principally from factors other than Jackson-Vanik.[98] More broadly, the public campaign for Soviet Jewish emigration served to raise awareness in the West of the freedom of movement issue—albeit somewhat ironically, given Israel's objection to Soviet Jewish resettlement in the United States rather than Israel[99]—and contributed to the West's insistence on placing the issue on the East-West agenda. This demand turned on its head the Westphalian principle of the prevalence of sovereignty over transnational human rights, and the unintended consequence of the Soviets' implicit acceptance of this radical idea, in "basket III" of the 1975 Helsinki Final Act, was to invite further undermining of the domestic legitimacy of the Soviet system itself.[100] As observed by the American official most directly involved in the United States' Soviet Jewish policy during the Reagan years, the Soviet

Jewish campaign was thus instrumental, however indirectly, in the eventual collapse of the Soviet empire.[101] Again, this development is not without a touch of irony, given Nativ's insistence on separating the struggle for Soviet Jewry from the general struggle for human rights in the USSR.[102]

It is important to remember that Israel was neither the sole nor even the most important author of the amendment and its passage. Soviet blunders like the education tax, Brezhnev's bungled June 1973 performance in Congress, and the conspicuous harassment of Soviet Jews created an important context for both the launching of Jackson-Vanik and the preservation of public opinion pressures in its favor. In addition, some elements of the Jackson coalition backed the amendment for reasons unrelated to Israel; the AFL-CIO, for example, regarded détente as immoral and imprudent and trade with the Soviet Union as detrimental to American labor.[103] Finally, the activist American Jewish movement to aid Soviet Jews had deep domestic roots. Jackson-Vanik struck a chord with the *American* element of American Jewish identity, as it was well suited to the psychological needs of Vietnam-era America. As Bowker and Williams explain, détente did not sit easily with a people who, at least up until Vietnam, had a sense of exceptionalism and of mission. Vietnam had destroyed the moral certitudes of American life and demolished the myths by which the United States had sustained itself throughout the Cold War. There was a need to fill the vacuum, but the Nixon-Kissinger détente seemed to put nothing in its place beyond a policy of expediency. In contrast, Jackson's Soviet Jewish campaign enabled America to retrieve the moral high ground it had lost in Vietnam[104] and appealed to two pillars of the American self-image: its identity as a "nation of immigrants" and a "redeemer nation." Jackson-Vanik struck a chord also with the *Jewish* element of American Jewish identity, emerging alongside the more general appearance of "identity and victimhood politics" in America.[105] It addressed a multitude of fundamental concerns about the identity and prospects of Jewish life in America, allowing bickering "New Left," liberal, and neoconservative Jews[106] to coalesce around the flag of individual freedoms; providing an opportunity for leaders of dwindling congregations to rejuvenate the community by engaging people in a Jewish solidarity cause;[107] and giving Jews of every stripe a chance to expunge at least some of their deep sense of guilt at American Jewish passivity during the Holocaust by responding actively to Jackson's morally unambiguous clarion call.[108] At a more tactical level, key American Jewish leaders felt compelled to toe the Jackson line because of the senator's dogged insistence[109] and the fear of a schism with their grassroots support base.[110]

Still, Israel's role, if not dominant, was significant. As Lazin writes, "the Israelis encouraged and even manipulated the involvement of American Jews and their organizations" to advance the amendment.[111] The campaign for Soviet Jewry in the West benefited greatly from the steady stream of reliable information on Soviet Jewish conditions provided by Nativ, and Israel's activity was probably decisive in making emigration the priority issue. Absent that activity, appeals to the Kremlin to end discrimination against Soviet Jews and respect their cultural and religious rights might have become the focal points of the campaign.[112] Israel's intervention with American Jewish leaders also helped to shore up the Jackson coalition at such critical junctures as the spring and fall of 1973. Why Israel assumed this role is the subject of the remainder of this chapter.

The Importance of Idealpolitik

In trying to understand what lay behind Israel's Soviet Jewish strategy, it becomes evident that Realpolitik calculations alone are not sufficient to explain the case, although they certainly can account for Israel's official posture of strict neutrality. From the Israeli perspective, open endorsement of Jackson-Vanik would have cast Jerusalem as a meddler in the legislative process of its superpower patron and as an impediment to détente, virtually guaranteeing the alienation of a president who had dramatically increased the scale of the American strategic commitment to Israel.[113] Conversely, siding with Nixon would have infuriated Jackson, not only a staunch supporter whose previous assistance included securing the delivery of F-4 Phantom jets to Israel, but also a presidential hopeful whose bid for the Democratic nomination was covertly supported by Rabin and Dinitz.[114] For the Meir government, engaged in a difficult election campaign during 1973 and then shaken to the core by the October War, the latter option would also have increased its vulnerability to attack from the right-wing opposition at home.[115] Projecting neutrality was a calculated way of navigating these stormy currents and reconciling incongruous policy goals.

The realist approach, however, *cannot* explain why this posture was complemented by hidden-hand intervention on behalf of Jackson-Vanik. Neither can an approach that stresses the primacy of domestic politics. The Israeli leaders and operatives in charge of Soviet Jewish policy, to their considerable credit, consistently withstood the temptation to reveal Israel's hand and score easy points domestically. They realized full well that such an exposure would have run the triple risk of unleashing the administration's wrath, placing American Jews in an untenable position, and provoking Soviet retaliation against Soviet Jews.[116] The Jackson-Vanik episode thus contradicts Kissinger's famous comment that Israeli foreign policy-making is always driven by domestic politics, while substantiating political scientist Aharon Klieman's assertion that Jerusalem often practices a subtle and skillful "diplomacy in the dark."[117]

To a small degree, the discreet Israeli efforts on behalf of Jackson-Vanik are attributable to coincidental factors, including the aforementioned breakdown of the normal chain of command during and immediately after the October War, as well as the simple fact that several champions of Jackson-Vanik happened to wield considerable influence in the Israeli corridors of power. One such figure was the minister without portfolio, Israel Galili, Golda Meir's confidant;[118] another was the prime minister herself. However, as noted by political scientist Shlomo Avineri in the more general context of Israeli Soviet Jewry policy, Israel's commitment to Jackson-Vanik cannot be wholly understood in terms of happenstance but belongs to the realm of fundamental ideological convictions.[119] A blend of mutually reinforcing cognitive and normative-emotional elements rendered the amendment ideologically attractive to Israeli leaders.[120] For the sake of analytical clarity, let us consider each element separately.

The cognitive element pertains to the feasibility of obtaining a steady flow of Jewish emigration from the Soviet Union (which, until 1974, meant the resettlement of most of these Jews in Israel). While Israeli principals valued the instrumental benefits of the potential influx of large numbers of relatively well-educated Soviet Jews—particularly the prospect of strengthening the Jewish demographic majority in the country[121]—purely functional and material calculations did not figure prominently in their commitment. Because Soviet Jewish immigration was deemed a rescue mission, they saw it mainly in ideological terms as a project expressive of the country's very raison d'être.[122] To illustrate, the Israeli and Jewish authorities in charge of immigration policy during the period in question refused to cut immigration numbers to match absorption capacity, despite mounting challenges of economic and social integration.[123]

For several reasons, Jerusalem deemed Jackson-Vanik the best available tool for advancing Soviet Jewish immigration goals. Their reasoning was based on widely held views about the determinants of Moscow's Jewish policy, derived despite the facts that the actual inner workings of the Kremlin remained obscure to both Israelis and Americans.[124] First, Israeli leaders came as early as 1970 to accept the argument of Soviet Jewish dissidents that only a public campaign could protect dissidents from the harshest forms of reprisals.[125] Second, Meir and her principal aides judged Moscow in such dire need of MFN and the other technological and economic benefits of détente as to be willing to liberalize emigration policy substantially.[126] Third and most important, Moscow's bowing to persistent public campaigns in the immediate past—in the aftermath of the 1970–1971 Leningrad trials and during the education tax episode a year later—led Israeli leaders into overconfidence regarding the efficacy of public pressure, to the point where they overlooked the danger that the Jackson-Vanik campaign could trigger a backlash.[127]

Demonstrating the normative and emotional appeal of Jackson-Vanik to Israeli leaders is trickier, since it took place at a less conscious and hence less detectable level. To do so, one has to step back and ponder how the Soviet Jewish saga affected the collective Israeli psyche.[128]

The leap in Soviet Jewish immigration to tens of thousands in 1971–1972 took the Israeli body politic by surprise. Capturing the imagination of Israelis, the development soon emerged in public discourse as an enchanting story that transcended the wheeling and dealing of mundane politics. All the ingredients of a fabled morality play were present, including a dichotomy between oppression in the Soviet Union and redemption in Israel, and victimized heroes experiencing trials and tribulations in the person of Jewish dissidents, or the "Prisoners of Zion," in national parlance. Moreover, the story resonated with Jewish connotations that infused it with psychological relevance and meaning. It invoked parallels with biblical exodus and the deliverance from slavery to freedom, as well as with David's struggle with Goliath. It also reminded people of more recent periods of Jewish helplessness, including that of the Yishuv (the Jewish community in Palestine during the British mandate) in the face of the Holocaust.[129] And it tapped a deep anti-Russian strain quite prevalent among the country's predominately Eastern European-born elite.[130]

Israel's top political echelon fully shared these sentiments. Eban spoke for the whole spectrum of Israeli Zionist parties when he dubbed Soviet Jewish emigration "the most exhilarating and exciting chapter in current Israeli history"[131]—an attitude evident in the prominence of the issue in the secret deliberations of the Knesset's high-profile Security and Foreign Affairs Committee, even in the immediate aftermath of the traumatic 1973 war.[132] Israeli decision-makers embraced Jackson-Vanik precisely because it was consistent, in several important ways, with this epic framing of Soviet Jewish emigration. First, the amendment's assertiveness contrasted with President Franklin Delano Roosevelt's meek response to the Holocaust.[133] Second, its moral clarity conformed to the unambiguous representation of the Soviet Jewry saga. Third, as political scientist Ben Mollov writes, it practiced coercive diplomacy vis-à-vis the Soviet authorities, in the (at least idealized) Jewish tradition of "speaking truth to power."[134] Fourth, it contributed to the fusion of the Jewish and universal human rights causes, by virtue of two factors: the mutual pro-Jackson-Vanik stance of the dissident physicist Andrei Sakharov and the bulk of Soviet Jewish dissidents,[135] and the elevation of a Jewish solidarity issue to the realm of public East-West negotiations. Finally and probably most significantly, support for Jackson-Vanik accorded with the Israeli leadership's understanding of Jewish cultural traditions and reinforced positive notions of Israel's identity and role on the world stage. It featured Israel as a sophisticated and resourceful actor capable of both advancing its national self-interest and pursuing what many regarded as the traditional Jewish mission of serving as "a light unto the nations."[136]

To further bear out the case of the causal effect of these ideas, norms, and emotions, and to show that Israeli leaders were not merely paying lip service to ideological conventions, let us focus briefly on the primary political agent until her resignation in April 1974 and departure from office the following June: prime minister Golda Meir.[137]

Meir chose to open her memoirs with a vivid recollection of herself as a young girl hiding out from a pending Russian pogrom.[138] The evidence suggests that sixty years later, the prime minister still retained a quest for personal and national invulnerability and an instinctive, atavistic distrust of Russian authorities of whatever stripe. For example, she deemed Soviet leaders irrevocably anti-Semitic and held out no hope for a genuine change of heart in the Kremlin with regard to either Soviet Jews or Israel;[139] and, when visiting the White House in 1969, she was delighted at the thought that at that very moment the Soviet foreign minister, Andrei Gromyko, was relegated to meeting Rogers instead of Nixon.[140]

Meir's empathy toward Soviet Jews was intensified by yet another formative emotional encounter: the gathering of large numbers of Soviet Jews to greet her, as Israel's first minister to Moscow, on the Jewish high holidays of 1948, in defiance of the Kremlin's stern warning.[141] During the next twenty years, Israel's inability to pry the Kremlin's doors open to Soviet Jewish emigration generated considerable frustration among Israeli policy-makers, Meir included.[142] For instance, as minister of foreign affairs, she asked the American Jewish establishment to give higher priority to the Soviet Jewry issue.[143] As prime minister, Meir regarded the first signs of Soviet Jewish immigration a miracle second only to the establishment of Israel[144] and privately termed the Soviet Jewish struggle "the campaign of our generation,"[145] a paramount "national mission" worthy of the commitment of every Israeli Jew.[146] On the very eve of the October War, she insisted on setting a personal example by going on a failed mission to convince the Austrian chancellor, Bruno Kreisky, to reopen the Jewish Agency transit camp for Soviet Jews at Schoenau Castle.[147] Finally, in spite of her rapport with Nixon, she did not fully trust the president or his administration to serve as effective guardians of Soviet Jewish interests.[148]

In aggregate, this overview of Meir's ideological and emotional disposition lends credence to Levanon's claim that ultimately the decision to covertly endorse Jackson-Vanik was Meir's own.[149] She agonized over the dilemma the amendment presented to her government and hoped for a compromise between the White House and Congress,[150] but at the end of the day, she endorsed behind-the-scenes support alongside official neutrality.

In sum, Jackson-Vanik was congruent with the basic emotional temperament and ideological goals of Golda Meir and other key Israeli policy-makers. This goes a long way in explaining why the country's leaders embraced the amendment and remained blind to the risk of Jackson-Vanik's overreaching. It also helps us understand why they were shocked by the Soviet repudiation of the trade agreement and by Jackson-Vanik's subsequent failure, at least in the short run, to open the gates of the Soviet Union to Jewish emigration.

In chapter 4, we will consider what this finding—that psychology and ideology were as important as Realpolitik in setting Israel's course—might mean for wider debates among scholars on the determinants of foreign policy. But first, in the coming chapter, we will shift our attention to the Soviet Jewish struggle on the American scene, with a double purpose in mind. First, complement our analysis of how Jackson-Vanik provided a foundation for the "conservative partnership"; and second, through a focus on Kissinger, furnish another example of the salience of ideology and psychology in this context, as Kissinger's failure to block Jackson-Vanik owed much to his hubris and inability to grasp that Jackson-Vanik suited the psychological needs of Vietnam-era America.

3

Kissinger, Soviet Jewish Emigration, and the Demise of Détente

It is an illusion to believe that leaders gain in profundity while they gain experience . . . the convictions that leaders have formed before reaching high office are the intellectual capital they will consume as long as they continue in office. . . . The public life of every political figure is a continual struggle to rescue an element of choice from the pressure of circumstance.

—Henry Kissinger, *White House Years*

This is the sober and uncharacteristically modest lesson Henry Kissinger drew from his attempt to put his conclusions as a historian to the test of reality, but it is hardly self-critical enough as far as his Soviet Jewish emigration record is concerned. Kissinger's actions on this file showed few signs of having been influenced by the insightful prescriptions for sound statecraft he had advanced while in academia. Rescuing little choice from the pressure of circumstance, his conduct saddled the administration with a counterproductive strategy and ended up undermining his most important policy goal, the advancement of détente.

Why did Kissinger fail to follow his insights through to their logical conclusions? In part, he was thwarted by the complications reality always presents to those seeking to implement preconceived designs and by overextension. But at least as salient were more personal factors: his limited ability to adjust to unexpected and challenging decision-making environments, his difficulty listening to the views of domestic advisers and adversaries, and his growing hubris after years of power and what he perceived as foreign policy successes.

As is the case with Israel's strategy on the Soviet Jewish emigration issue, no study has yet made Kissinger's policy in the area its principal concern. This is due in part to the heated polemic between Kissinger and his antagonists, which has blurred the historical picture. But at least as important have been rigid disciplinarian boundaries and a lack of dialogue between scholars operating in different subfields:[1] the literature on Jackson-Vanik concentrates on Congress;[2] the writing on Soviet Jewish emigration tends to emphasize the role of American Jewish lobbies and individuals;[3] the sizeable Kissingerology industry has been preoccupied with the strategic aspects of détente, triangular diplomacy, Vietnam and the Arab-Israeli dispute, as have Nixon studies and general accounts of the administration's foreign policy;[4] and examinations of U.S.-Israeli relations in the 1970s and more specific studies of Israel's place in American domestic politics have generally ignored the Soviet Jewry dimension.[5]

Of course, Kissinger hardly bore exclusive responsibility for the emigration-related deterioration of relations with the Soviet Union, which as we have already seen, he tenaciously sought to avert. That the Soviet Jewish issue exploded in the administration's face was partly due to factors beyond Kissinger's control, such as Watergate and Senator Jackson's inflexibility, the latter fed not only by a genuine sense of mission but also by presidential aspirations and aides who were bent on "educating Kissinger" that the very prospect of compromise would only serve to harden Moscow's stance.[6] Israel, as the previous chapter documents, also played a key role in the behind-the-scenes machinations that built momentum behind Jackson-Vanik and soured relations with Moscow. And the Soviet rulers themselves bore much of the responsibility for an outcome that both they and the White House wanted to avoid. Displaying "mirror imaging," they could not imagine an American President who was not a supreme ruler, believing at least until mid-1973 that Nixon could impose his will on American public opinion, the press, and Congress.[7] For example, when Kissinger sought, during the early stages of MFN discussions, to inform Brezhnev of the necessary legislative steps, Brezhnev retorted: "but you yourselves write the laws, it is for you to change them."[8] On American policy, Moscow applied Marxist dogma, ascribing inflated importance to American economic motives and paying disproportionate attention to business interests.[9] Moreover, Soviet representatives often behaved boorishly, losing ground in Congress and the public at large by making intimidating comments and employing anti-Semitic innuendo.[10] To all appearances, the Kremlin took little advantage of Soviet ambassador Anatoly Dobrynin's subtler grasp of American policy currents.[11]

Nonetheless, the fact that Kissinger was not the sole author of the clumsy domestic and international politics that marked the Soviet Jewish emigration debate does not negate the importance of his role. Dominant by nature and design, Kissinger's standing as Nixon's principal foreign policy aide and a key architect of détente meant that his imprint on the Soviet

Jewish emigration policy's conceptualization, implementation, and outcome was very significant.

In the coming pages, we will seek—in line with historian Philip Zelikow's advice—to judge Kissinger not so much by policy outcomes, but rather in terms of the degree to which this historically conscious actor succeeded in following his own model of statesmanship.[12] In addition, we will identify factors shaping Kissinger's behavior, assessing their relative significance and considering what could have been done differently, given contemporaneous circumstances.

Kissinger the Scholar's Advice to the Statesman

Few policy-makers came to power more preoccupied than Kissinger with the challenge of mastering the environment. This seasoned student of Metternich, Castlereagh, and Bismarck had been, in his academic career, palpably torn between, on the one hand, a nearly romantic belief in the inspired statesman's capacity to shape history by transcending both circumstance and conventional wisdom and, on the other hand, a realization that happenstance often makes a mockery of even the most finely calibrated policy.[13]

To reconcile these convictions, Kissinger developed recommendations aimed at rendering the policy realm more predictable and thus, more susceptible to the statesman's creativity. Leaders, he asserted, must develop a clear sense of direction informed by a vision and a profound yet agile conceptualization of the factors and forces at play.[14] This "philosophical deepening," sorely lacking in the American foreign policy tradition in Kissinger's judgment,[15] would provide a compass for the ship of state. This, however, was not enough. To reach the destinations pointed toward by the compass, Kissinger stressed, required that the captains of the state steer the course with imagination, flexibility, and prudence.

Drawing upon these precepts, Kissinger peppered his analyses of past and contemporary statesmen with a recurrent set of cautionary guidelines for the practitioner of international diplomacy. As early as his undergraduate thesis, he admonished leaders that "freedom derives . . . from a recognition of limits" of their country's power as well as their own.[16] Sober perspective is key to the fulfillment of vital tasks in the diplomatic game: "Mastery in adapting to the requirements of the moment,"[17] timely discernment of both opportunities to exploit and risks to avoid, and keeping a range of alternatives open as a means of adjusting to the unpredictable.[18]

Kissinger's model of statecraft, especially his "doctrine of limits,"[19] evinced considerable reflection and sophistication—though that sophistication was not always sufficient to fully eliminate tensions between some of his core tenets. Notably, he postulated that only when the major powers share an adherence to some basic "rules" of the *international* game—the most important of which is strict noninterference in one another's domestic affairs—can international stability obtain,[20] but also maintained that in order to garner the necessary domestic support, a policy must be broadly congruent with the "*national* experience."[21] Such tensions notwithstanding, Kissinger arrived on the scene of Soviet Jewish emigration policy equipped with complex insights into the sorts of problems he was to encounter.

It is tempting to read Kissinger's prescriptions as, in part, an exercise in anticipatory self-restraint; sometimes, it almost seems as if Kissinger the scholar foresaw, and sought to check, certain patterns of behavior that would characterize Kissinger the leader. The apostle of international stability as the ultimate guarantor against nuclear destruction acknowledged that "the statesman is confronted with what must always upset his calculations: that it is not balance which inspires men but universality, not safety but immortality."[22] The architect of centralized foreign policy-making was attentive to the fragility of structures dependent on individuals.[23] The policy-maker who later publicly dismissed as illegitimate any Soviet Jewish emigration policy course but his own[24] faulted Bismarck for not comprehending that the requirements of the national interest are often ambiguous and "statesmen might differ in understanding [these requirements]."[25] The elitist expert-turned-statesman termed domestic legitimacy, in one of his most familiar maxims, the "acid test" of a policy[26] and urged leaders to contemplate timely political concessions in order to protect the social sphere[27] and harmonize their vision with the people's experience:[28] in Kissinger's words, "if the sweep of [the statesman]'s conceptions exceeds the capacity of his environment to absorb them, he will fail regardless of the validity of his insights."[29]

Kissinger the Statesman's Early Behavior

With respect to the Soviet Jewish emigration issue, Kissinger the senior official diverged from Kissinger the scholar's advice from early in his tenure. True, he still suggests otherwise: in a recent assessment in *Diplomacy* of the administration's record, he echoes his idealized notion of carefully conceived policy, writing that "as a diplomatic subject, the issue of Jewish emigration from the Soviet Union had been the brainchild of the Nixon Administration."[30] Archival evidence, however, flies in the face of this assertion, unmasking it as possibly disingenuous and certainly self-serving and inaccurate. The first three years of the Nixon presidency actually saw a reactive, reluctant administration that treated Soviet Jewish emigration in ad hoc fashion and addressed it only because of conspicuous anti-Semitism in the Soviet Union and growing domestic concern.[31]

To be sure, as far as 1969 and 1970 are concerned, extenuating circumstances go a long way to explaining why the Soviet Jewish question received little executive attention. Prior to 1969, the issue was hardly on the agenda of U.S.-Soviet relations, though American principals, beginning with some in the Eisenhower administration, including Nixon, did raise it with the Kremlin on a few occasions, and awareness of it within the foreign policy bureaucracy was slowly growing.[32] Squeaking into office with the barest of pluralities, facing Democratic control of both houses of Congress, and seeking to articulate a new policy in a time of deep national crisis,[33] the Nixon team was bound to set its sights elsewhere. As we have seen, it was only in the closing months of 1970 that the dramatic Leningrad trials catapulted the plight of Soviet Jews into the international limelight[34] and by that point, Vietnam had sapped much of the Nixon team's attention and energies. As Richard Melanson and others remind us, any scrutiny of the administration's record must acknowledge just how draining was the challenge of confronting simultaneously a bloody war abroad and a society in turmoil at home.[35]

In terms of the substance of policy, the executive's early reticence is also partly understandable. Throughout this period, virtually no observer anticipated the subsequent emergence of the Soviet Jewish emigration question to the center stage of superpower diplomacy and, of course, Israel and American Jewish leaders were themselves hewing to a low-key approach.[36] These constraints, however, were not so overwhelming as to predetermine the administration's policy. Kissinger's hand was apparent in charting a course of avoidance and delay. As early as mid-1969, Nixon's overburdened national security adviser did acknowledge the problem of Soviet Jewish oppression, if not its depth, though his shortsightedness on the latter count can be attributed in part to inadequate CIA and State Department reports.[37] But Kissinger's partial awareness only served to buttress his efforts to contain the political and diplomatic importance of the issue, and by the end of the year, he had explicitly declined to commit the administration to the principal of freedom of emigration from the Soviet Union. Obviously seeking to retain latitude, this policy reflected Kissinger's conviction that the norm of noninterference applies most fully to superpowers like the Soviet Union.[38]

More personal factors were also involved. Sporadic tête-à-tête discussions in the oval office suggest that at one level, the topic irked Kissinger because it placed him in a precarious situation with Nixon.[39] Attaining his predominant decision-making position in fits and starts and rather dependent on Nixon's favor,[40] the national security adviser was, as we saw in chapter 1, worried that competitors for bureaucratic influence might take advantage of any policies that could be construed as too pro-Jewish to undermine his standing with the president. This sensitivity contributed to Kissinger's determination to minimize contacts with Jewish leaders and take a lead role on "Jewish issues" such as Soviet Jewish emigration. Also salient were Middle East policy calculations. Kissinger shrewdly predicted that the Soviet Jewish problem might evolve into a rallying point for American Jews. Significant presidential involvement on behalf of Soviet Jews would run the risk, he warned, of drawing Moscow and the Arabs closer together and tying the administration's hands in the Middle East, without bringing about a Jewish exodus from the Soviet Union.[41]

Several early measures Kissinger took in the general Soviet policy sphere also deeply affected the administration's posture on the Jewish emigration issue. Intent on keeping a tight grip on the threads of policy, alongside Nixon, Kissinger minimized the involvement of Nixon's liaison to the Jewish community, Leonard Garment, and some State Department officials, such as under secretary of state for political affairs U. Alexis Johnson. This reduced prospects for a full airing of policy options, since Garment and, to a lesser extent, Johnson, contemplated a forthright broaching of the Soviet Jewish question with Moscow.[42] As early as the first months of 1969, Kissinger also established the secret back channel with Moscow, through which he assured Moscow of the administration's acceptance of Soviet predominance in Eastern Europe, notwithstanding "isolated critical public comments" made for domestic political reasons. The Kremlin, in all probability, concluded that Washington could be relied upon to steer equally clear of what it regarded a sensitive domestic issue, the Jewish question.[43]

Compounding the effect of these measures were, by mid-1971, Kissinger's emerging propensity to underrate the impact of the Soviet Jewish problem on domestic public opinion (revealing, again, a gap between astute theoretical insights and blind spots in practice). Although the impact on public opinion of the Leningrad trials did not go unnoticed by figures such as Garment and Representative Gerald Ford,[44] Kissinger, along with his bitter rival, Rogers, and Nixon himself, preferred to downplay the issue. Despite his efforts behind the scenes to get the Leningrad death sentences commuted, Kissinger continued to dismiss the Soviet Jewish question as subordinate to matters of high politics as the prospects of triangular diplomacy and détente loomed on the horizon. Congressional, Jewish, and general public displays of discontent with what was perceived as executive indifference failed to incite the national security adviser to earnestly take the matter up with Moscow.[45]

Thus, in part deliberately and in part unintentionally, Kissinger's conduct at this early stage restricted the range of options available to the administration. Leaving a vacuum, it also invited Congress and interested lobbies to intervene.

Raising Expectations and Underestimating the Threat of Jackson-Vanik

The next two years, through April 1973, were the heyday of détente. The relationship with the Soviet Union, domestic support, and the popularity and leverage of the Nixon-Kissinger team all peaked. The same period represented a second, crucial phase in Kissinger's handling of the Soviet Jewish question. Kissinger could have utilized the dividends of détente to at least partly defuse the issue. But he fumbled, ignoring some of his own key maxims. Through the 1972 elections, instead of prudence, the administration fomented a "crisis of rising expectations," both within the ranks of the Soviet Jewish emigration movement and in Moscow. And the months thereafter were, in historian Paula Stern's apt phrase, "a period of malign neglect"[46]—just the opposite of the carefully calibrated action advocated by Kissinger the scholar.

Let us examine the domestic front first. It is true that, as the May 1972 summit with Soviet leaders approached, Nixon and Kissinger worried in private about the possibility that the public's expectations would spiral out of control, both regarding the general gamut of superpower relations and the specific topic of Soviet Jewish emigration.[47] It is also true that it was Nixon rather than Kissinger who employed such hyperbole as "a full generation of peace"[48] and who behaved publicly in such a fashion as to leave Jewish audiences with the impression that the president would use his good offices in Moscow to improve the lot of Soviet Jews.[49] The temptation to oversell détente for short-term electoral gain, it seems, overcame Nixon's judiciousness as well as his gut distrust of the Jewish voter and the media's (and his own) previously dismissive attitude toward the notion that Jews might support Republican candidates.[50] In the end, however, the Soviet Union's decision to levy the August 1972 education tax on would-be immigrants made a mockery of any professed advances the Nixon administration was making on the Soviet Jewish emigration front. The whole episode cost Nixon, and Kissinger especially, some points with the Jewish community, although it obviously prevented neither Nixon's improved electoral showing in this sector nor his landslide victory.[51]

The most lasting effect of the episode was, of course, the introduction of Jackson's amendment, with all that followed. In some respects, the administration had fostered its own vulnerability on this front. First, Jackson did not invent the idea of trade "linkage," but merely transformed a notion devised by the administration itself.[52] Second, Kissinger himself conceded in 1975 that when Nixon negotiated the trade agreement in 1972, the Soviets "were never even told there was a possibility of congressional difficulty."[53] Third, Nixon and Kissinger's attempt to alert the Soviets to the adverse domestic ramifications of the exit tax was short-lived, prompted less by concern over the fate of détente than by urgent American Jewish and Israeli appeals and the drive to defeat McGovern.[54] Thereafter, Nixon and Kissinger's interest dwindled noticeably, as they mistakenly believed the matter would fade away with the passing of the election season.[55] As Stern argues, Nixon and Kissinger thus missed a crucial opportunity to take advantage of détente's popularity and Nixon's huge mandate to derail the Jackson amendment.[56]

The documentation suggests that Kissinger's downplaying of the issue at this point was partly intentional. Consistently emphasizing Moscow's status sensitivity, he was convinced that the best chance of Soviet backtracking on the exit tax lay in giving the Soviets "some months to dig out . . . if there is a confrontation they cannot possibly yield to what they see as interference in their domestic affairs."[57] Nonetheless, much of Kissinger's conduct is attributable more to overextension and ineptitude than design. During this period, Nixon and Kissinger were so preoccupied with the Vietnam Paris peace talks that they simply neglected other subjects. Somewhat less well recognized is the dynamic set in motion by an extended period of power. Kissinger's growing arrogance was plainly evident in his notorious November 1972 "lone cowboy" interview with Oriana Fallaci.[58] The celebrated architect of détente was in a euphoric state of mind that hampered his judgment. Consequently, he failed to heed advance warnings about congressional agitation, was surprised when a senator hijacked his instrument of manipulating trade incentives to shape Soviet behavior, and was dismayed by its application in the personally discomfiting context of Soviet Jewry.[59] The occasional perceptive assessment notwithstanding,[60] Kissinger remained more sanguine than many Nixon aides about the Jackson challenge, partly because he was swept up in the administration's success, partly because of his innate disdain of Congress, and partly because, at that point, he still viewed Soviet Jewish emigration as a marginal issue that could not possibly develop into a major impediment to such a grand design as détente.[61]

Hubris was also manifest in one of Kissinger's most significant missteps: consistent exaggeration, with his Soviet interlocutors, of the executive's capacity to override Congress and deliver the MFN status pledged in the 1972 trade agreement. One may certainly empathize with the delicate balancing act Kissinger was forced to perform in this context, since exuding confidence in the political viability of an agreement comprises an indispensable instrument in the diplomat's toolkit. But Kissinger overplayed his hand. Sensitive to Moscow's growing concern about Jackson-Vanik, but trapped by his own rhetoric and probably unable to seriously contemplate the amendment's passage, he kept reassuring the Kremlin through March 1974, by which point doubt had long since surfaced in the minds of his aides, Soviet counterparts, and the embattled president himself.[62] By committing himself so completely to the defeat of Jackson-

Vanik, Kissinger risked the administration's credibility, as well as his own, well beyond the point of necessity.[63]

The Unsuccessful Fight against the Amendment

The third stage, the year following April 1973, saw Kissinger succumbing more and more to the temptation of risking the long-term prospects of détente for short-term gain. What little remained of the administration's Soviet Jewish policy latitude did not survive the pressure cooker of Watergate and the October War.

By April 1973, when Nixon sent Congress the Trade Reform Act and Jackson and seventy-six other senators reattached the Jackson amendment to it, the administration could no longer be accused of ignoring the amendment. Nixon and Kissinger launched a determined campaign to win American public opinion over to the logic of quiet diplomacy.[64] They failed, partly because their increasingly intense efforts behind closed doors to affect Soviet practices failed to produce visible results,[65] and partly because of several self-defeating behaviors. First, they adopted heavy-handed methods in an attempt to split the Jewish community, achieving little but the antagonism of important Jewish leaders.[66] Second, rather than dealing with Jackson directly, Nixon and Kissinger operated through some "losing horses" like Max Fisher, a well-known Nixon hand who was ultimately found to exert little influence on the Jewish rank-and-file,[67] and Ambassador Dinitz, who as we have seen was destined to be eclipsed, on the Soviet Jewish policy scene in the United States, by Nativ's largely pro-Jackson officials.[68] Third, Kissinger did not translate his perceptive grasp of the requirements of the moment into practice. For example, on 2 August 1973, Kissinger reiterated his "acid test": "No foreign policy—no matter how ingenious," he said, "has any chance of success if it is born in the minds of a few and carried in the hearts of none."[69] In his first major address as secretary of state, five weeks later, Kissinger further observed that "the need for national dialogue has never been more urgent."[70] However, his insinuations on the same occasion that the Jackson forces were pursuing a shallow and dangerous policy revealed Kissinger's inability to actually engage in a substantive, respectful dialogue and win domestic support through persuasion.[71] Ironically, this attitude repeated one of the faults Kissinger had earlier identified in Bismarck's behavior. More importantly, it was viewed by key opinion-makers as vindicating the charges of imperial callousness and dubious morality that had begun to shadow the Nixon team.[72]

When the October War broke out, Kissinger's skills as a diplomat-statesman were severely tested. Hardly an experienced player on the

Middle East arena[73] and largely left to his own devices by a besieged president, Kissinger found himself overseeing a web of high-risk, interrelated games that required a delicate equilibrium between contradictory policy objectives. Kissinger's challenges were extremely complicated: how to effect a military stalemate that would render the Middle East ripe for diplomacy. How to exclude Moscow from the area and preserve détente. How to convince the oil-rich Arab states that relying on Soviet patronage would lead them nowhere, while simultaneously safeguarding Israel's security and making Jerusalem see the benefit of negotiated settlement. How to refute Jackson's double indictment that, first, Moscow's conduct prior to and during the war demonstrated the pointlessness of détente, and, second, that détente had worked to Israel's disadvantage. Kissinger scored unevenly on the first three challenges and suffered a serious setback on the last.

To a considerable extent, Kissinger's wounds on the home front were self-inflicted. Granted, as Isaacson compellingly demonstrates, the week-long delay in the provision of military resupplies to Israel was only partially traceable to Kissinger's office.[74] Yet the secretary's maneuvers, shrewdly leaked to the press by Jackson, sufficed to tarnish his image in the eyes of key Jewish leaders.[75] His attempt to strike a package deal around Jackson-Vanik added insult to injury. Kissinger may well have been as sincerely concerned about Israel's fate as he was determined to pursue détente and secure American dominance in the Middle East.[76] By this stage, however, many Jewish leaders did not trust him, which helps explain the equivocation of the National Conference on Soviet Jewry and the Jewish leadership's ultimate retreat from the deal. The distrust also helped Jackson win new recruits for his assault on détente, notably Jewish neoconservatives such as Norman Podhoretz.[77]

From late 1973, then, Kissinger was perceived as an honest broker by neither important American Jewish leaders nor Kremlin influentials. The squandering of this asset weakened his hand when, a few months later, he embarked on negotiations aimed at finding a compromise that would satisfy both Jackson and Moscow—negotiations that seemed to meet success but collapsed by late 1974.[78] The failure to secure an agreement was in large part due to Soviet behavior. Generous gestures on the Kremlin's part might still have swayed public sentiment in the United States away from condemnation and toward endorsement of compromise. Instead, despite appeals by the administration, and Brezhnev's half-hearted willingness to respond, the Soviets committed heavy-handed blunders that contributed substantially to the undermining of domestic support for détente in the United States. They dragged their feet regarding Soviet Jewish hardship cases,[79] and they continued to visibly harass Soviet Jews, as well as high-profile dissidents like celebrated author

Alexander Solzhenitsyn and Sakharov. Such actions naturally facilitated the drive of both Henry Jackson and prominent Jewish and non-Jewish Soviet dissidents to couch Soviet Jewish policy in the general context of human rights violations. Most influential was a public letter Sakharov penned to the United States Congress, drawing a tight connection between the repression in the Soviet Union and the importance of the Jackson amendment, which he endorsed. Soon, liberal groups that heretofore had supported détente and objected to trade restrictions with the Soviet Union reversed course and an increasingly isolated administration was thrown on the defensive. This agitated climate of opinion guaranteed that the Soviet Jewish issue would remain entangled in the fierce political battles that surrounded Nixon's waning months in office.[80]

The Jackson team undermined the negotiations by often pursuing a relatively rigid line that key American Jewish leaders felt compelled to toe.[81] The senator himself, as his otherwise sympathetic biographer concedes, was inflexible and could or would not listen to the doubts even hard-line Sovietologists expressed about the utility of his approach.[82] Most questionable was Jackson's tendency to trumpet in the spotlight sensitive aspects of the dialogue with Kissinger,[83] as well as Soviet concessions secured in confidential discussions. A conspicuous example of the latter came at the very moment that a deal finally seemed all but sealed. On 18 October 1974, Jackson arrived at the White House to exchange with Kissinger letters that stipulated the terms of the deal. Controlling the later meeting with the press, Jackson referred to the agreement as a "historic understanding in the era of human rights" and implied that the Soviets had capitulated to a campaign he had been waging. He even drew specific attention to a figure of annual Soviet Jewish emigration (60,000) never officially approved by Moscow. Humiliating Moscow further, he defied the clear Soviet objection to an official release of the letters.[84] Such behavior may have merely reflected intoxication in the moment of victory, but may also be interpreted, as Kissinger and others have since contended, as proof that Jackson, seeking an issue to promote his presidential aspirations rather than a solution, had all along been negotiating in bad faith.[85] In sum, while the evidence at hand casts no doubt on Jackson's genuine and passionate commitment to the Soviet Jewish cause, it does portray him as resembling Kissinger in one crucial sense—having trouble subordinating personal ambition to the goal of securing a workable solution to the Soviet Jewish problem.

Yet, whatever role Moscow and Jackson played in the breakdown of negotiations, mediator Kissinger must also be held partly accountable. Three principal flaws in his strategy stand out. First, a whole year elapsed between the administration's launching of an active campaign to block Jackson-Vanik (April 1973) and the initiation of an ongoing dialogue between Kissinger and Jackson (March 1974). The delay was consequential, if only because the negotiations started in earnest when the drama of Nixon's downfall was written on the wall and was bound to dominate any policy maneuver in Washington. The summer of 1973 saw Kissinger reluctant to face the strong-willed Jackson.[86] Only after Nixon prodded him directly did Kissinger approach the senator,[87] but that overture was cut short by the October War, which sparked a heated controversy between the two men about the morality of détente, as well as leading to an American nuclear alert, in the wake of which Jackson publicly taunted Moscow. This behavior caused Kissinger to conclude that the senator could not be trusted to remain discreet in the Soviet context.[88] For months thereafter, Kissinger procrastinated, despite repeated advice by subordinates that only his personal involvement could moderate Jackson's (and hence, the Jewish community's) position and advance the legislative process—or, failing that, at least refute "future complaints" that the secretary's evasion of Jackson had undermined the prospects for striking an emigration-trade deal.[89]

Second, if Kissinger's suspicion of Jackson on the grounds of diplomatic indiscretion is somewhat understandable, not so Kissinger's excessive resort to a devious divide-and-rule tactic once the negotiations got underway. He portrayed Jackson to the Israelis as disingenuous. He exerted (via Max Fisher) pressure on Jackson through an appeal to the Washingtonian's Jewish financial backers. He sought to isolate Jackson from his Jewish base and from like-minded Jewish senators.[90] Jackson felt cornered and responded in kind.[91] Kissinger's maneuvers backfired, eroding whatever confidence existed between the senator and the administration.[92] An adversarial relationship developed between the Kissinger and Jackson teams,[93] as well as between the two men. By August 1974, as his involvement in the mediation effort intensified to the point of consuming much of his time, Kissinger confessed to his aides: "The more I see Scoop the less I like him . . . I used to like him a lot."[94] The whole affair suggests that Kissinger was less adept a diplomat at home than abroad. Partly because of his arrogant maltreatment of Jackson, the negotiations deteriorated into a struggle to score points between two bitterly suspicious rivals.

Third, the apologetic tone that consistently permeated Kissinger's broaching of the Soviet Jewish issue with his Soviet interlocutors misled Moscow, compounding the Kremlin rulers' own inability to accurately gauge the wave of anti-Soviet sentiment in American public opinion that their Soviet Jewish practices helped foment.[95] Kissinger should have presented a more forthright picture of American opinion trends to Moscow. While certainly not music to Moscow's ears, it could have increased the prospects of ultimate compromise by nudging Brezhnev to intensify efforts to end harassment.

Kissinger's apologetic tone stemmed from a profound belief in the primacy of sovereignty, recognition of Moscow's acute concern with saving face, as well as from some impatience with the growing success of Soviet dissidents in communicating their case effectively to the American people.[96] It did *not* reflect disregard for the turning of domestic opinion against him. Kissinger *was* becoming painfully aware of his failure to pass his own "acid test." This was not for the lack of trying: from mid-1973 onward, he sought to educate Americans about the need to reject Jackson-Vanik, by way of delivering eloquent public speeches and granting background briefings to a few reporters of choice.[97] To no avail: the polls demonstrated that the man in the street consistently sided with Jackson. Congress was echoing the voice of the people.[98]

At the end of the day, as efforts to strike a deal collapsed, relations with Moscow chilled, and Jackson's amendment became law, Kissinger the Statesman might, were he sufficiently reflective, have detected an air of disappointment from Kissinger the Scholar.

Explaining Kissinger's Failure

The sources of Kissinger's failure to legitimize his Soviet Jewish policy with American Jews and the general public merit close consideration, for they go to the heart of Kissinger's role in détente's demise. While Kissinger's domestic difficulty has been extensively investigated in the literature,[99] it is still worth exploring the roots of this particular difficulty. More than the October War drove Kissinger and the Jewish community apart. Tensions derived also from the fact that they drew sharply divergent lessons from the Holocaust. Kissinger's firsthand encounter with Hitler's Germany triggered a life-long pursuit of international stability as a remedy against catastrophe. Given a choice of order or justice, he often said, he would choose order.[100] Conversely, a deep sense of guilt at an ineffectual "cacophony of voices" in Roosevelt's days drove the otherwise pluralistic Jewish community as one toward the Soviet Jewry movement and Jackson's clear-cut solution.[101] Aggravating this split was Nixon's attempt to realign American politics by forging a "majority of the resentful." As Richard Melanson argues, this divisive and confrontational strategy backfired, since it antagonized "elitist" opinion-shapers who might otherwise have been strong supporters of détente.[102] Among Jewish leaders in particular—some of whom sensed anti-Semitic hints in Nixon's anti-elitist messages—the result was guardedness, if not outright antipathy, toward the administration's Soviet policies.

Why did Jackson-Vanik strike a chord with the American people at large? From the time of the events to the mid-1990s, Kissinger conveniently argued this was nothing but a historical accident (in his words, an "eclipse of the sun") occasioned by the ambitious Jackson's shrewd exploitation of Watergate and sustained by a typically shallow American

understanding of international affairs. Even with his later acknowledgment that détente was ill-suited to the psychological needs of Vietnam-
era America, it is not clear that Kissinger has ever fully understood the
nature of the domestic equation.[103] The problem was not simply an un-
fortunate political configuration, or a lack of sophistication in the audience, even though these factors played a role. As we saw in chapter 2, the
Soviet Jewish campaign enabled Americans to regain a sense of moral purpose lost in the jungles of Vietnam and the compromises of détente.
Kissinger's championing of "unsentimental" policy-making made it hard
for him to appreciate this psychological dimension of the campaign.

What could Kissinger have done differently? Recent archival disclosures substantiate some familiar criticisms of Kissinger's conduct on the
domestic front. As Robert Schulzinger once observed, Kissinger was "out
of touch with the way modern democratic states conduct their diplomacy."[104] He should have anticipated that in a pluralistic political system, "linkage" would be difficult to control once unleashed. He could
have devised a more inclusive modus operandi.[105] While centralization
and secrecy may have minimized leaks and increased cohesion, they also
meant that the president and his senior foreign policy adviser were given
not only sole credit but also sole burden for U.S.-Soviet relations. By iso-
lating themselves from the bureaucracy and Congress, Nixon and
Kissinger overstretched themselves and missed opportunities to acquire a
subtler sense of the broad decision-making context. Several illustrations
of potentially avoidable mistakes demonstrate the severity of this problem.
At a critical juncture in early 1973, Nixon and Kissinger overlooked the
sound advice of Kissinger aide Helmut Sonnenfeldt and State Department
officials to alert Moscow to the extent to which the exit tax was fanning
anti-Soviet sentiment in the United States.[106] They also failed to delegate
substantive negotiating authority to such a capable emissary as secretary
of the treasury George P. Shultz.[107] Later, Kissinger decided to keep secret Soviet minister of foreign affairs Andrei A. Gromyko's 26 October
1974 rejection of the Kissinger-Soviet-Jackson deal, exposing himself to
charges of deception[108] and, as Kissinger later acknowledged, leading congressional leaders, including Jackson, to the false impression that Moscow
would eventually yield more ground if Congress kept pressing.[109] Finally,
Kissinger disregarded warnings from others in the administration and consequently, in late 1974, was caught by surprise when the Soviets—angered
by the Stevenson amendment's ceiling of $300 million over four years on
new export-import bank credit commitments to Moscow—suspended
negotiations on the emigration-trade deal.[110]

Also missed were opportunities for domestic coalition building. If,
for example, he had properly consulted potential allies such as Ways and
Means chairman Wilbur Mills, the president's trade representative

William Eberle, or the State Department's chief liaison with Congress, A. Linwood Holton regarding the trade negotiations with Moscow, they might have done more to counter Jackson-Vanik.[111] Instead, Kissinger not only methodically excluded State Department officials,[112] but also kept even his own aide, Sonnenfeldt, partly in the dark.[113] As well, the projection of greater empathy toward Jackson's concerns and those of the Jewish community could have done much to mitigate the polarization that ensued and might even have left room for domestic compromise and the partial disentangling of the emigration issue from détente. Finally, Kissinger (and Nixon) could have been much more attentive to the risk that a culture of suspicion and Byzantine infighting at the top would erode the procedural legitimacy of détente, which would in turn undermine the strategy's substantive legitimacy.[114]

Why did a statesman who arrived in office with such an impressive intellectual arsenal—a realization that power was finite and that creativity was required to make it productive, an intuitive sense of the pitfalls of hubris, a recognition of his own limits in understanding what "can be sold to the American people"[115]—fail, in the Soviet Jewish policy sphere, to follow these insights through to their logical conclusions, and instead end up practicing what historian Ronald W. Pruessen has termed "intellectual brinkmanship"?[116] Although he was partly thwarted by the obstacles reality inevitably throws in the way of those seeking to implement preconceived designs and by simple overextension, at least as salient was his vulnerability to what he himself once called the "aphrodisiac of power." Brimming with confidence after the breakthroughs of 1972, Kissinger's bad habits grew worse.[117] Never lacking in vanity or manipulativeness, he increasingly neglected his own doctrine of limits and adaptability in favor of a more aggressive, rigid, and egocentric approach. More and more, he limited foreign policy influence to a chosen few, exuded disdain for domestic politics as a separate and inferior sphere, adhered strictly to the notion that sovereignty is the sole proper organizing principle of international life, and endorsed the view that the exalted ends of foreign policy justify the application of foul means. The gathering clouds of Watergate and the October War only accelerated Kissinger's retreat into isolation and arrogance. This was certainly evident in the domain of Soviet Jewish emigration policy, where Kissinger's inflexibility and machinations not only undermined his ability to serve as an honest broker, but even frustrated such an eminent realist as Hans Morgenthau.[118]

Eventually, what Kissinger regarded as the debacle of Jackson-Vanik's passage did prompt him to pay greater attention to domestic currents and lobbies, as well as place human rights on the American foreign policy agenda.[119] But this was too little, too late. As Kissinger himself once noted, a statesman cannot hoard opportunities for use at a later date. The foundations of détente in Washington *and* Moscow were already unraveling. Of course, the Soviet Jewish policy tangle was but one of a complex web of developments that led to the demise of détente. Of particular import were a string of policies Moscow pursued in the Middle East: the massive air supply operation of military hardware to the Arab belligerents during the war (that preceded and largely triggered the American airlift of supplies to Israel); defense minister Andrei Grechko's depiction of the war, two days after the Arabs had launched a surprise attack, as proof of the aggressive nature of imperialism; and, in the aftermath of war, Moscow's cheering up of the Arab oil embargo and increased backing of radical Arab regimes. These policies projected a confrontational stance that placed the supporters of détente in the United States on the defensive.[120]

Yet, the dynamic that developed between Moscow and Washington around the Soviet Jewish struggle clearly served to undercut the support base for détente in both countries. Much as the continued harassment of Jews provided fuel for the conservative campaign against détente in the United States, the administration's fumbling around the Soviet Jewish emigration question allowed ideological conservatives within the Soviet apparatus to argue that rapprochement with the West was dangerous for the regime, since it allowed the United States a Trojan horse inside Soviet society.[121]

True, that question had presented Kissinger with difficult policy dilemmas: how to walk the tightrope between irritable Kremlin leaders, agitated American Jews, and lurking political rivals. How to reconcile the contradiction inherent in the task of securing *public* support for *quiet* diplomacy. How to strike a balance between the imperatives of sovereignty, human rights, and reducing the risk of nuclear catastrophe. How to integrate the emigration issue into larger and more complex policy puzzles, particularly the MidEast and superpower relations. These dilemmas would have tested the resourcefulness of any policy-maker, and Kissinger, by late 1973, had to cope with them during a time of social turmoil at home and darkening horizons abroad. But these caveats are not excuses. Kissinger's inability to adjust to the ascendancy of a nontraditional question, his failure to secure choice from circumstances, and his practice of "intellectual brinkmanship"—all in contrast to his earlier advice to statesmen—made a bad situation worse. With his well-established tendency to talk about limits in theory but ignore them in practice aggravated by a growing conceit, the architect of détente misperceived and mishandled an issue that, to his surprise, had enough resonance to hasten the end of détente itself.[122]

The tragic phenomenon of an incisive intellect overpowered by ambition and pride is by no means unique to Kissinger; indeed, it is a common human response to the possession of great power. The Kissinger example does provide an important cautionary note: whatever their other qualities, there seems to be little in the training of political scientists or historians that automatically equips them to resist the effects of power, provide clear-headed advice to the prince, or even become effective princes themselves. It is with an eye to broader lessons of this sort that we shift our focus back from the Soviet Jewry policy game to the broad tapestry of American-Israeli relations.

4

Nixon's Final Months, the Legacy of the Period, and the Lessons of the Case

At this point in the discussion, it is imperative to conclude the storyline by systematically examining the nature of the bilateral dialogue in the aftermath of the October War. The American-Israeli relationship chilled appreciably during Nixon's last months in office. This was partly due to the pressure cooker of the October War, as both sides felt that coordination and mutual consideration left much to be desired.

Of course, Golda Meir and her colleagues felt very much indebted to Nixon personally for the airlift of supplies.[1] Their gratitude did not extend to Kissinger, however, whom they suspected of stalling the airlift in order to avert a decisive Israeli victory and thus improve the prospects of a diplomatic settlement under American sponsorship after the war—a suspicion Nixon did little to refute.[2] Moreover, Israel's political and military leadership deeply resented the American drive during the last days of the war to salvage the Egyptian Third Army. From their perspective, this move not only deprived Israel of the possibility of victory; it also betokened insensitivity to the trauma the Israeli society experienced and to the sacrifice the Israeli leadership had made by discretely complying, on the eve of war, with the American demand not to preempt.[3]

The Israeli frustration over perceived ingratitude was reciprocated by the president and his secretary of state. Nixon and Kissinger felt the Israelis took for granted both their declaration of a nuclear alert as a means of checking possible unilateral Soviet military intervention in the war and their resistance to the Arab oil boycott. On a more personal level, Kissinger believed that the undermining of Israeli (and American Jewish) trust in him on account of his conduct during the war was unwarranted. After all, he was not only the key figure behind the nuclear alert, and bought Israel time to

67

complete the encirclement of the Egyptian Third Army, but he also ignored Nixon's instruction during the last days of the war to sound out Brezhnev about an imposed superpower settlement of the Arab-Israeli conflict.[4]

Kissinger's shuttle diplomacy only intensified the mutual frictions born of the war, as Israeli and American policy-makers parted over their objectives in the disengagement process. The Israeli leaders sought a consolidation of the ceasefire and the repatriation of Israel's prisoners of war. They could hardly, however, swallow any broader settlement that involved cessation of territory and signaled political compromise. The ordeal of the war deeply undermined the capacity of the Labor Party to govern, slashing the size of its parliamentary coalition, eroding its popular legitimacy and rendering the party's leaders too paralyzed to endorse any bold diplomatic initiatives.[5] Meir was too immersed in unflinching hatred of the enemy, guilt over the failure to anticipate the surprise attack, and bewilderment in the wake of mounting domestic pressure on her to accept responsibility and resign.[6] Her relatively inexperienced successor, Rabin, was also soon immobilized. He was hamstrung by the mere one-vote margin his cabinet enjoyed in the Knesset, by the disintegration of the party's veteran leadership, by the economic dislocations caused by the war, by the loss of popular faith in government, and, finally, by a perpetual need to assert authority within his own party over formidable rivals.[7]

Israel's reticence, however, ran counter to Kissinger's strategic game plan for the region. He was intent on projecting to the Arab interlocutors that the administration could be relied upon to play honest broker. This posture partly reflected a personal lesson drawn from the recent past: Kissinger now believed that the administration's decisive tilt in favor of Israel and embrace of the Arab-Israeli status quo between 1971 and 1973 had been a grave mistake that had helped push Sadat toward launching the war.[8] More importantly, the posture was geared to weakening Soviet influence in the Middle East. Kissinger strove to demonstrate to Sadat and other relatively moderate Arab leaders that only through the good offices of the United States could they begin to realize their dream of reclaiming territories lost to Israel during the 1967 War.[9]

Moreover, Kissinger was confident that gradual diplomatic progress under exclusive American auspices served not only America's but also Israel's best long-term interests. He did his utmost to convince American Jews and Israelis that this track, with the Soviets quiescent and the Europeans and Japanese sidelined, represented Israel's only hope of reaping any benefits from the crucible of the bitter war. The record suggests that he genuinely believed that the failure of his shuttle mission would spell disaster for Israel, inviting the involvement of intermediaries favorable to the Arabs, and turning what he perceived to be volatile American public opinion against Israel, with the Arabists in the State Department and American oil companies riding the wave of the Arab oil boycott.[10] The first order of the day for Israel, he lectured, was to buttress shuttle efforts through both largesse in the negotiating process and support for détente, since it and the related promise of economic carrots to Moscow had helped to co-opt Moscow and facilitate American ascendancy in the region.[11] Too aggrieved to be persuaded, the Israelis bargained tenaciously over every minute detail in the negotiations. More than ever, they also openly doubted the utility of détente as a vehicle for restraining Moscow, suggesting Soviet complicity in the surprise attack.[12] Embittered and fatigued, Kissinger accused Israel's leaders of blindness to the danger of Israeli isolation and ungratefulness for, specifically, the administration's having resisted (despite détente) Soviet (and European) pressures to take part in the diplomatic exercise and, more generally, the administration's bold plunge into the deep and untested diplomatic waters of the Middle Eastern conflict, an unprecedented move that committed the prestige of the country as well as Nixon and Kissinger's own.[13]

The American-Israeli divisions over the substance of negotiations were compounded by squabbles over authority and credit. Kissinger aborted the first experiment in direct Israeli-Egyptian negotiations—the "Kilometer 101 talks" between generals Aharon Yariv and Mohamed Abd al-Ghani el-Gamasy—partly because he insisted on proving that an American role was essential for sustained diplomatic progress,[14] but also partly because he was typically suspicious of independent negotiation channels and determined to hold the reins of diplomacy in his own hands.[15] Despite his jealousy over the public accolades accorded to his secretary, Nixon craved the success of the shuttle no less. His need for respite from the agony of Watergate and hope for a measure of reflected glory partly explain the unmitigated pressure he applied on the Israelis during the critical stage of the Syrian shuttle in May 1974, sending threatening letters to the Israelis and even ordering deputy national security adviser Brent Scowcroft to cut off all aid to the country unless Jerusalem complied.[16]

The sudden surge of acrimony between American and Israeli leaders, illustrated by this Nixon instruction, suggests the salience of factors beyond divergence in strategic outlook and drive for personal prestige. One has to explore the bilateral emotional milieu. Clearly, by 1974, a sense of mutual disappointment settled in, amplified by vivid memories of the "honeymoon" prior to the war. Witness, for instance, Kissinger's warning to Nixon on the eve of the latter's June 1974 visit to Israel not to expect newly appointed prime minister Rabin to be nearly as responsive or self-assured as he had been during his tenure as ambassador to Washington, or Kissinger's disparaging assessment of deputy prime minister Yigal Allon.[17]

The Jewish dimension added another edge. Meir was probably concerned not to further alienate a secretary of state then still in office when she observed in her 1975 memoirs: "As for his being Jewish, I don't think it either aided or hindered [Kissinger] in all those months of negotiation. But if he was emotionally involved with us, such an involvement never reflected itself for one moment in anything he did to us or did on our behalf."[18] The documentary record, however, suggests otherwise. As historian Jeremi Suri has recently demonstrated, Kissinger did not welcome the focus on his Jewishness that was an unavoidable by-product of the spectacle of Middle Eastern shuttle diplomacy; he was too anxious about his own acceptance in American society. As we have seen, he had always tried to deemphasize this component of his identity, which was in his eyes a source of vulnerability that Nixon, his bureaucratic rivals in Washington, the Arabs, and even his own coreligionists were out to exploit.[19] In his dealings with Jerusalem, Kissinger initially attempted to turn the Jewish link into an asset, presenting it as a guarantee of his ultimate commitment to Israel's survival.[20] More often than not, however, he found out that the reverse was taking place: partly because of his religion, whatever credit he may once have had with the Israelis was rapidly dissipating. He was greeted, while visiting Israel, with protesters carrying pointed banners and polarized press reports highlighting his Jewishness. Israeli opinion polls of the period found that he was both the most admired and the most disliked public figure. This public agitation was matched by the heated tone of debate behind closed doors, in which Kissinger openly told his Israeli discussants that they were trying to bring him down.[21] The diplomatic discourse clearly transcended a dispute between the secretary of state of a superpower and the leaders of the superpower's client state; it was turning into a no-holds-barred quarrel in the family with Kissinger cast in the role of a troublesome and renegade member, a painful experience for both sides that, by the time of Nixon's resignation, spilled over into influential books and articles in both Israel and the United States.[22]

All the elements of American-Israeli friction, including the Jewish complication, manifested themselves during Nixon's June 1974 visit to Israel. During the eight months since the October War, the image of Israel had markedly deteriorated in Nixon's eyes. Deeming Israel the party most responsible for slowing the pace of diplomatic progress in the Middle East, feeling besieged by a presumably Jewish-controlled media on account of Watergate, and growing increasingly exasperated by congressional support for the Jackson-Vanik Amendment and mounting public opposition to détente, Nixon reverted to his old image of Israel as aligned with his enemies—a force conspiring with American Jews to undermine both the administration's foreign policy and his own domestic standing.[23] By the time he arrived in Israel as part of a hastily prepared Middle Eastern swing designed principally to boost his rapidly waning legitimacy at home, the tone had already been set by promises he had given to Arab leaders and by anti-Semitic innuendoes that were reported to be on the White House tapes. The public reception in Israel contrasted sharply with the huge crowds that turned out to greet Nixon during his visit to Egypt. Nixon, for his part, embarrassed his hosts by initially refusing to pay the standard visit to the Holocaust memorial Yad Vashem, and then declining to put on a yarmulke once he got there.[24] The tense undercurrent found expression in Nixon's private meetings with Israeli leaders, where he said that

> the days when Israel felt very comfortable with a relationship . . . where we supported Israel . . . were going to be Israel's best friend . . . where your immediate warlike neighbors were considered enemies of the United States, those days [are over]: some might say in this country and many of our very good friends in the Jewish community in the United States say it now: let's go back to the old days. I don't think it is policy . . . time will run out.[25]

Obviously, this first visit by an American president to Israel did not ameliorate Nixon's vindictive mood: in his instructions to treasury secretary William E. Simon before the latter's July 1974 visit to Israel, he minced no words:

> I want you to be very hard-line in Israel. . . . I don't want any pandering to the Israelis. . . . when discussing long-term Israeli assistance, fuzz it up. It is ridiculous to give $6 billion to them and only a dribble to the Arabs, especially with the current Israeli attitude on negotiations.[26]

The friction of 1974 in American-Israeli relations, then, had its origins in two sets of causes. It was certainly due to the transformed policy-making environment, internationally as well as regionally, following the October War and the partly related growing uneasiness about détente within the United States. These are the sorts of strategic considerations we are most accustomed to identifying when assessing the trajectory of international relations. Yet, on a deeper level, it was also very much the child of prewar trends. First, the mutual disenchantment was intensified by memories of intimate partnership. Second, and somewhat ironically, Israel's 1974 alignment with anti-détente American conservatives, so infuriating for Nixon and Kissinger, was to a considerable degree a culmination of Israel's "conservative turn," a development the administration had been encouraging just a few years earlier. Third, Nixon's proclivity to cast Jews as his personal enemies, clouding his view of Israel at the outset of his tenure, resurfaced with a vengeance toward the end of his term. It seems apt, then, to characterize the evolution of Nixon's personal Israeli orientation as traveling full circle, from suspicion to embrace to suspicion again: indeed, the negative turn was not lost on Israel's officials. Recently declassified documentation reveals that Israeli principals welcomed Nixon's resignation, viewing him as too driven by personal commitment to détente and an anti-Jewish vendetta.[27]

From Jerusalem's longer-term perspective, however, Nixon's ultimate exasperation toward Israel was insignificant in comparison with the positive impact of the Nixon years on subsequent American-Israeli relations. The legacy of the Nixon years for the American-Israeli relationship was not one of estrangement but of an enduring bond. Diplomatically, with all their grumbling about Washington's increased sensitivity to the objectives of Arab moderates, Israel's leaders could not but welcome the Nixon administration's success at undercutting the Soviet role in the peace process. In terms of material backing, the dramatic leap in American civil and military assistance to Israel, authored by Nixon in late 1971 in large part in response to Israel's "conservative turn," has since become a political fixture underwritten by both parties. And politically, as Israel's conservative choices increasingly allied it with more conservative elements in American politics, Israel's stock in the American political market soared. This has been the case because the shifting of Israel's support base to the right occurred in tandem with the relative ascendancy of conservatism within the American political system. The loss of support from many on the left and some liberals, most of them avowed Democrats,[28] was more than compensated for by the staunch backing of neoconservatives, who were increasingly joining the ranks of the GOP, and evangelist Christians, the original backbone of the party's right wing.[29] Israel could now count on influential strongholds within both political parties. Moreover, the turn against Israel in American public opinion, predicted by Kissinger and even desired by a few of his closest aides, did not materialize.[30] Not long after entering office, President Ford became the first of many post-Nixon American presidents to learn a sobering lesson about the limits of executive latitude when it came to "disciplining" Israel. Following the collapse of Israeli-Egyptian talks in March 1975, Ford officially announced the reassessment of America's Middle Eastern policy. For six months, the administration refused to sign new arms deals with Israel. The president contemplated abandoning the step-by-step approach in favor of an alternative less palatable to Israel, a comprehensive peace plan that might entail Soviet participation. Yet, he soon backed off and approved the resumption of the step-by-step strategy, realizing that a policy departure would be politically counterproductive: the American public was not enthusiastic about such a move, and seventy-six senators sent Ford a letter urging him to be "responsive to Israel's economic and military needs."[31] Ford's willingness to take a hard line on aid to Israel did last through the first part of the 1976 election campaign. Yet, by the fall, when Governor

Jimmy Carter of Georgia, the Democratic candidate, was enjoying a huge lead in the polls, Ford and Carter began trying to outdo each other as the better friend of Israel.[32]

In sum, Israel emerged from the Nixon years with its special place in American foreign policy entrenched. This was partly due to a convergence of international, regional, and American domestic circumstances beyond Israel's control. However, in illuminating the considerable acumen Israeli leaders exhibited in effecting a "conservative turn" and backing Jackson-Vanik without publicly appearing to do so, our study shows that this important historical development owes much to Israel's own doing.

Lessons

The story of U.S.-Israeli relations in the Nixon years offers rich lessons for students in four fields: American history, Israeli history, American-Israeli relations, and foreign policy-making and international affairs.

For students of American history and politics, the pattern revealed in Nixon's Israeli policy serves as an important corrective to the current literature's tendency to treat the Nixon administration's Vietnam policy and Middle Eastern policy separately. The evidence illustrates the degree to which Vietnam concerns informed the president's Middle Eastern policy decisions. For example, Nixon's ambivalent reaction to Israel's aerial bombings of the Egyptian heartland during the War of Attrition echoed his Vietnam conduct. In both policy contexts, he was arguably torn between his instinct for brinkmanship and his awareness that the climate of opinion at home placed limits on military adventurism.[33] More importantly, Nixon's initial consideration of trading Israeli concessions for Soviet assistance in Vietnam stemmed in part from his perception of Israel as being under the sway of perceived domestic enemies—Democrat, American Jewish "weak reeds" on Vietnam. As we have seen, the Meir government's outspoken support of Nixon's Vietnam policy played a crucial role in assuaging this suspicion and deepening Nixon's commitment to Israel. Thus, far from being distinct policy domains, Vietnam and the Middle East were, in the early 1970s, closely linked.

Similarly, for students of Israeli history and politics, the book's findings demonstrate that the American-Israeli relationship, so crucial for Israel, can be significantly affected by Israeli policy choices *outside* the Middle East. Golda Meir and Yitzhak Rabin's decision to break away from earlier Israeli ambiguity and declare Israel's support for Nixon's Vietnam stand was deliberately designed to curry favor with Nixon, and worked. Also, the study takes issue with the common hypothesis that Israel's leaders have been so Israelo-centric and obsessed with security objectives as to pay mere lip service to the ideal of Jewish solidarity. Jerusalem's Jackson-Vanik record illustrates exactly the opposite: ostensible caution that camouflages an assertive intervention deemed crucial for salvaging a community in trouble, an intervention counter to an American president's explicit demands. The study thus corroborates the view that the lot of Jewish communities in distress can weigh quite heavily on at least some Israeli policy-makers.[34]

For students of American-Israeli relations, our study shows that the origins of the "special relationship" are multifaceted, and in some respects different from those most often pointed to by scholars. Three distinct approaches to the roots of the special relationship stand out in the literature.[35] The first, and the dominant one as far as Nixon's case is concerned, ascribes primacy to the perception of strategic partnership and mutual interests.[36] Our examination of the evidence suggests that in Nixon's case, this constituted a *necessary yet insufficient* factor. Nixon's perception of Israel as a strategic asset, following the Black September episode, began to trigger a shift in his policy toward Israel, but it proved inadequate in itself to generate a comprehensive and enduring commitment. The second approach stresses intangible bases of affinity—such as guilt feelings about American inaction during the Holocaust, a natural affinity between democracies, American mistrust of the Arabs, and a sense of mutual Judeo-Christian cultural origins.[37] Nixon, however, appears not to have been primarily driven by this motive.

The third approach, skillful practice of interest-group politics by Israel and her American Jewish champions, merits close attention, not least because the argument has recently been advanced in controversial fashion by political scientists John J. Mearsheimer and Stephen M. Walt, who argue that Israel and the American Jewish leadership have orchestrated a relentless and well-coordinated campaign designed to tilt American policy in Israel's favor.[38] With regard to the Nixon years, the emerging picture runs counter to this argument in one key respect. Israel indeed made several policy choices that importantly altered Nixon's image of Israel. However, Israel adopted these policies not *in concert* with American Jews but *despite* American Jewish disapproval.

In terms of the process involved, Rabin was too much a product of the classical Zionist negation of the Diaspora to cooperate with American Jewish establishment organs. He clashed frequently with the American Israel Public Affairs Committee (AIPAC) and preferred to blaze his own paths of access to the White House.[39] In practical terms, Meir's late-1969 decision to announce Israel's support for Nixon's Vietnam policy created noticeable fissures in Israeli-American Jewish relations. From the Israeli perspective, the disproportionate American Jewish participation in the antiwar movement amounted to a selfish exercise in moral purity oblivious to the injurious consequences of the movement to Israel's security and even, in the long run, its very survival.[40] For their part, a significant number of American Jews resented what they regarded as unwarranted intrusion in American domestic affairs, at one of the most sensitive moments in the course of the heated domestic debate about the war.[41] Rabbi Arthur Hertzberg was agitated enough to ask Meir publicly not to place him in the impossible position of having to choose between Israel and the younger American Jewish generation, for, in that case, he would have to choose his "children".[42] Probably even more unwelcome to American Jews was Rabin's virtual endorsement of Nixon during the 1972 presidential race. They resented the Israeli "instruction" as condescending and viewed Rabin's motion as undercutting American Jewry in the most sensitive area imaginable—the paramount objective not to be vulnerable to charges of double loyalty.[43] Most analysts of the 1972 elections agree that Nixon more than doubled his 1968 share of the Jewish vote chiefly because of McGovern's sloppy campaigning and American Jewish identification with Nixon's domestic agenda. American Jewish approval of his Israeli policy also played a part, but Rabin's prodding made little difference, if any.[44]

The consolidation of the special relationship was, of course, related to a growing Israeli bond with the conservative and neoconservative forces in American society. Several studies identify the 1977 rise of the right to power in Israel as the critical event in the emergence of this bond.[45] The evidence presented in this book suggests that the convergence of perspectives between the Israeli political elite and American conservatives began earlier, around a hawkish stand on Vietnam, a commitment to Soviet Jewish emigration, and a more general distrust of the Soviet Union.

For students of foreign policy-making and international history more generally, this study provides relevant insights on a number of perennial issues.

First, Israel's choice to support Nixon on Vietnam demonstrates that even a regional "client state" cannot confine its foreign policy horizons to its region, but rather, must keep an eye on the global context and on the nonregional preoccupations of its patron.

Second, the Israeli-U.S. relationship between 1971 and 1973 illustrates the risks associated with too close a convergence of outlooks; namely, a climate of horizontal "groupthink" *across* borders, a phenomenon generally overlooked in the literature.[46] The partnership that developed between the few American and Israeli policy-makers who conducted the relationship grew *too* intimate in the pre-October War period, producing a climate of conformity conducive to a mutual reinforcement of error and contributing to the failure of policy-makers in both countries to perceive developments of considerable consequence. To be sure, whether a more conciliatory American and Israeli policy line could have prevented the 1973 war is a matter of speculation and dispute, and will remain so at least until the declassification of relevant Egyptian records,[47] but we can safely conclude that the blind led the blind regarding the possible outbreak of the war[48] and the eruption of the oil crisis.[49]

Third, Kissinger's failure in the Soviet Jewish emigration context illustrates many of the well-known dilemmas faced by statesmen: the perils of euphoria, excessive secrecy, and overcentralization after an extended period in office; and the risk of cognitive closure entailed in overadherence to realist premises. Kissinger's conduct was hampered in part by his slow appreciation of the degree to which presumed matters of "low politics," such as Soviet Jewish emigration, might undermine such a grand design, "high-politics" construct as détente.

Fourth, Nixon and Kissinger's Soviet Jewish emigration policy, and détente more generally, illustrate a most difficult challenge for policymakers engaged in conflict reduction efforts: how to reconcile the expectations of one's domestic audience and those of erstwhile rivals. Recurrent and often consequential, this challenge merits some elaboration here.

Let us turn first to the intricate calibration task inherent in inducing one's rival into a viable modus vivendi, without having the rival's expectations spiral out of control. The study shows that Nixon and Kissinger pledged MFN status to the Soviets in 1972 without taking adequate account of possible congressional opposition. Later, Kissinger proved particularly slow to communicate the seriousness of the legislative obstacle to Moscow, partly because of his Realist convictions, partly because of hubris, and partly because he was so wedded to détente as to be trapped in wishful thinking that Jackson-Vanik would not come to pass.[50] Recently declassified documents reveal that in the Chinese context as well, both Nixon and Kissinger fell victim to the temptation of breaking the ice by making grand promises in advance. During his first, confidential meeting with Chinese foreign minister Zhou Enlai, Kissinger surprised his opposite number by hinting that the United States would in future be amenable to a return of Taiwan to Chinese Communist control. Largely because of residual backing for the Republic of China in the American body politic, the Nixon-Kissinger and Ford-Kissinger teams never made good on this promise, and the Chinese disappointment at Nixon and Kissinger's failure to deliver figured in the slowing of American-Chinese rapprochement between 1973 and 1976.[51] Both the Soviet Jewish emigration and the Taiwan cases underscore the perils involved in trying to soften up a rival: offering carrots may be crucial for turning a rival into a partner in conflict reduction, but the very "can-do" mentality that enables such inducements implies inattention to the obstacles ahead and can lead, over the longer term, to considerable exasperation for the partner.

This brings us to the management of domestic expectations. In his voluminous postmortem assessments of détente, Kissinger has consistently

rejected the charge that détente was oversold to the American public—
or, at least, that he should be held accountable for any overselling. Time
and again, his writings refer, as proof, to the annual reports to Congress
drafted by his NSC staff and himself, which, he argues, cautioned against
the expectation that détente would bring about a mellowing of Soviet ideological convictions. For him, drama-seeking reporters were to blame for
the fact that these reports did not influence public opinion.[52]

Newly declassified records lend some credence to Kissinger's view-
point. Showing that Kissinger knew he was "no expert on what might be
sold to the American public,"[53] the evidence shifts the principal blame to
the president, who failed to act on his own premonition on the eve of the
1972 Moscow summit that public embellishment of détente could lead to
inflated expectations at home:[54] On the last day of the summit, Nixon
signed the Basic Principles agreement, which emphasized the imperative
of conducting mutual relations on the basis of peaceful coexistence, and
then, during the following months, proceeded to brand détente as herald-
ing a full "generation of peace."[55]

Most importantly, in addition to shifting the focus to Nixon, the new
evidence confirms the predominant scholarly judgment that these actions
helped to create a set of expectations, both in Moscow and the United
States, which undermined détente later on.[56] When the Soviets accused
Nixon and Kissinger of unilateral diplomacy in the aftermath of the 1973
war, they fortified their case by contending that American conduct violated the letter and sprit of the Basic Principles agreement. American unilateralism in the Middle East, some scholars argue, invited Soviet
unilateralism in Southeast Asia and greater adventurism elsewhere.[57] And
Nixon's exalted rhetoric paved the way for a domestic backlash in 1974,
including passage of Jackson-Vanik, when the Soviets seemed not to live
up to Nixon's public vision.

The question remains, why Nixon did not make a determined effort to
keep the lid on expectations. Most scholars agree that the president signed
the Basic Principles agreement hastily. Dismissing the agreement as insignificant, he underrated the importance Moscow accorded to it as a
token of equal status[58] and failed to anticipate that the agreement would
later on turn into a weapon in the hands of opponents at home.[59] As for
playing détente up as ushering a more peaceful era in international relations, Nixon succumbed to the temptation of scoring easy electoral points
as the 1972 elections approached.[60] The temptation to employ grand rhetoric grew for Nixon because of the combination of pressing electoral need
and an agonizing war effort that tore at the fiber of the American body
politic: as in other policy spheres, we must turn to the affect of Nixon's preoccupation with Vietnam as a key explanation of Nixon's choices. Merely
a month before the summit, Nixon misinterpreted the North Vietnamese

attack on the South as part and parcel of a global Soviet test of American resolve.[61] He ordered the military to launch fierce retributions, knowing full well that this response might derail the summit.[62] He remained obsessed with Vietnam right up to the summit.[63] There are some evidentiary clues indicating that on the very eve of elections, when the North Vietnamese seemed far more amenable to negotiations than before, Nixon's anxiety about Vietnam turned into self-satisfaction. He now believed that his application of military and diplomatic (through the Soviets) pressure on the North Vietnamese had paid off. He found special vindictive pleasure in positing himself as the harbinger of peace and thus stealing the thunder of his liberal rivals at home.[64] Ultimately, then, an important unifying theme of this study is that Nixon's preoccupation with Vietnam was the key determinant of his Soviet, Israel, and domestic policies.

Finally and most generally, this book offers a fifth lesson regarding the very nature of policy-making. The illumination of nonstrategic dimensions of the American-Israeli dynamic during the Nixon years provides a degree of support for recent developments in the fields of both international history and international relations, including a certain "ideational turn" and a growing acknowledgment of the impact of emotions on policy-making.[65] As historian Jeremi Suri writes, the distinction between domestic and foreign politics is largely artificial.[66] For Nixon, Meir, and Kissinger, the domestic and the foreign intertwined inseparably to form their policy-making environment; moreover, their emotional dispositions and fundamental ideological convictions put blinders on them, shaping the American-Israeli relationship in critical ways.[67] Nixon's Israel policies were significantly affected by his self-perception as the voice of the "silent majority," laid low by petty foes who could not appreciate his grand designs. It wasn't until he was convinced that Israel was not under the sway of American Jews and his other perceived domestic enemies that the "special relationship" could come into its own.[68] Meir's deep devotion to the Soviet Jewish cause blinded her to the probability that public pressure on the Soviet Union might backfire. And Kissinger's deep commitment to averting American decline and nuclear catastrophe, as well as weaning the United States from a pattern of swinging between crusading overextensions and defiant isolationism,[69] hindered his ability to grasp that, by late 1973, Americans and Israelis alike came to prefer what they perceived as a morally unambiguous, values-based foreign policy over détente. Our study has shown how both the leaders and the led formulate their foreign policy preferences not only on the basis of straightforward cost-benefit analysis, but also in accordance with their understanding of their country's fundamental raison d'être.

NOTES

Introduction: Beyond Geostrategy

1. Douglas Little, *American Orientalism: The United States and the Middle East since 1945* (Chapel Hill: University of North Carolina Press, 2002), 106; William B. Quandt, *Decade of Decisions: American Policy toward the Arab-Israeli Conflict, 1967–1976* (Berkeley: University of California Press, 1977), 122; Jussi Hanhimäki, *The Flawed Architect* (Oxford: Oxford University Press, 2004), 96–98; Moshe Yager et al., eds., *Ministry for Foreign Affairs: The First Fifty Years* (Jerusalem: Keter, 2002), 273 (Hebrew); and Yaacov Bar-Siman-Tov, "A Special Relationship?" *Diplomatic History* 22:2 (Spring 1998): 245.

2. For overviews of the "special relationship" discourse, see Gabriel Sheffer, Introduction, *U.S.-Israeli Relations at the Crossroads*, ed. Gabriel Sheffer (London: Frank Cass, 1997), 6; Peter L. Hahn, "Special Relationships," *Diplomatic History* 22:2 (1998): 263–272.

3. Compare, for instance, the angry criticism of George Lenczkowski, *American Presidents and the Middle East* (London and Durham: Duke University Press, 1990), and Edward Tivnan, *The Lobby: Jewish Political Power and American Foreign Policy* (New York: Simon and Schuster, 1987), with the defensive accounts of Nixon aides, William Safire, *Before the Fall: An Inside View of the Pre-Watergate White House* (Garden City, N.Y.: Doubleday, 1975), Leonard Garment, *Crazy Rhythm: My Journey from Brooklyn, Jazz and Wall Street to Nixon's White House* (New York: Times Books, 1997), and, of course, Henry Kissinger, *White House Years* (Boston: Little, Brown, 1979) and *Years of Upheaval* (Boston: Little, Brown, 1982). For an excellent analysis of the historiography of Nixon's image, see David Greenberg, *Nixon's Shadow: History of an Image* (New York: Norton, 2003).

4. Quandt, *Decade of Decisions*, 73; Nixon Presidential Materials Project (College Park, Md.) (hereafter NPP), NSC Country Files-Middle East, Box 644, Folder 1, Saunders to Kissinger, 22 October 1969; NPP, NSC VIP Visits, Box 921, Folder 4, Saunders to Kissinger, 4 November 1969.

5. For instance, even Kissinger was only partially briefed about the private meeting Nixon held with prime minister Golda Meir on 26 September

1969. Avner Cohen and William Burr, "Israel Crosses the Threshold," *The Bulletin of the Atomic Scientists* 62:3 (2006): 27.

6. Examples include Cohen and Burr, "Israel Crosses the Threshold," 22–30; Claire Diagle, "The Russians Are Going: Sadat, Nixon and the Soviet Presence in Egypt, 1970–1971," *Middle East Review of International Affairs* 8:1 (2004): 1–15.

7. NPP, NSC, Institutional Files, Box H–34, Folder 5, NSC review group, 18 February 1969.

8. NPP, Kissinger telcons, Box 3, Folder 5, Kissinger-Elliot Richardson (telcon), 9 December 1969; NPP, NSC, Saunders Files-Middle East Negotiations, Box 1169, Folder 11, Kissinger to Nixon (memo), 11 November 1969; Kissinger, *White House Years*, 559; Quandt, *Decade of Decisions*, 78.

9. For the Israeli government, Nixon's fixation with supposed Jewish influence proved a double-edged sword, as it underlay the president's March 1970 decision to hold Israel's request for one hundred A-4 Skyhawk and twenty-five F-4 Phantom jets in abeyance. See Kissinger, *White House Years*, 565–567; National Archives II (College Park, Md.) (hereafter cited as NA), H. R. Haldeman Diary, CD version, Entry 26 February 1970; Israel State Archive, Jerusalem (hereafter ISA), RG 93, 7792/A8, Dinitz to Gazit, 4 April 1973.

10. NPP, Nixon Tapes, Tape 628/2, Nixon-Meir-Kissinger-Rabin discussion, 2 December 1971; Quandt, *Decade of Decisions*, 146–147; NPP, Kissinger telcons, Box 13, Folder 1, Nixon-Haldeman, 25 January 1972.

11. See, for instance, NA, Haldeman Diary, CD version, Entry 17 May 1971.

12. For Nixon's early suspicion of Israel, see NPP, NSC Country Files-Middle East, Box 612, Folder "Israeli aid," Nixon to Kissinger, 17 March 1970. For his newly found confidence in Israel, see Nixon-Graham conversation, 1 February 1972, in *The White House Tapes: Eavesdropping on the President*, ed. John Prados (New York: The New Press, 2003), 243–244; Safire, *Before the Fall*, 577; ISA, RG 130:20, Foreign Ministry Files (FM) 5294/11, Nixon to Meir, 22 March 1973; NPP, Kissinger telcons, Box 14, Folder 2, Nixon-Kissinger, 6 May 1972; NA, Haldeman Diary, CD version, Entry 1 February 1972.

13. The most recent crop in the literature covers a different time frame and relies much more on oral histories than Israeli and American government documentation. See Fred A. Lazin, *The Struggle for Soviet Jewish Emigration in American Politics: Israel versus the American Jewish Establishment* (Lanham: Lexington Books, 2005) and Pauline Peretz, "The Action of Nativ's Emissaries in the United States: A Trigger for the American Movement to Aid Soviet Jews, 1958–1974." *Bulletin du Centre de Recherché Français de Jérusalem* 14 (Spring 2004): 112–128.

14. For a polemic argument in this vein, see G. Martin, *A Matter of Priorities: Labor Zionism and the Plight of Soviet Jewry, 1917–1996* (Jerusalem: Diamond Books, 1996), esp. 93, 109. For scholarly arguments, see Robert G. Kaufman, *Henry Jackson: A Life in Politics* (Seattle: State University of Washington Press, 2000), 269; Aharon Klieman, *Statecraft in the Dark* (Boulder, Colo.: Westview Press, 1988), 44; Daniel J. Elazar, *Community and Polity: The Organizational Dynamics of American Jewry*, 2nd edition (Philadelphia: Jewish Publication Society of America, 1995), 111; Efraim Inbar, "Jews, Jewishness and Israel's Foreign Policy," *Jewish Political Studies Review* 2:3–4 (Fall 1990): 169.

15. See Nehemia Levanon, *"Nativ" Was the Code Name* (Tel Aviv: Am Oved, 1995) (Hebrew), 382; Peretz, "Nativ's Emissaries," esp. 126–127; Lazin, *The Struggle*, 51–53.

16. ISA, FM 5294/11, Elizur to foreign ministry director general, 21 March 1973; Levanon, *"Nativ,"* 400–401; ISA, RG 93, 4996/1, Gazit to Dinitz, 27 April 1973; ISA, RG 60, 8163/4, Meir to Knesset Security and Foreign Affairs Committee, 4 May 1973.

17. The most detailed account of Kissinger's role has long been Paula Stern's *Water's Edge: Domestic Politics and the Making of American Foreign Policy* (Westport, Conn.: Greenwood, 1979). It draws on Stern's interviews with practitioners and on her own firsthand involvement in Jackson-Vanik's legislative history as legislative assistant to Senator Gaylord Nelson (D-Wisconsin).

18. See NPP, HAK Office Files, Box 67, Folder "Map Room August 72–May 73 1 of 3," Sonnenfeldt to Kissinger, 15 December 1972; NPP, HAK Office Files, Box 71, Folder "Gromyko 1973," Kissinger memo for files, 28 September 1973.

19. For the close and covert collaboration between Nativ and Henry Jackson's aide Richard Perle, see Levanon, *"Nativ."*

20. Janice Stein and Richard N. Lebow, *We All Lost the Cold War* (Princeton: Princeton University Press, 1994), 166–172; Raymond Garthoff, *Détente and Confrontation: American-Soviet Relations from Nixon to Reagan* (Washington, D.C.: Brookings, 1994 edition), 404–412; Vladislav M. Zubok, *A Failed Empire: The Soviet Union in the Cold War from Stalin to Gorbachev* (Chapel Hill: University of North Carolina Press, 2007), 239; The National Security Archive, George Washington University, "The October War and U.S. Policy," *Electronic Briefing Book 98*, ed. William Burr (7 October 2003) (hereafter cited as nsarchive), documents 3, 14.

21. Garthoff, *Détente and Confrontation*, 449; Robert O. Freedman, *Soviet Policy toward the Middle East since 1970* (New York: Praeger, 1975), 169–170; Lebow and Stein, *We All Lost*, 287–288.

22. See Alfred Gottschalk, "Perspectives," in *The Yom Kippur War: Israel and the Jewish People*, ed. Moshe Davis (New York: Ayer Co.,

1974), esp. 37; Kissinger-Jewish intellectuals (memcon), 6 December 1973, reprinted in Zaki Shalom, "Kissinger and the American Jewish Leadership after the 1973 War," *Israel Studies* 7:1 (Spring 2002): 198–208.

23. NPP, NSC HAK Office Files, Box 68, Folder "Map Room D," Sonnenfeldt to Kissinger, 16 November 1973; Stein and Lebow, *We All Lost*, 285–288.

24. NA, RG 59, Records of HAK, Box 10, Folder "nodismemcons October '74," Kissinger-Dinitz (memcon), 5 October 1974.

25. Hanhimäki, *Flawed Architect*, 303–304; NA, NSC HAK Office Files, Box 76, Folder "sec. Kissinger's Pre-summit trip to Moscow March 24–28," Kissinger to Nixon, 26 March 1974.

Chapter 1. Joining the Conservative Brotherhood

*NPP, NSC Country Files-Middle East, Box 612, Folder "Israeli aid." Nixon to Kissinger, 17 March 1970. Excerpts of the same memo, excluding the first sentence, can also be found in Richard Nixon, *RN: The Memoirs of Richard Nixon* (New York: Grosset and Dunlap, 1978), 479–480.

1. Quandt, *Decade of Decisions*, 81.

2. Nixon, press conference, 27 January 1969, in *The Nixon Presidential Press Conferences* (New York: Coleman, 1978), 3.

3. Nixon, press conference, 4 March 1969, in *Presidential Press Conferences*, 30.

4. Ibid., 24.

5. NPP, Kissinger telcons, Box 3, Folder 5, Kissinger-Elliot Richardson, 9 December 1969; NPP, NSC Saunders Files-Middle East Negotiations, Box 1169, Folder 11, Kissinger to Nixon (memo), 11 November 1969; Kissinger, *White House Years*, 559; Quandt, *Decade of Decisions*, 78. This was an exercise in wishful thinking on Nixon's part, since the Soviets could not bully the North Vietnamese into accepting a compromise solution in Southeast Asia, and it is very doubtful that they had wished to do so. See Hanhimäki, *Flawed Architect*, 49.

6. NPP, NSC Country Files-Middle East, Box 644, Folder 2, Nixon to Kissinger and Rogers, 22 February 1969. Of course, the very issuance of this directive indicates that Nixon was anything but indifferent to this factor, as is demonstrated later in this chapter.

7. See Nancy B. Tucker, "Taiwan Expendable? Nixon and Kissinger Go to China," *The Journal of American History* 92:1 (2005): 109–135.

8. Cohen and Burr, "Israel Crosses the Threshold." Since this very recent article exhausts the issue until further evidence comes to light, my discussion of the nuclear element is confined to placing it within the context of explaining Nixon's Israeli policy shift.

9. ISA, RG 60, 8163/2, Meir to Knesset Security and Foreign Affairs Committee, 16 March 1973; NPP, RG 59, Records of HAK, Box 136, Folder 2, Nixon-Golda et al. (memcon), 1 November 1973.

10. The State Department disseminated this American position among the parties on October 28, eliciting a strong Israeli rejection. For details, see Quandt, *Decade of Decisions*, 89–92; Yitzhak Rabin, *The Rabin Memoirs* (Boston: Little, Brown, 1979), 123–125.

11. Quandt, *Decade of Decisions*, 98.

12. Rabin, *Memoirs*, 141–142.

13. Ephraim Karsh, "Israel," in *The Cold War and the Middle East*, ed. Yezid Sayigh and Avi Shlaim (Oxford: Clarendon, 1997), 168.

14. Direct evidence to this effect is lacking. The case for this point is based on the rare convergence of opinion between Kissinger's memoirs and the most authoritative account to date that draws on State Department sources. See Kissinger, *White House Years*, 564; David A. Korn, *Stalemate: The War of Attrition and Great Power Diplomacy in the Middle East, 1967–1970* (Boulder, Colo.: Westview Press, 1992), 148.

15. NPP, Kissinger telcons, Box 5, Folder 8, Nixon-Kissinger, 8 June 1970. See also Odd Arne Westad, *The Global Cold War: Third World Interventions and the Making of Our Times* (Cambridge: Cambridge University Press, 2005), 195.

16. NPP, Kissinger telcons, Box 2, Folder 6, Kissinger-Attorney General Mitchell, 11 September 1969.

17. NPP, NSC Institutional Files, Box H-34, Folder 5, NSC Review Group, 18 February 1969.

18. NPP, Kissinger telcons, Box 1, Folder 4, Kissinger-Rogers, 13 March 1969; NPP, NSC Country Files-Middle East, Box 644, Folder 2, Saunders to Kissinger (memo), 19 March 1969.

19. Korn, *Stalemate*, 154.

20. Cited in Ibid., 156.

21. Ibid., 149.

22. Kissinger, *White House Years*, 348.

23. Soviet opposition apparently derived less from substantive issues and more from the fact that the Rogers Plan had become a unilateral American initiative. See Galia Golan, *Soviet Policies in the Middle East from World War Two to Gorbachev* (Cambridge: Cambridge University Press, 1990), 72.

24. NPP, NSC Saunders Files-Middle East, Box 1169, Folder 10, Rogers to Nixon (memo), 14 October 1969. See also NA, RG 59, Box 1824, Folder "pol 27 Arab-Israeli 11/15/69," Rogers to Nixon (memo), 16 November 1969; NPP, Kissinger telcons, Box 3, Folder 4, Kissinger-Sisco, 4 December 1969. The minority view within the State Department, particularly Yost and a number of midlevel INR figures, argued that Arab

endorsement of the plan might be possible if only the United States would be seen to apply concerted pressure on Israel. See NA, RG 59, Box 1824, Folder "pol 27 Arab-Israeli 11/15/69," Pierce (INR) to Open Forum Panel, 20 November 1969; NPP, NSC Saunders Files, Middle East Negotiations, Box 1170, Folder 1, Yost to Kissinger, 9 July 1969.

25. Nixon was one of the original proponents of the Domino Theory. See Jeffrey Kimball, "Peace with Honor: Richard Nixon and the Diplomacy of Threat and Symbolism," in *Shadow on the White House: Presidents and the Vietnam War, 1945–1975*, ed. David L. Anderson (Lawrence, Kans.: University Press of Kansas, 1993), 153.

26. See, for instance, Nixon, *RN*, 479; NPP, Kissinger telcons, Box 9, Folder 1, Nixon-Kissinger, 13 December 1969.

27. NPP, Kissinger telcons, Box 5, Folder 3, Nixon-Kissinger, 13 December 1969. In October and again in November 1969, day-long protests called moratoriums drew hundreds of thousands to Washington, San Francisco, and other cities, and marked the antiwar movement's zenith. See Greenberg, *Nixon's Shadow*, 87–91.

28. NPP, Kissinger telcons, Box 2, Folder 7, Nixon-Kissinger, 27 September 1969. See also NA, RG 59 Office Files of Rogers, Box 4, Folder "White House Correspondence 1969," Nixon to Rogers, 11 January 1969; NA, Haldeman Diary, CD version, Entry 27 October 1969.

29. NPP, Kissinger telcons, Box 5, Folder 3, Nixon-Kissinger, 13 December 1969.

30. NPP, NSC Country Files-Middle East, Box 645, Folder 5, Kissinger to Nixon, 2 October 1969.

31. Garment, *Crazy Rhythm*, 192.

32. ISA, FM, 4156/3, Bitan to Avidar, 23 December 1969.

33. NPP, Kissinger telcons, Box 2, Folder 7. Meir-Kissinger and Kissinger-Nixon, 27 September 1969.

34. Burr and Cohen, "Crossing the Threshold," 26.

35. NPP, NSC Country Files-Middle East, Box 604, Folder 2, Nixon to Kissinger, 22 September 1969, and Laird to Kissinger, 22 August 1969. See also Safire, *Before the Fall*, 566.

36. NPP, NSC Country Files-Middle East, Box 612, Folder "Israeli Aid." Kissinger-Nixon (telcon), 10 March 1970.

37. Kissinger, *White House Years*, 565–567; NA, Haldeman Diary, CD version, Entry 26 February 1970; ISA, RG 93, 7792/A8, Dinitz to Gazit, 4 April 1973.

38. NPP, Kissinger telcons, Box 4, Folder 6, Kissinger-Garment, 12 March 1970; NA, Haldeman Diary, CD version, Entry 18 March 1970.

39. Rabin, *Memoirs*, 116; Karsh, "Israel," 171.

40. Richard B. Parker, *The Politics of Miscalculation in the Middle East* (Bloomington: Indiana University Press, 1993), 156–157; and Dima

P. Adamsky, "How American and Israeli Intelligence Failed to Estimate the Soviet Intervention in the War of Attrition," in *The Cold War and the Middle East: Regional Conflict and the Superpowers*, ed. Nigel Ashton (London and New York: Routledge, 2007), 113–135.

41. For the different appraisals of Soviet motives, compare: Parker, *Politics of Miscalculation*, esp. 125; Isabella Ginor, "Under the Yellow Arab Helmet Gleamed Blue Russian Eyes: Operation KAVKAZ and the War of Attrition, 1969–1970," *Cold War History* 3:1 (2002): 127–156; and Dima P. Adamsky, "Zero Hour for Bears: Inquiring into the Soviet Decision to Intervene in the Egyptian-Israeli War of Attrition, 1969–1970," *Cold War History* 6:1 (February 2006): 113–136.

42. See Parker, *Politics of Miscalculation*, 160; Ephraim Inbar, *Rabin and Israel's National Security* (Washington, D.C.: Woodrow Wilson Center Press, 1999), 40.

43. NPP, NSC Countries-Middle East, Box 612, Folder "Israeli Aid," Nixon-Kissinger (telcon), 10 March 1970.

44. NPP, NSC Countries-Middle East, Box 612, Folder "Israeli Aid," Kissinger memo on conversation with Rabin and Nixon, 18 March 1970; Rabin, *Memoirs*, 134.

45. For Nixon's brinkmanship instinct in Vietnam, see: Melvin Small, "Containing Domestic Enemies: Richard M. Nixon and the War at Home," in *Shadow on the White House*, ed. Anderson, 137; and Kimball, "Peace with Honor," 160.

46. Small, "Containing Domestic Enemies," 143; Quandt, *Decade of Decisions*, 99; NPP, Kissinger telcons, Box 5, Folder 8, Nixon-Kissinger, 8 June 1970.

47. NPP, NSC Countries-Middle East, Box 606, Folder 1, Rabin-Kissinger (memcon), 25 April 1970; NPP, Kissinger telcons, Box 5, File 9, Kissinger-Nixon, 11 June 1970.

48. NPP, Kissinger telcons, Box 5, Folder 2, Rogers-Kissinger, 9 April 1970.

49. NPP, NSC Saunders Files-Middle East Negotiations, Box 1186, Folder 5, Sisco to American Embassy, Moscow, 9 July 1970. Israel also began to realize it had no military answer to the Egyptian SA-3 missiles. See Rabin, *Memoirs*, 136; Yaacov Bar-Siman-Tov, *The Israeli-Egyptian War of Attrition, 1969–1970* (New York: Columbia University Press, 1980), 183.

50. NPP, Kissinger telcons, Box 5, Folder 9, Nixon-Kissinger, 11 June 1970; ISA, RG 72, 11455/C3, Dinitz Papers, Gazit to Dinitz, 11 August 1970.

51. NPP, Kissinger telcons, Box 6, Folder 2, Kissinger-Garment, 14 July 1970; NPP, Country Files-Middle East, Box 654, Folder 3, Kissinger-Rogers (telcon), 7 August 1970.

52. Karsh, "Israel," 173; NPP, Kissinger telcons, Box 5, Folder 6, Nixon-Richardson, 22 May 1970. The letter was addressed to Rogers, signaling Nixon's success at diverting domestic criticism to the secretary of state.

53. For the text of Nixon's address, see Quandt, *Decade of Decisions*, 100–101.

54. Korn, *Stalemate*, 263.

55. Ibid., 266.

56. ISA, FM 4156/2, Ben Aharon to Foreign Office, 26 March 1969, and Bitan to Elizur, 27 May 1969; NPP, NSC VIP Visits, Box 921, Folder 3, Barbour to SecState, 20 May 1969. The quote is from Barbour's telegram. See also Gideon Rafael, *Destination Peace: Three Decades of Israeli Foreign Policy* (Jerusalem: Idanim, 1981), 165–167 (Hebrew version).

57. ISA, FM 4156/2, Raviv to Elizur, 4 April 1969; NPP, NSC Country Files-Middle East, Box 644, Folder 2, Saunders to Kissinger, 19 March 1969; Rabin, *Memoirs*, 115.

58. NA, RG 59, Office Files of William P. Rogers, Box 1, Folder "memcons," Rogers-Presidents of Major American Jewish organizations (memcon), 15 April 1969; ISA, FM, 4155/8, Evron to Bitan, 17 May 1968; Yager et al. eds., *Ministry for Foreign Affairs*, 271; Judith A. Klinghoffer, *Vietnam, Jews and the Middle East: Unintended Consequences* (New York: St. Martin's Press, 1999), 57. For a convincing argument that Lyndon Johnson's support for Israel flowed in large part from likening Israel to his home territory of Texas, see Robert D. Johnson, *Lyndon Johnson and Israel: The Secret Presidential Recordings* (Tel Aviv: S. Daniel Abraham Center for International and Regional Studies, 2008).

59. ISA, FM, 4156/2, Argov to Bitan, 26 March 1969.

60. Argov persisted in calling for a confrontation with the administration, contributing to his falling from Rabin's grace. See ISA, FM, 4156/2, Argov to foreign office, 28 May 1969; ISA, RG 72, 11455/C4, Dinitz Papers, Argov to Dinitz, 6 August 1970; ISA, RG 72, File 11455/C2, Dinitz Papers, Argov to Gazit, 24 March 1971.

61. ISA, RG 43, 7071/1, Rabin to Bitan, 3 July 1968; ISA, FM, 4155/9, Rabin to Eban, 8 September 1968.

62. ISA, FM, 4155/11, Argov to Bitan, 25 December 1968; Rabin, *Memoirs*, 102–104; Inbar, *Rabin and Israel's National Security*, 37–38; I. L. Kennen, *Israel's Defense Line: Her Friends and Foes in Washington* (Buffalo, N.Y.: Prometheus Books, 1981), 219; ISA, RG 43, Rabin to Gazit, 15 May 1972; ISA, RG 43, 7052/21, Rabin to Dinitz, 15 February 1972.

63. Inbar, *Rabin and Israel's National Security*, 41.

64. ISA, FM, 4156/2, Bitan to Rabin, 21 April 1969, and Knesset Security and Foreign Affairs subcommittee deliberations, 20 May 1969;

NPP, Kissinger telcons, Box 1, Folder 5, Kissinger-Garment, 14 March 1969; ISA, RG 43, 7071/1, Rabin to Meir, 10 November 1969; Rabin, *Memoirs*, 111–115.

65. ISA, FM, 4156/2, Eban to Rabin and Argov, 30 April 1969.

66. Golda Meir, *My Life* (Jerusalem: Steimatsky, 1975), 2. See also Mordechai Namir, *Israeli Mission to Moscow* (Tel Aviv: Am Oved, 1971), 52 (Hebrew).

67. Meir, *My Life*, 203–204; ISA, FM, 4550/3, FM to Washington Embassy, 14 January 1970; Meir to journalist James Reston, *New York Times*, 27 December 1970.

68. ISA, FM 4156/2, Raviv to Elizur, 4 April 1969.

69. ISA, FM, 4156/2, Elizur to Rabin, 30 April 1969; See also Abba Eban, *Abba Eban: An Autobiography* (New York: Random House, 1977), 463.

70. NPP, NSC VIP Visits, Box 921, Folder 3, Barbour to Rogers, 20 May 1969; NPP, NSC, Box 604, Folder 1, Rabin-Saunders (memcon), 26 May 1969.

71. See Cohen and Burr, "Israel Crosses the Threshold," 27.

72. See, for instance, NPP, NSC Country Files-Middle East, Box 606, Folder 2, Meir to Nixon (letter), 12 March 1970; NPP, NSC Name Files, Box 815, Folder "Garment," Garment to Haldeman, 21 November 1970.

73. Rabin, *Memoirs*, 120–121; NPP, Kissinger telcons, Box 9, Folder 1, Kissinger-Rabin, 28 February 1970.

74. ISA, RG 72, 11455/C3, Dinitz Papers, Eban to Dinitz, 17 March 1970.

75. Rabin, *Memoirs*, 127.

76. NPP, NSC Country Files-Middle East, Box 606, Folder 3, Meir-Barbour (memcon), 23 March 1970. At least until the aftermath of the 1973 war, Nixon fully endorsed the Meir government's determination to retain control over the Golan Heights. See NPP, Kissinger telcons, Box 3, Folder 4, Kissinger-Sisco, 4 December 1969; NPP, Kissinger telcons, Box 9, Folder 1, Kissinger-Sisco, 27 February 1971.

77. Eban, *Autobiography*, 465–466; ISA, RG 43, 7071/1, Rabin to Eban, 17 November 1969.

78. Rabin, *Memoirs*, 139; NPP, Kissinger telcons, Box 10, Folder 5. Kissinger-Sisco, 22 June 1970; NA, RG 59, Office Files of Rogers, Box 3, Folder "Personal papers of Rogers," Rabin to Kissinger (memcon), 22 June 1970.

79. NPP, NSC Country Files-Middle East, Box 608, Folder "Israel vol. VII 2 of 2," Nixon to Congressman MacGregor (memcon), 10 September 1970.

80. NPP, NSC Country Files-Middle East, Box 607, Folder 7, Sisco to Barbour, 7 August 1970. See also Quandt, *Decade of Decisions*, 106.

81. NPP, Kissinger telcons, Box 9, Folder 5, Kissinger-Rabin, 22 March 1971.

82. Quandt, *Decade of Decisions*, 128.

83. NPP, Kissinger telcons, Box 9, Folder 1, Nixon-Kissinger, 24 February 1971.

84. NPP, Kissinger telcons, Box 9, Folder 1, Kissinger-Sisco, 27 February 1971.

85. Little, *American Orientalism*, 106; Quandt, *Decade of Decisions*, 122; Hanhimäki, *Flawed Architect*, 96–98; Yager et al., eds., *Ministry for Foreign Affairs*, 273; and Bar-Siman-Tov, "A Special Relationship?," 245.

86. Rabin, *Memoirs*, 148.

87. NPP, NSC Country Files-Middle East, Box 607, Folder 7, Sisco to Barbour, 25 September 1970; Nixon Tapes, Tape 628/16, Nixon-Meir-Rabin meeting, 2 December 1971.

88. To illustrate, the quantum leap in economic and military aid to Israel took place between 1970 and 1971: $159.3 million for 1970 and $1,286 million for 1971. See Organsky, *The $36 Billion Bargain: Strategy and Politics in U.S. Assistance to Israel* (New York: Columbia University Press, 1990), 143.

89. NPP, Haldeman Diary, CD version, Entry 11 March 1971; NPP, HAK Office Files, Box 129, Folder 1A, Haldeman memo on Nixon-Rogers-Haldeman meeting, 22 April 1971.

90. Diagle, "The Russians Are Going." Overlooking Kissinger's role, Diagle somewhat overplays Rogers's general influence over Nixon; yet, for those few months, his case is validated by Nixon's choice not to inform Kissinger about Rogers's meetings with Sadat. See Quandt, *Decade of Decisions*, 144. For a similar conclusion, see Salim Yaqub, "The Politics of Stalemate: The Nixon Administration and the Arab-Israeli Conflict, 1969–1973," in *The Cold War and the Middle East: Regional Conflict and the Superpowers*, ed. Nigel Ashton (London and New York: Routledge, 2007), 46–47.

91. Excerpt of a quotation in Diagle, 8.

92. NPP, Haldeman Diary, CD version, Entry 17 May 1971.

93. NPP, NSC Country Files-Middle East, Box 657, Folder "nodis July–Sept. 71, 1 of 2." NSC meeting, 5 August 1971.

94. Gad Yaacobi, "The Attempt to Reach an Interim Agreement with Egypt in 1971–1972 and Its lessons," in *The October War: A Reassessment*, ed. Yaacov Bar-Siman-Tov and Haim Opaz (Jerusalem: Davis Institute,1999), 46 (Hebrew); ISA, FM, 4549/8, Ramati-Brosh, 9 July 1971; ISA, RG 43, 6689/C36, Rafiah-Gazit, 1 August 1971; NPP, Box 658, Folder "nodis Oct.–Dec. 71 3 of 3," Meir-Rogers (memcon), 4 December 1971.

95. NPP, Nixon Tapes, Tape 628/2, Nixon-Meir-Kissinger-Rabin discussion, 2 December 1971.

96. NPP, Nixon Tapes, Tape 528/9, Nixon-Douglas Home discussion, 30 September 1971. For a similar interpretation of Sadat's motives, see Adeed Dawisha, "Egypt," in *The Cold War and the Middle East*, ed. Sayigh and Shlaim, 36; Mordechai Gazit, "Egypt and Israel: Was There a Peace Opportunity Missed in 1971?," *Journal of Contemporary History* 32:1 (1997): 105.

97. Quandt, *Decade of Decisions*, 146–147; NPP, Kissinger telcons, Box 13, Folder 1, Nixon-Haldeman, 25 January 1972.

98. Kissinger, *White House Years*, 1289; NPP, NSC Country Files-Middle East, Box 609, Folder 2, Saunders to Kissinger, 28 October 1971. Eban was so methodically kept out as to embarrass even Rabin's successor Dinitz. See ISA, RG 93, 7792/A8, Dinitz to Gazit, 4 July 1973. On the U.S. side, particularly uninformed was the American embassy in Tel Aviv, all the more so after the replacement of Barbour with Kenneth Keating. See William D. Morgan and Charles S. Kennedy, eds., *American Diplomats: The Foreign Service at Work* (New York: iUniverse, 2004), 144; ISA, RG 93, 7792/A8, Shomron-Dinitz, 27 July 1973.

99. Hanhimäki, *Flawed Architect*, 97; Lebow and Stein, *We All Lost* , 174–175.

100. On the Rogers Plan, see Abraham Ben-Zvi, *The United States and Israel: The Limits of the Special Relationship* (New York: Columbia University Press, 1993), 85; NA, RG 59, Central Foreign Policy Files 1967–1969, Box 1824, Folder "pol 27 Arab-Isr. 11/15/69," #6454 Moscow to State, 20 November 1969; ISA, FM, 5294/9, Atherton to Evron, 22 April 1972.

101. Compare: Rabin, *Memoirs*, 120; ISA, RG 43, 7071/1, RG 43, Tekoah to FM, 25 June 1969; NPP, WHSF: POF: Annotated News Summaries, Box 30, Folder 9, Nixon Handwriting, 29 September 1969; NPP, Haldeman Diary, CD version, Entry 18 September 1970; NPP, Nixon Tapes, Tape 771/1, Nixon-Kissinger conversation, 6 September 1972.

102. NPP, President's Personal Files, Box 51, Folder 21, Nixon notes in preparation for meeting Meir, 25 September 1969; NPP, Kissinger telcons, Box 6, Folder 1, Nixon-Kissinger, 7 July 1970.

103. NPP, NSC Saunders Files-Middle East Negotiations, Box 1169, Folder 11, Kissinger to Nixon (memo), 11 November 1969; NPP, NSC Institutional Files, Box H-25, Folder "NSC meeting 10 December 1969," Kissinger memo, 10 December 1969; NPP, NSC Country Files-Middle East, Box 645, Folder 1, Kissinger-Nixon, 16 June 1970.

104. NPP, Haldeman Diary, CD version, Entry 17 September 1970.

105. See, for instance, Nixon's grudging remarks about this to Mitchell, NPP, Nixon Tapes, Tape 576/6, Nixon-Mitchell discussion, 18 September 1971.

106. See, for instance, NPP, Kissinger telcons, Box 8, Folder 2, Kissinger-Sisco, 14 December 1970; NPP, NSC Country Files-Middle East,

Box 606, Folder 1, Saunders's handwritten remarks to Haig at the margins of a document titled "Economic and Military Assistance to Israel," 10 March 1970. Sisco was naturally concerned lest he would end up "the fall guy" in the duel between Kissinger and Rogers, but he persevered to stay on as assistant secretary when Kissinger replaced Rogers in late 1973. See NPP, Kissinger telcons, Box 11, Folder 10, Kissinger-Sisco, 9 October 1971.

107. Kissinger telcons, Box 11, Folder 5, Rabin-Kissinger, 5 October 1971; Garment, *Crazy Rhythm*, 190.

108. NA, Haldeman Diary CD version, Entry 11 March 1971; Nixon Tapes, Tape 628/2, Kissinger-Nixon discussion, 2 December 1971; Hanhimäki, *Flawed Architect*, 25.

109. NPP, Nixon Tapes, Tape 628/2, Kissinger-Nixon discussion, 2 December 1971. For the best discussion available of Kissinger's precarious and defensive position regarding his Jewishness, see Jeremi Suri's recent studies, *Henry Kissinger and the American Century* (Cambridge: Harvard University Press, 2007), esp. 209–210, 252; and "Henry Kissinger, the American Dream, and the Jewish Immigrant Experience," *Diplomatic History* 32:5 (November 2008), esp. 726–729.

110. Klieman, *Statecraft in the Dark*, 46; ISA, RG 72, 11455/C3, Dinitz Papers, Gazit to Dinitz, 30 November 1970.

111. ISA, RG 72, 11455/C3, Rabin to Dinitz, 2 June 1971; ISA, RG 93, 7792/A–8. Rabin to Dinitz, 27 December 1972; Eban, *Autobiography*, 465.

112. NPP, Kissinger telcons, Box 18, Folder 6, Kissinger-Rabin, 18 January 1973.

113. ISA, RG 43, Rabin to Eban and Bitan to Argov, both dated 2 November 1969.

114. NPP, Nixon Tapes, Tape 628/16, Meir-Nixon-Kissinger-Rabin meeting, 2 December 1971; Rabin, *Memoirs*, 161–163. For a detailed description of what he regards as "Israeli concessions," see Gazit, "Egypt and Israel," 103.

115. NPP, Kissinger telcons, Box 9, Folder 7, Nixon-Kissinger, 29 September 1971.

116. NA, Haldeman Diary, CD version, Entry 17 January 1972.

117. Betty Glad and Michael Link, "President Nixon's Inner Circle of Advisors," *Presidential Studies Quarterly* 26:1 (1996): 23. The year between mid-1972 and the eruption of Watergate saw many Israelis worried by the prospect that Nixon would replace Kissinger. See, for instance, ISA, FM 5294/10, Evron to Eban, 31 August 1972; ISA, RG 93, File 7792/A8, Gazit to Dinitz, 3 June 1973.

118. NPP, WHSF: POF: Annotated News Summaries, Box 37, Folder 2–7 December 1971, 6 December 1971; Elizur, "Security Without Peace," in Yager et al., eds., *Ministry for Foreign Affairs*, 308.

119. NPP, Haldeman diary, CD version, Entry 23 January 1972.

120. Most students of Nixon agree on this point. See, for instance, William Bundy, *A Tangled Web: The Making of Foreign Policy in the Nixon Presidency* (New York: Hill and Wang, 1998), 519–520; Small, "Containing Domestic Enemies," 133–142. For a mild counterargument, see Joan Hoff, *Nixon Reconsidered* (New York: Basic Books, 1994).

121. The only major study covering the nexus between Jerusalem, Washington, American Jewry, and Vietnam hardly goes beyond the Johnson years. See Klinghoffer, *Jews*.

122. NPP, NSC Country Files-Middle East, Box 608, Folder "Israel vol. VIII 1 of 3," Kissinger-Rabin (memcon), 22 December 1970. For three other occasions, see NPP, NSC Country Files-Middle East, Box 607, Folder 3, Barbour to Rogers, 23 July 1970; ISA, RG 93, 4996/A1, Dinitz to Idan, 24 March 1973; ISA, RG 43, 7052/3, Gazit to Dinitz, 14 June 1973. The Soviet Union had broken diplomatic relations with Israel during the June 1967 Six-Day War, and, unlike the United States, could not talk to both sides of the Arab-Israeli conflict.

123. On the status of Israeli-Vietnamese relations at the time, see ISA, FM, 4189/39, Horam to Erel, 24 April 1968. I thank Professor Joseph Heller for alerting me to this point.

124. Klinghoffer, *Jews*, 58.

125. Ibid., 66–69; Arlene Lazarowitz, "Different Approaches to a Regional Search for Balance: The Johnson Administration, the State Department, and the Middle East, 1964–1967," *Diplomatic History* 32:1 (January 2008): 40; Rostow-Harman memcon, 3 May 1966, in *FRUS 1964–1968*, Vol. 18, Arab-Israeli Dispute, 1964–1967, 581.

126. ISA, FM, 4156/3, Bitan to Rabin, 6 November 1969, and Bitan to Rabin, 13 November 1969; NA, Country Files-Middle East, Box 605, Folder 1(A), Davis to Elliot, 12 November 1969; Joseph Alsop, "Salute to Nixon Makes 'Kid' March Heartache," *Washington Post*, 17 November 1969.

127. See: Knesset Deliberations, 26 November 1969, Vol. 56, 80–85; NPP, NSC Country Files-Middle East, Box 607, Folder 2, Garment to Haldeman, 26 May 1970.

128. See, for instance, ISA, FM, 4159/10, Bitan to Herzog, 14 December 1969.

129. ISA, FM, 4156/3, Bitan to Rabin, 6 November 1969; ISA, RG 43, 7040/13, 9 November 1969.

130. See ISA, FM, 4157/5, Rabin to Eban, 10 July 1968.

131. ISA, RG 43, 740/13, Argov to Dinitz, 7 November 1969.

132. ISA, RG 43, 7071/1, Argov to Dinitz, 19 November 1969.

133. NPP, NSC Name Files, Box 815, Folder "Garment," Garment to Haldeman, 14 October 1969; Safire, *Before the Fall*, 567. To the best of my knowledge, Safire's memoir is the only source that advances this

study's argument that Nixon's Israeli policy was importantly shaped by his perception of Meir's conduct in non-Middle Eastern contexts.

134. SA, FM 5294/9, Elizur to Rabin, 23 May 1972.

135. ISA, RG 43, 7040/13, Argov to Bitan, 18 November 1969; Small, "Containing Domestic Enemies," 140; Richard Nixon, *In the Arena: A Memoir of Victory, Defeat and Renewal* (New York: Simon and Schuster, 1990), 332; and Richard Nixon, *No More Vietnams* (New York: Arbor House, 1985), 115; ISA, FM, 4156/3, Ben-Haim to Prime Minister's Office, 7 October 1969. This last message actually relays the very positive impression Meir left on Nixon regarding Vietnam during their meeting in September 1969.

136. Safire, *Before the Fall*, 577; ISA, FM 5294/11, Nixon to Meir, 22 March 1973; NPP, Kissinger telcons, Box 14, Folder 2, Nixon-Kissinger, 6 May 1972; NA, Haldeman Diary, CD version, Entry 1 February 1972.

137. See Melanie McAlister, *Epic Encounters: Culture, Media and the U.S. Interests in the Middle East since 1945* (Berkeley: University of California Press, 2005), 170–171, 174–175.

138. *Washington Post*, 11 June 1972, A1.

139. NPP, NSC Country Files-Middle East, Box 609, Folder 2, Clawson to Haldeman, 14 June 1972.

140. ISA, FM 5295/8, Rabin to FM, 18 July 1972.

141. NPP, NSC Country Files-Middle East, Box 609, Folder 2, Clawson to Haldeman, 14 June 1972; NPP, Kissinger telcons, Box 14, Folder 2, Nixon-Kissinger, 6 May 1972.

142. Inbar, *Rabin*, 39; NPP, Kissinger telcons, Box 16, Folder 2, Rabin-Kissinger, 25 September 1972.

143. ISA, FM 4548/6, Elizur to Brosh, 1 December 1971; NPP, NSC Name Files, Box 815, Folder "Garment," Garment to Haldeman, 21 November 1970; New York Public Library DOROT section, New York City (hereafter cited as NYPL), *The Politics of American Jews* collection, Sy Kennen, Oral History.

144. ISA, FM 4156/2, Elizur to Argov, 27 July 1969; NPP, NSC Presidential Correspondence, Box 756, Folder 6, Meir to Graham, 11 March 1970; NPP, NSC Countries-Middle East, Box 609, Folder 2, FBI Director to Kissinger, 13 August 1971. Meir also favored a Graham visit to Israel. ISA, RG 43, 7042/1, Dinitz to Rabin, 6 March 1972.

145. Nixon-Graham conversation, 1 February 1972, in *The White House Tapes*, ed. Prados, 243–244. Nixon professed not to care about his standing with Jewish voters, but during 1971 his campaign strategists, at least, believed this could prove a key swing factor. NYPL, *The Politics of American Jews* collection, Rita Hauser Oral History.

146. ISA, RG 93, 7792/A8, Rabin to Dinitz, 27 December 1972.

147. NPP, Kissinger telcons, Box 17, Folder 10, Nixon-Kissinger, 16 January 1973. See also Kissinger telcons, Box 14, Folder 10, Nixon-Kissinger, 29 June 1972. Indeed, Rabin appears to have been the most influential among several Israeli ambassadors in Washington who figured importantly in the shaping of the relationship. For the general phenomenon, see Shlomo Gazit, "The Role of the Foreign Ministry and the Foreign Service," in Yager et al., eds., *Ministry for Foreign Affairs*, 1090.

148. ISA, RG 93, 7792/A8, Dinitz to Rockefeller, 16 May 1973; ISA, RG 93, 4496/A2 Dinitz to Gazit, 23 August 1973, and Shalev to Gazit, 10 September 1973. After the Yom Kippur War, when the American-Israeli relationship ran into grave problems, this would come to haunt Dinitz.

149. ISA, RG 93, 7792/A8, Max Fisher-Meir meeting, 27 May 1973.

150. ISA, RG 93, 7792/A8, government meeting protocol, 3 June 1973, and Dinitz to Gazit, 5 June 1973.

151. ISA, RG 60, 8163/4, Rabin to Knesset Security and Foreign Affairs Committee, 30 March 1973.

152. ISA, FM, 5294/11, Elizur to foreign ministry director general, 21 March 1973; Levanon, *"'Nativ' was the Code Name"*, 400–401; ISA, RG 93, 4996/1, Gazit to Dinitz, 27 April 1973; ISA, RG 60, 8163/4, Meir to Knesset Security and Foreign Affairs Committee, 4 May 1973.

153. NPP, NSC Presidential/HAK memcons, Box 1026, Folder 20, Meir-Nixon (memcon), 1 March 1973.

154. ISA, FM, 5294/13, Elizur to Dinitz, 2 September 1973; NPP, Kissinger telcons, Box 12, Folder 10, Kissinger-Nixon, 15 January 1972. See also ISA, RG 93, 7792/A8, Gazit to Dinitz, 10 May 1973.

155. Rabin, *Memoirs*, 165–167; NPP, WHSF: POF: Annotated News Summaries, Box 37, Folder 2–7 December 1971, 6 December 1971; ISA, RG 43, 7052/21, Rabin to Dinitz, 19 March 1972, and 17 April 1972.

156. ISA, RG 93, 4996/A2, Gazit to Dinitz, 14 June 1972, and Gazit to Dinitz, 15 June 1973; NPP, Kissinger telcons, Box 20, Folder 7, Kissinger-Dinitz, 14 June 1973.

157. ISA, RG 93, 7792/8, Gazit to Dinitz, 8 April 1973. For Sadat's perspective, see Anwar Sadat, *In Search of Identity* (London: Collins, 1978), 229.

158. ISA, FM 5295/8, Periodical summary (probably authored by Military Intelligence), 3 July 1972, Rabin to Foreign Office, 18 July 1972; ISA, RG 60, 8163/4, Rabin testimony before the Knesset Security and Foreign Affairs Committee, 30 March 1973.

159. Eban, *Autobiography*, 486; ISA, FM, 5295/9, foreign ministry symposium on American policy, 26 March 1973; ISA, RG 93, 7792/A8, government session minutes, 16 September 1973.

160. ISA, RG 43, 7062/8, government session minutes, 13 March 1973.

161. NPP, NSC Country Files-Middle East, Box 658, Folder "nodis vol. V 2 of 2," Zurhellen (American chargé d'affaires)-Allon discussion, 5 March 1973.

162. Rafael, *Destination Peace*, 246–249 (Hebrew); Eban, *Autobiography*, 479.

163. ISA, FM, 5294/9, Eban-Rogers-Sisco (memcon), 21 April 1972; nsarchive, document 4; NPP, NSC Countries-Middle East, Box 610, Folder "Israel vol. 12," Sisco interview on Israeli television, 1 August 1973.

164. NPP, NSC Countries-Middle East, Box 610, Folder "Israel vol. 12," Kissinger-Keating (memcon), 13 August 1973; ISA, RG 93, 4996/A2, Dinitz to Gazit, 11 July 1973; ISA, 7792/A8, Dinitz to Kidron, 3 August 1973.

165. ISA, RG 93, 7792/A8, Rabin to Dinitz, 30 December 1972.

166. This aspect of the story is well covered in the literature and, essentially not in scholarly dispute, requires no detailed recounting here. See Quandt, *Decade of Decisions*, 143–164; Mordechai Bar-On, in Yager et al., eds., *Ministry for Foreign Affairs* (Hebrew), 274–275; Hanhimäki, *Flawed Architect*, 305–306; commentary by former ambassador to Egypt Herman Elits, in Leon Freidman and William F. Levantrosser, eds., *Cold War Patriot and Statesman: Richard M. Nixon* (Westport, Conn.: Greenwood Press 1993), 141–144; Lebow and Stein, *We All Lost*, 179; ISA, RG 43, 7055/8, memcon Kissinger-Meir, 28 February 1973.

167. Quandt, *Decade of Decisions*, 129.

168. NPP, Country Files-Middle East, Box 610, Folder "Israel Vol. 11," Kissinger to Nixon, n.d. (around October 1972).

169. ISA, FM 5294/4, Ben-Aharon to Foreign Office, 13 December 1972; ISA, FM, 5294/9, Rabin to Gazit, 19 July 1972.

170. This important episode has only begun to receive scholarly attention. For a convincing argument that the lack of American responsiveness strengthened Sadat's resolve to go to war as a means to break the stalemate, see: Uri Bar-Joseph, "Last Chance to Avoid War: Sadat's Peace Initiative of February 1973 and Its Failure," *Journal of Contemporary History* 41:3 (July 2006): 545–556.

171. ISA, RG 93, 7792/A8, Dinitz to Meir, 29 May 1973.

172. Quandt, *Decade of Decisions*, 161.

173. ISA, RG 93, 4996/A2, Dinitz to Gazit, 30 September 1973.

174. NPP, Presidential/HAK memcons, Box 1027, Folder 3, Kissinger-Scowcroft-PFIAB (memcon), 3 August 1973.

175. The Israeli embassy was far less concerned about these speeches than was the Israeli foreign ministry. Compare: ISA, FM 5294/13, Shalev to Evron, 12 September 1973, and Evron to Shalev, 14 September 1973.

176. ISA, RG 93, 4996/A2, Dinitz to Gazit, 30 September 1973; Quandt, *Decade of Decisions*, 162; Kissinger, *Years of Upheaval*, 296.

177. Stein and Lebow, *We All Lost*, 166–172; Garthoff, *Détente and Confrontation*, 404–412; Zubok, *Failed Empire*, 239.

178. Stein and Lebow, We All Lost the Cold War, 285–288.

179. See: Gottschalk, "Perspectives," in *The Yom Kippur War*, ed. Moshe Davis, esp. 37; Murray Friedman, *The Neoconservative Revolution: Jewish Intellectuals and the Shaping of Public Policy* (Cambridge: Cambridge University Press, 2005), 125; Kissinger-Jewish intellectuals (memcon), 6 December 1973, reprinted in Zaki Shalom, "Kissinger and the American Jewish Leadership after the 1973 War," *Israel Studies* 7:1 (2002): 198–208.

180. Meir, *My Life*, 365; NA, RG 59, Records of HAK, Box 136, Folder 2, Nixon-Kissinger-Golda Meir (memcon), 1 November 1973; NA, RG 59, Records of HAK, Box 2, Folder "November–December 1973 Folder 2," Kissinger-Golda Meir (memcon), 11 November 1973.

181. Anatoly Dobrynin, *In Confidence: Moscow's Ambassador to Six Cold War Presidents* (Seattle: University of Washington Press, 2001), 302–305.

182. NPP, NSC HAK Office Files, Box 129, Folder 3, Nixon-Secretary of the Treasury Simon (memcon), 9 July 1974.

Chapter 2. Israel, Soviet Jewish Emigration, and Idealpolitik

*An earlier, much abbreviated version of this chapter appeared as "Idealpolitik in Disguise: Israel, Jewish Emigration from the Soviet Union, and the Nixon Administration, 1969–1974," *International History Review* 29:3 (September 2007): 550–572.

1. Avi Pickar, "The Beginning of Selective Immigration in the 1950s," *Iyunim Bitkumat Israel* 9 (1999): 338 (Hebrew); Debra Hacohen, *Immigrants in Turmoil: The Great Wave of Immigration to Israel and Its Absorption, 1948–1953* (Jerusalem: Yad Ben-Zvi, 1994) (Hebrew), 120–121.

2. Pickar, "The Beginnings of Selective Immigration," 347.

3. Uri Bialer, "Top Hat, Tuxedo and Cannons: Israeli Foreign Policy from 1948 to 1956 as a Field of Study," *Israel Studies* 7:1 (2002): 19.

4. Levanon, *"Nativ,"* 216, 238; Yoram Dinstein (Israeli consul to New York, 1966–1970) conversation with author, Tel Aviv, 14 August 2003.

5. See Mike Bowker and Phil Williams, *Superpower Détente: A Reappraisal* (London: Sage, 1988), 164; Garthoff, *Détente and Confrontation*, 518; Dobrynin, *In Confidence*, 334; Zubok, *Failed Empire*, 234; NPP, Kissinger Office Files, Box 68, Folder "Dobrynin-Kissinger

Vol. 19," 28 September 1973; memcon Kissinger-Brezhnev, 24 October 1974, in William Burr, *The Kissinger Transcripts* (New York: The New Press, 1998), 330–331.

6. Benjamin Pinkus, "Israel's Activity on Behalf of Soviet Jews," in *Organizing Rescue: Jewish National Solidarity in the Modern Period*, ed. S. I. Troen and B. Pinkus (London: Frank Cass, 1991), 373; Henry Kissinger, *Diplomacy* (New York: Touchstone, 1994), 752.

7. For a sample of this multifaceted controversy, see Kissinger, *Years of Upheaval*, 250–255, 984–985; Fred Neal, *Détente or Debacle* (New York: W. W. Norton 1979); Henry M. Jackson Papers, University of Washington Libraries, Seattle, Washington (hereafter cited as Jackson Papers), Seattle, Accession No. 3560–28, Box 1, Folder 15, Letter Soviet Jewish dissidents to Jackson, 10 April 1974; William Korey, "Jackson-Vanik and Soviet Jewry," *The Washington Quarterly* 7:1 (1984): 116–128.

8. Pinkus, "Israel's Activity," 373.

9. Ya'acov Ro'i, Introduction, to Z. Khanin and B. Morozov, *Traitors to Mother Russia: Jewish Emigration through Soviet Eyes* (Tel Aviv: Tel Aviv University Press, 2005), 21 (Hebrew).

10. Among the most critical collections still out of public reach are the Kissinger Papers at the Library of Congress and the papers of Nativ

11. As noted in the introduction to this volume, the recent crop of literature on the issue covers a different time frame and relies much more on oral histories than governmental Israeli and American documentation. See Lazin, *The Struggle*, and Peretz, *Le Combat pour les Juifs Soviétiques: Washington—Moscou—Jérusalem 1953–1989* (Paris: Armand Colin, 2006).

12. William Orbach, *The American Movement to Aid Soviet Jews* (Amherst, Mass.: University of Massachusetts Press, 1979), 45; Arie Boaz, *Unseen Yet Always Present: The Life Story of Shaul Avigur* (Tel Aviv: Ministry of Defense, 2001), esp. 299 (Hebrew); ISA, FM, 4606/17, Baruch to Netzer, 23 June 1970; Dinstein conversation with author, Tel Aviv, 14 August 2003.

13. Dinstein conversation with author, Tel Aviv, 14 August 2003; Meir Rosenne (Nativ emissary at New York 1961–1966, and officer at Nativ Tel Aviv headquarters, 1966–1969) conversation with author, Jerusalem, 23 January 2006. Binyamin Eliav served, inter alia, as Nativ emissary at New York, 1960–1961, and head of Nativ's operations in the West, 1961–1966. For details on Nativ's early years, see Boaz, *Avigur*; Levanon, *"Nativ"*; Levanon, "Israel's Role in the Campaign," in *A Second Exodus: The American Movement to Free Soviet Jews*, ed. M. Freedman and A. D. Chernin (Hanover, N.H., and London, 1999), 71–83; Peretz, "Nativ's Emissaries."

14. Pinkus, "Israel Activity"; Levanon, *"Nativ,"* 193, 244, 433, 296, 385; Boaz, *Avigur*, 294–295; ISA, RG 77, 7339/34, Israeli government directive, 3 April 1970.

15. Jerusalem, Central Zionist Archive (hereafter cited as CZA), RG Z5, 14068, Tekoah press conference, 27 January 1970.

16. Pinkus, "Israel Activity," 394.

17. Lazin, *Struggle*, 32.

18. ISA, FM 4606/17, Baruch to Netzer, 23 June 1970.

19. Rosenne conversation with author, 23 January 2006; ISA, FM 4605/10, Dinstein to Levanon, 2 March 1970; ISA, RG 77, 7339/34, Netzer to Prime Minister Meir, 15 December 1969; ISA, FM 4605/10, Caspi (New York) to FM, 14 April 1970. Somewhat ironically, Kazakov (Ya'acov Kedmi) was destined to become Nativ's director in the 1990s.

20. Levanon, *"Nativ,"* 343; CZA, J124/748, immigration absorption minister Nathan Peled to Prisoners of Zion Organization Chairperson, 13 December 1971; CZA, J124/747, Prisoners of Zion Organization Chairperson to Council for Soviet Jewry Chairperson, 5 February 1973.

21. Dinstein conversation with author; Levanon, *"Nativ,"* 347.

22. ISA, FM, 4606/3, Israeli Los Angeles consulate to FM, 30 December 1970; Noam Chomsky ad, *New York Times*, 3 December 1970.

23. NPP, HAK Office Files, Box 71, Folder "Gromyko 70," Acting Secretary Irvin to Nixon, 21 October 1970; ISA, FM 4607/1, Baruch to FM, 14 December 1970.

24. NPP, NSC subject files, Box 342, Folder "HAK's evening notes, Dec.70–Jan.71," Embassy Moscow to Secstate, 31 December 1970; NPP, NSC, Country Files-Europe, Box 714, Folder "USSR Volume VII," Eliot to Kissinger, 6 January 1971.

25. ISA, FM, 4606/4, Gazit to New York Consulate, 3 January 1971.

26. CZA, S100/1075, Jewish Agency board meeting, 21 December 1970; ISA, FM, 4607/2, Consulate New York to FM, 28 January 1971.

27. CZA, S100/1076, Jewish Agency board meeting, 14 January 1971.

28. CZA, Z6/1151, Goldmann to prime minister Levi Eshkol, 19 November 1968; CZA, S62/913, Golda Meir statement, 7 May 1970; Boaz, *Avigur*, 297; Levanon, *"Nativ,"* 164–165.

29. ISA, 3 February 1971, 4607/3, Washington Embassy to FM; CZA, S100/1076, Levanon to Jewish Agency board meeting, 4 January 1971.

30. For an admonition against walking out of the shadows, see, for instance, ISA, FM, 4607/3, Israeli Washington embassy to Israeli consul general in Atlanta, 9 March 1971.

31. ISA, FM, 5370/1, Eran to FM, 17 March 1972.

32. NPP, NSC Country Files—MidEast, Box 609, Folder "September 1971–September 1972," Kissinger-Eban (memcon), 24 April 1972; NPP, Leonard Garment Papers, Box 119, Folder "Soviet Jewry '72 (3 of 4)," Maass-Stein-Fisher Statement, 25 April 1972.

33. ISA, FM 5370/1, Evron to Eban, 7 April 1972; CZA, Z5/14093, Richard Maass to NCSJ membership, 11 November 1971.

34. NA, Haldeman diary (CD version), 2 January 1972 and 12 June 1972.

35. Robert O. Freedman, ed., *Soviet Jewry in the Decisive Decade* (Durham, N.C.: Duke University Press, 1984), 44; Zubok, *Failed Empire*, 233. Gromyko and Dobrynin apologetically relayed the bureaucratic explanation to Kissinger. NPP, Kissinger telcons, Box 16, Folder 4, Kissinger-Rabin, 4 October 1972.

36. Particularly KGB chairman Yuri Andropov. See Boris Morozov, ed., *Documents on Soviet Jewish Emigration* (Portland: Frank Cass, 1999), Introduction, 20, and politburo meeting, 20 March 1973, 170–176; Dobrynin, *In Confidence*, 268–269; Petrus Buwalda, *They Did Not Dwell Alone: Soviet Jewish Emigration from the Soviet Union, 1967–1990* (Washington, D.C.: Woodrow Wilson Center Press, 1997), 90–91.

37. See "The New Serfdom," *New York Times* editorial, 29 August 1972. Stern's point that Jackson's amendment was more an initiative than a response to the exit tax seems well founded but overstated. *Water's Edge*, 21.

38. CZA, Z5/14139, Jerry Goodman to NCSJ membership, 6 September 1972.

39. Several Nativ operatives (and Israeli cabinet ministers) believed the tax should be paid, recalling the long-standing and largely successful Israeli practice of offering dollars to induce Jewish emigration from Eastern Europe. See: NYPL, *Soviet Jewry in America* series, Yehoshua Pratt 1989 Oral History; Levanon, *"Nativ,"* 395; Bialer, "Top Hat, Tuxedo and Cannons," 35–36; Dalia Ofer, "Immigration and *Aliya*: New Aspects of Jewish Policy," *Cathedra* 75 (April 1995): 154.

40. NPP, NSC Presidential Correspondence 1969–1974, Box 756, Folder "Israel–Prime Minister Golda Meir 1971–1972," Haig to Kissinger, 31 August 1972.

41. NPP, NSC Country Files-Middle East, Box 610, Folder "Israel Vol. 11," Rogers-Allon (memcon), 16 December 1972.

42. Jerusalem, Hebrew University at Mount Scopus Davis Building, the Abba Eban Center for Israeli Diplomacy, Eban Archive, file C-0031-F-0283, Eban on *Face the Nation* 27 September 1972.

43. ISA, FM, 5370/2, Eban to Rabin, 18 August 1972, and Gazit to Rabin, 12 October 1972.

44. CZA, S100/1076, *Jewish Agency board*—Levanon Meetings, 4 January and 14 January 1971; New York City, National Conference on Soviet Jewry Archive (hereafter cited as NCSJA), RG I-181, Box 5, Folder "Maass Richard," Maass-Levanon meeting, 13 September 1972.

45. Peretz, "Nativ's Emissaries," 121; Levanon, "Israel's Role," 77; ISA, FM, 4607/2, Unsigned letter to Netzer (Nativ headquarters), January 1970.

46. NA, Subject-Numeric, Box 3010, Folder "ref USSR," Ambassador Barbour to secstate 3271, 23 May 1972; NPP, WHSF:SMOF: Haldeman, Box 105, Folder "Garment," Garment to Haldeman,

17 November 1972. See also Peter Golden, *Quiet Diplomat: A Biography of Max M. Fisher* (New York: Cornwall Books, 1992), 260, 271.

47. NPP, NSC VIP visits, Box 922, Folder "Israel (Golda Meir's visit 1 March 1973)," Dep. of State to Nixon, 24 February 1973.

48. NYPL, *The Politics of American Jews* Collection, Richard Maass Oral History, 5 June 1974; NPP, Kissinger telcons, Chronological File, Box 15, Folder 9, telcon Kissinger-Peterson, 7 September 1972.

49. NA, Haldeman diary (CD version), 16 September 1972; NPP, HAK Office Files, Box 74, Folder "Trip to Moscow Sept. 1972," memcon Kissinger-Brezhnev, 12 September 1972.

50. See NPP, NSC Presidential/HAK memcons, Box 1027, Folder "memcons Apr.–Nov.1973," memcon Nixon-Senate Commerce Committee, 8 May 1973.

51. NPP, NSC Presidential/HAK memcons, Box 1026, Folder 23, Golda-Nixon-Kissinger-Rabin (memcon), 3 March 1973; NPP, Nixon Tapes, Cabinet Room tape 123/1, Nixon-Jewish leadership meeting, 19 April 1973.

52. NPP, Kissinger telcons, Dobrynin File, Box 27, Folder 10, Kissinger-Dobrynin, 22 April 1973; ISA, RG 43, 7045/2, Dinitz to Gazit, 19 April 1973.

53. Rowland Evans and Robert Novak, "Nixon's Warning," *Washington Post*, 9 July 1973; ISA, RG 93, Dinitz Papers, 4996/2, Dinitz to Gazit, 24 September 1973.

54. ISA, RG 93, 4996/2, Dinitz to Gazit, 30 September 1973.

55. ISA, FM, 5370/6, Knesset secretary report on Foreign Relations and Security Committee deliberations, 25 September 1973, and Israeli Policy Statement 342, 5 October 1973; Knesset minutes, 2 June 1973, Volume 67, 3277.

56. NPP, NSC Presidential/HAK memcons, Box 1026, Folder 23, Golda-Nixon-Kissinger-Rabin (memcon), 3 March 1973.

57. ISA, RG 60, 8163/4, Meir to Knesset Security and Foreign Affairs Committee, 4 May 1973.

58. ISA, RG 93, 4996/2, Dinitz to Gazit, 24 September 1973; CZA, S62/744, message from the "Action Committee of Soviet Newcomers in Israel" to Golda Meir, 20 June 1973; ISA, RG 60, file 8163/3, Knesset Security and Foreign Affairs Committee deliberations, 25 February 1973.

59. Levanon, *"Nativ,"* 400–401.

60. The present writer shared this experience with Pauline Peretz. See Peretz, "Nativ's Emissaries," 127; Lazin, *Struggle*, 27.

61. NYPL, Pratt Oral History, 1989; Dinstein conversation with author, Tel Aviv, 13 August 2003. Quite naturally, the anti-Jackson voices within Nativ hardly receive a hearing in Levanon's memoir.

62. ISA, RG 93, 4996/1, Gazit to Dinitz, 27 April 1973.

63. ISA, FM, 5294/11, Elizur to foreign ministry director general, 21 March 1973.

64. ISA, RG 60, 8163/7, Meir to Knesset Security and Foreign Affairs Committee, 21 September 1973.

65. New York City, American Jewish Committee Archives (hereafter cited as AJC), BGX series, Box 25, Folder "Soviet Union Trade," bookbinder note for record on meeting with Israeli officials at embassy, 19 March 1973; Stern, *Water's Edge*, 76.

66. CZA, S62/744, Charlotte Jacobson to Louis Pincus, 4 April 1973.

67. ISA, RG 93, 4996/1, Gazit to Dinitz, 3 May 1973; ISA, FM, 5370/2, Shomron to FM, 15 June 1973.

68. Stern, *Water's Edge*, 78–79; NYPL, *Soviet Jewry in America* series, Levanon Oral History; ISA, FM, 5296/16, Arad to Evron, 19 September 1973; NCSJA, Box 5, Folder "Maass," Maass memo for the record, 23 June 1973.

69. ISA, RG 60, 8163/2, Levanon to Knesset Security and Foreign Affairs Committee, 6 February 1973; CZA, S62/744, Decter to Jerry Goodman and NSCJ publication, "Summary of Soviet Jewish Emigration Data," both dated 22 June 1973.

70. ISA, RG 93, 4996/2, Dinitz to Gazit, 30 September 1973, and Dinitz to Gazit, 1 October 1973.

71. NPP, Kissinger telcons, Chronological File, Box 22, Folder 3, Nixon-Kissinger, 17 September 1973; NPP, Kissinger telcons, Chronological File, Box 22, Folder 6, Kissinger-Jackson, 1 October 1973.

72. Isaacson, *Kissinger*, 516–517; NA, RG 59, Records of HAK, Box 3, Folder "nodis letters HAK 1973–1977," Kissinger-Dinitz (memcon), 8 October 1973; Henry Kissinger, *Crisis: The Anatomy of Two Major Foreign Policy Crises* (New York: Simon and Schuster, 2003), 87.

73. NA, RG 59, Records of HAK, Box 136, Folder 2, Nixon-Kissinger-Golda Meir (memcon), 1 November 1973; NCSJA, Box 6, Folder "J. Goodman 1973," Goodman File for Record, 10 November 1973; memcon Kissinger-Jewish leaders, 27 December 1973, reprinted in Zaki Shalom, "Kissinger and the American Jewish Leadership after the 1973 War," *Israel Studies* 7:1 (Spring 2002): 209–217.

74. Meir, *My Life*, 358, 381; NA, RG 59, Records of HAK, Box 136, Folder 2, Nixon-Golda et al. (memcon), 1 November 1973; Rafael, *Destination Peace*, 264 (Hebrew). While the prime minister coped comparatively well with the disaster, she contemplated suicide several times during the war. See U. Bar-Joseph, *The Watchman Fell Asleep* (Lod: Zmora-Bitan, 2001), 394 (Hebrew).

75. NYPL, *Soviet Jewry in America* series, Y. Rager Oral History, 8 June 1990.

76. ISA, RG 60, 8163/4, Rabin to Knesset Security and Foreign Affairs Committee, 30 March 1973, and Eban to Knesset Security and Foreign Affairs Committee, 30 April 1973; ISA, FM 5294/7, Rabin to Dinitz, 20 April 1972; ISA, FM 5370/2, Eban to FM, 18 September 1972. The friction between Nativ and the foreign ministry dated back to Golda Meir's own tenure as foreign minister in the 1950s. See Boaz, *Avigur*, 267.

77. See: Simcha Dinitz, "The American-Israeli Dialogue during the War," in *The Yom Kippur War*, ed. Bar-Siman-Tov and Opaz (Jerusalem: Davis Institute, 1999), 157.

78. NA, RG 59, Box 1, Folder "nodis memcons Sept–Dec.73," Kissinger-Jewish group (Morris Abram, Saul Linowitz) meeting, 8 February 1974; NCSJA, RG I-181, Box 6, Folder "J. Goodman 1973," Goodman file for record, 10 November 1973.

79. NYPL *Soviet Jewry in America* series, Rager Oral History; Lazin, *Struggle*, 73 note 160; author's interview with former NCSJ executive secretary Jerry Goodman, New York City, 6 February 2003.

80. CZA, S62/776, Minutes of the Executive of the WZO-American section, 19 March 1974; NYPL, *Oral History of the American Jewish Committee* series, Maass 1980 Oral History.

81. Memcon Kissinger-Jewish intellectuals, 6 December 1973, reprinted in Zaki Shalom, "Kissinger and the American Jewish Leadership after the 1973 War," *Israel Studies* 7:1 (Spring 2002): 198–208; AJC, BGX collection, Folder "Soviet Trade," David Geller to Elmer Winter, 11 January 1974; NYPL, *Soviet Jewry in America* series, Eugene Gold Oral History, 10 January 1990; Lebow and Stein, *We All Lost*, 288.

82. Isaacson, *Kissinger*, 615.

83. In retrospect, Kissinger's concern was misplaced. See NPP, NSC Presidential/HAK memcons, Box 1027, Folder "Memcons HAK Apr.–Nov. 73 1 of 5," memcon Bipartisan leadership meeting, 27 November 1973; Eitan Gilboa, *American Public Opinion Towards Israel and the Arab-Israeli Conflict* (Lexington, Mass.: Lexington Books, 1987), 60–65.

84. NA, RG 59, Records of HAK, Box 2, Folder "nodismemcons Jan-June 74 Folder 3," memcon Kissinger-Meir, 15 January 1974; NA, RG 59, Records of HAK, Box 6, Folder "nodismemcons Feb. 74," Kissinger-Dinitz (memcon), 9 February 1974. The quote is from the February 9 memo.

85. CZA, S100/1086, Charlotte Jacobson report to Jewish Agency board, 26 June 1974, and Levanon report to Jewish Agency Board, 29 July 1974.

86. NA, RG 59, Box 7, Folder "nodismemcons March 1974 f.2," Kissinger-Meir memcon, 8 May 1974; NA, RG 59, Records of HAK, Box 8, Folder "nodis memcons May 74 Folder 10," memcon Kissinger-Golda-Dinitz, 29 May 1974.

87. NA, RG 59, Records of HAK, Box 4, Folder "nodismemcons Jan 74 Folder 3," memcon Kissinger-Allon-Dinitz, 2 October 1974; NA, RG 59, Records of HAK, Box 22, Folder "classified external memos December 74 April 75 Folder 2," Kissinger-Rabin-Allon (memcon), 13 October 1974; NA, RG 59, Records of HAK, Box 10, Folder "nodismemcons October '74," memcon Kissinger-Dinitz, 5 October 1974.

88. NA, RG 59, Records of HAK, Box 4, Folder "nodismemcons Jan 74 Folder 3," Kissinger-Allon-Dinitz (memcon), 2 October 1974.

89. NA, RG 59, Records of HAK, Box 9, Folder "nodismemcons July 1974 Folder 1," memcon Kissinger-Allon, 31 July 1974. Rejected by Kissinger, Allon's litmus test notion was endorsed in the 1980s by then-secretary of state George Schultz. See Ro'i's introduction to *Traitors to Mother Russia*, 32.

90. CZA, S100/1086, Jewish Agency board meeting with American Jewish leaders, 26 June 1974; ISA, RG 60, File 8163/7, Dinitz to Knesset Security and Foreign Affairs Committee, 17 September 1973.

91. CZA, S100/1086, Levanon report to Jewish Agency board, 29 July 1974; CZA, S82/44, Pedhazur message, 20 November 1974; Levanon, *"Nativ,"* 402; NA, RG 59, Records of HAK, Box 4, Folder "nodismemcons Jan 74 Folder 3," memcon Kissinger-Allon-Dinitz, 2 October 1974.

92. Levanon, *"Nativ,"* 402.

93. CZA, S82/44, Sapir (Jewish Agency chairperson) to Jacobson, 19 December 1974, and to New York, 22 December 1974.

94. Levanon, *"Nativ,"* 403. For a table of Soviet Jewish emigration figures, see Lazin, *Struggle*, 309.

95. Dobrynin, *In Confidence*, 304; Rabin, *Memoirs* (Hebrew edition) (Tel Aviv: Maariv, 1979), 427–428; NA, RG 59, Records of HAK, Box 12, Folder "nodis memcons August 75," memcon Rabin-Allon-Kissinger-Sisco, 26 August 1975.

96. ISA, FM 5370/1, Rabin to FM, 21 April 1972; ISA, FM 5296/15, Rivlin to Dinitz, 4 April 1973; ISA, FM 5370/2, Levanon to Gazit, 20 June 1973; CZA, S62/735, Bert Gold, "Who Speaks for the Jews?" AJC Annual Meeting Address, 4 May 1972; Charles Liebman, *Pressure without Sanctions* (Rutherford: Fairleigh Dickinson University Press, 1977), 238–244; Rabin, *Memoirs*, 397.

97. See A. Herzberg, "Israel and the Diaspora: A Relationship Reexamined," in *U.S.-Israeli Relations at the Crossroads*, ed. Sheffer, 177; and Lazin, *Struggle*, passim.

98. See D. Forsythe, *Human Rights and U.S. Foreign Policy: Congress Reconsidered* (Gainesville, Fla.: University Press of Florida, 1988), 75. For an authoritative overview of Soviet policy-making in this context, see Ro'i's introduction to *Traitors to Mother Russia*.

99. I thank an anonymous reader of an earlier version of this chapter published in the journal *International History Review* for drawing my attention to this irony.

100. J. M. Hanhimäki, "Ironies and Turning Points: Détente in Perspective," in *Reviewing the Cold War: Approaches, Interpretations, Theory*, 2nd edition, ed. O. A. Westad (London: Frank Cass, 2001), 335–338; Buwalda, *They Did Not Dwell Alone*, 115–116; Dobrynin, *In Confidence*, 346–347. For recent and persuasive analyses of how the "Helsinki affect" influenced dissidents and policymakers in the Soviet Union, see D. C. Thomas, "Human Rights Ideas, the Demise of Communism, and the End of the Cold War," *Journal of Cold War Studies* 7:2 (Spring 2005), esp. 117–123; Svetlana Sarvanskaya, "Unintended Consequences: Soviet Interests, Expectations and Reactions to the Helsinki Final Act," in *Helsinki 1975 and the Transformation of Europe*, eds. Oliver Bange and Gottfriend Niedhart (Oxford: Berghahn Books, 2008), 175—190; Vladislav M. Zubok, "The Soviet Union and Détente in the 1970s," *Cold War History* 8:4 (November 2008), esp. 441–444.

101. See Richard Shifter, "The Impact of the United States on Soviet Emigration Policy," in *Russian Jews on Three Continents: Migration and Resettlement*, ed. Ya'acov Ro'i et al., (London: Frank Cass, 1997), esp. 88.

102. Gold, "Who Speaks for the Jews"; Levanon, *"Nativ,"* 193.

103. Kaufman, *Jackson*, 267; NA, RG 59, Records of the Counselor, Box 9, Folder "trade bill August 1974," Sonnenfeldt to Kissinger, 16 September 1974; NPP, NSC-Presidential-HAK memcons, Box 1027, Folder "April–Nov 1973 (3 of 5)," Meany-Lovestone-Kissinger meeting, 14 September 1973.

104. Bowker and Williams, *Superpower Détente*, 155, 161. For a partial concession of this point by one of Kissinger's most trusted lieutenants, see Peter Rodman OH, 22 May 1994, Association for Diplomatic Studies and Training (ADST) Oral History Collection.

105. NYPL, *Soviet Jewry in America* collection, David Geller Oral History; Peter Novick, *The Holocaust in American Life* (Boston: Houghton Mifflin, 1999), 188–190.

106. For a recent analysis of intra-Jewish frictions, explicitly sympathetic to the Jewish role in the neoconservative movement, see Friedman, *The Neoconservative Revolution*, esp. chapters 6–8.

107. Beit Berl, Israel, Labor Party Archives (hereafter cited as LPA), file 2-21-1971-103, Louis Pincus at Ha'maarach Party Convention, 4 April 1971; ISA, FM, 4550/7, Brosh to Gazit, 15 July 1971.

108. Murray Freedman, "The Jewish Community Comes of Age," introduction to *A Second Exodus*, ed. Murray Freedman and Alfred Chernin (Hanover, N.H., and London: Brandeis University Press), 6–7; NYPL, *Soviet Jewry in America* collection, Eugene Gold Oral History, 1990.

109. ISA, FM, 5370/2, Shomron to FM, 27 April 1973; NA, RG 59, Subject-Numeric Files, Box 1114, Folder "FT US-USSR 1/1/73," memcon Goodman-Meyer Rashish, 10 October 1973. See also I. M. Destler, "Congress," in *The Making of America's Soviet Policy*, ed. J. Nye Jr. (New Haven: Yale University Press, 1984), 55.

110. Peretz, "Nativ's Emissaries," 126; CZA, S100/1086, Jacobson report to Jewish Agency board, 26 June 1974.

111. Lazin, *Struggle*, 7.

112. Peter Hagel and Pauline Peretz, "States and Transnational Actors: Who's Influencing Whom? A Case Study in Jewish Diaspora Politics During the Cold War," *European Journal of International Relations* 11:4 (2005): 467–493, esp. 485.

113. ISA, RG 60, 8163/4, Meir to Knesset Security and Foreign Affairs Committee, 4 May 1973; ISA, RG 93,4996/1, Gazit to Dinitz, 25 May 1973.

114. Kaufman, *Jackson*, 263; ISA, FM, 5370/2, Shomron to FM, 27 April 1973; ISA, RG 93, 4996/1, Gazit to Dinitz, 27 April 1973.

115. ISA, RG 93, 4996/2, Gazit to Dinitz, 14 June 1973.

116. ISA, FM 5370/1, Caspi to FM, 14 April 1970, and Shomron to FM, 1 February 1972; Knesset minutes, 12 June 1973, Vol. 67, pp. 3276–3277; Knesset minutes, 19 July 1973, Vol. 68, pp. 4447–4451.

117. Klieman, *Statecraft in the Dark*.

118. NA, Records of HAK, RG 59, Box 10, Folder "nodismemcons Feb 75 Folder 4," Rabin-Kissinger memcon, 11 February 1975; Levanon, *"Nativ,"* 401. Another advocate, though less influential with the prime minister, was Yigal Allon. See Knesset minutes, 1 July 1970, Vol. 58, p. 2316; NA, RG 59, Records of HAK, Box 9, Folder "nodismemcons July 1974 Folder 1," Allon-Kissinger memcon, 31 July 1974; ISA, RG 43, 7031/5, Rafiah to FM, 1 August 1974; Anita Shapira, *Yigal Allon: Spring of His Life* (Tel Aviv: Hakibutz Hameuchad, 2004), 481 (Hebrew).

119. See Shlomo Avineri, "Ideology and Israel's Foreign Policy," *Jerusalem Quarterly* 37 (1986): esp. 13.

120. The distinction between the cognitive and normative dimensions of policy legitimacy draws on A. L. George, "Domestic Constraints on Regime Change in U.S. Foreign Policy: The Need for Policy Legitimacy," in *Change in the International System*, ed. O. R. Holsti, R. M. Siverson, A. L. George (Boulder, Colo.: Westview Press, 1980), 233–262. George dissects the problem of legitimizing a policy domestically rather than the problem under scrutiny here— why policy-makers find a certain policy line attractive.

121. See, for instance, ISA, FM, 3427/23, Tekoah to foreign minister, 7 December 1963. I thank Professor Joseph Heller for drawing my attention to this point.

122. According to historian Dalia Ofer, the shift from a selective-pragmatic view of *aliya* to a view that enshrined it on a merging of secu-

rity and ideological grounds dates back to the 1930s. See Dalia Ofer, "The Aliya, the Diaspora and the Yishuv," *Cathedra* 43 (March 1987): 70.

123. LPA, file 2-910-1970-63, Address by immigration absorption minister Nathan Peled to the Public Committee for Absorption, 6 July 1971; CZA, S100/1085, Jewish Agency executive board meeting, 13 November 1973.

124. NPP, NSC Country Files-MidEast, Box 609, Folder "Sept71–Sep.72," Alexis Johnson to Barbour, 19 June 1972; ISA, FM 5370/2, Washington to FM, 31 August 1972; Levanon, *"Nativ,"* 292, 343, 362.

125. ISA, FM 4606/17, Netzer to Baruch, 21 June 1970; NYPL, *Soviet Jewry in America* series, Dorothy Fosdick Oral History.

126. ISA, RG 60, 8163/6, Meir to Knesset Security and Foreign Affairs Committee, 22 June 1973; ISA, RG 106, Golda Meir Papers, 833/15, Eban to Meir, 3 February 1974.

127. Knesset minutes, 6 January 1971, Vol. 59, 892; NPP, NSC: HAK Office Files, Box 141, Folder "Israel," State Contingency Talking Points Briefing Paper to Nixon's visit to Israel, June 1974 (no exact date).

128. The following attempt to gauge the influence of ideology draws partly on the recent example set by Thomas, "Human Rights Ideas."

129. Knesset minutes, 6 January 1971, Vol. 59, p. 892; Knesset minutes, 12 June 1973, p. 3274. For a similar analysis of the sources of Israeli obligation to Soviet Jewry, see Pinkus, "Israel Activity," 378–379.

130. For the harboring of this sentiment by even relatively dovish figures, see CZA, Z6/1151, Levi Eshkol-Nahum Goldmann correspondence, 19 November 1968; Rafael, *Destination Peace*, 212, 240 (Hebrew).

131. Knesset minutes, 11 May 1971, Vol. 60, p. 2377.

132. See ISA, RG 60, 8163/10, Levanon's report to the committee, 29 October 1973.

133. Levanon, *"Nativ,"* p. 401.

134. This was one reason why eminent political scientist Hans J. Morgenthau endorsed Jackson-Vanik. See Benjamin M. Mollov, "Jewry's Prophetic Challenge to Soviet and Other Totalitarian Regimes According to Hans J. Morgenthau," *Journal of Church and State* 39:3 (Summer 1997): 561–575; Gerald Ford Library, Ann Arbor, Michigan (hereafter GFL), Ford Vice Presidential Papers, Box 150, Folder "Jews," Militch to Ford, 14 March 1973; Hans J. Morgenthau, "Henry Kissinger, Secretary of State: An Evaluation," *Encounter* [Great Britain], 43:5 (1974): 57–61.

135. Kissinger, *Years of Upheaval*, 988; Stern, *Water's Edge*, 84–86.

136. Isadore Twersky has observed that many prominent Jews were ill at ease with Zionism on the grounds that it would transpose Judaism from "glorious eternity into dull temporality." See Isadore Twersky, "Survival, Normalcy, Modernity," in *Zionism in Transition*, ed. M. Davis (New York: Herzl Press, 1980), 353–354. For Israeli leaders, Jackson-Vanik arguably provided an antidote to this line of criticism.

137. Amos Eran, Israeli embassy liaison with the American Congress through 1972, and Shlomo Avineri, foreign ministry director general in 1975–1976, testified to Meir's emotional attachment to the Soviet Jewish cause. Author discussions with Eran (by phone, 24 October 2002) and Avineri (Jerusalem, 20 September 2005).

138. Meir, *My Life*, 2. See also Namir, *Israeli Mission to Moscow*, 52 (Hebrew).

139. Meir, *My Life*, 203–204; ISA, FM, 4550/3, FM to Washington embassy, 14 January 1970; Meir to journalist James Reston, *New York Times*, 27 December 1970.

140. Meir, *My Life*, 327.

141. Ibid. , 205–207; LPA, file 4-37-1972-76, Meir address to Israeli youth at the seminar "Absorption and the Social Gap," 10 March 1972.

142. Uri Bialer, *Between East and West: Israel's Foreign Policy Orientation 1948–1956* (Cambridge: Cambridge University Press, 1990), 74–76.

143. Hagel and Peretz, "States and Transnational Actors," 478.

144. LPA, file 4-37-1972-76, Meir address to Israeli youth at the seminar "Absorption and the Social Gap," 10 March 1972.

145. ISA, FM 5296/13, FM to Washington embassy, 1 June 1972.

146. LPA, file 2-28-1971-4, Meir to Ha'maarach steering committee, 28 October 1971.

147. Meir, *My Life*, 347.

148. ISA, RG 93, 4996/1, Gazit to Dinitz, 27 April 1973; ISA, RG 93, 4996/2, Gazit to Dinitz, 3 June 1973.

149. Levanon, *"Nativ,"* 400–401.

150. ISA, RG 93, 4996/1, Gazit to Dinitz, 27 April 1973; ISA, RG 60, 8163/4, Meir to Knesset Security and Foreign Affairs Committee, 4 May 1973.

Chapter 3. Kissinger, Soviet Jewish Emigration, and the Demise of Détente

1. Notable yet partial exceptions to this rule are Bowker and Williams, *Superpower Détente*, chapter 7; Garthoff, *Détente and Confrontation*, 505–516; and Isaacson, *Kissinger*, chapter. 27.

2. Kaufman, *Henry Jackson*.

3. Orbach, *The American Movement to Aid Soviet Jews*; Freedman, ed., *Soviet Jewry in the Decisive Decade, 1971–1980*; Friedman and Chernin, eds., *A Second Exodus*; Ro'i et al., eds., *Russian Jewish Emigration on Three Continents*.

4. See, for example, Garthoff, *Détente and Confrontation*; Wilson, *Nixon Reconsidered*; Herbert Parmet, *Richard Nixon and His America* (Boston: Little, Brown, 1990); Bundy, *A Tangled Web*; Burr, *The Kissinger Transcripts*.

5. Ben-Zvi, *The United States and Israel: The Limits of the Special Relationship*; Nimrod Novik, *The United States and Israel: Domestic Determinants of a Changing U.S. Commitment* (Boulder, Colo.: Westview Press, 1986); Quandt, *Decade of Decisions*; Kenneth Stein, *Heroic Diplomacy: Sadat, Kissinger, Carter, Begin and the Quest for Arab-Israeli Peace* (New York: Routledge, 1999).

6. NPP, Garment Papers, Box 118, Folder "Soviet Jewry Current 1971 (2 of 2), Letter Jackson to Shakespeare, 26 March 1971; NCSJA, RG I-181, Box 31, Folder "Senate," Jackson address at Yeshiva University, 4 June 1973; AJC, BGX series, Box 25, Folder "Soviet Union Trade," Bookbinder to Bert Gold memo, 16 March 1973; Jackson Papers, Accession No. 3560-28, Box 1, Folder 10, memo Richard Perle to Jackson, 5 March 1974; Jackson Papers, Accession No. 3560-28, Box 1, Folder 11, memo Perle to Jackson, 14 March 1974. The citation is from the March 5 Perle memorandum.

7. NPP, NSC Country Files-Europe, Box 715, Folder 13, memo Kissinger to Nixon, 5 April 1971; NPP, HAK Office Files, Box 74, Folder "trip to Moscow Sept. 1972," memcon Brezhnev-Kissinger, 11 September 1972; NPP, HAK Office Files, Box 75, Folder "Kissinger conversations at Zavidovo May 5–8 1973," memcon Brezhnev-Kissinger, 8 May 1973; NPP, HAK Office Files, Box 75, Folder "meetings with Brezhnev memoranda from Kissinger," memo Kissinger to Nixon, 14 June 1973; NPP, HAK Office Files, Box 71, Folder "Gromyko 73," memo Kissinger for Files, 28 September 1973.

8. NPP, HAK Office Files, Box 72, Folder "Kissinger conversations in Moscow April 20–24," memcon Brezhnev-Kissinger, 22 April 1972.

9. NA, RG 59, Subject-Numeric Files, Box 1114, Folder "FT US-USSR 3/10/72," Beam to State 17111, 15 November 1972; NA, RG 59, Subject-Numeric Files, Box 1114, Folder "FT US-USSR 1-1-73," Amembassy Moscow to State, 16 March 1973; NPP, HAK Office Files, Box 68, Folder "Dobrynin-Kissinger Vol. 19," Brezhnev-Kendall meeting, 28 September 1973.

10. Victor Zorza, "To Force an End to Exit Tax on Jews," *Washington Post*, 15 March 1973; NSCJA, RG I-181, Box 62, Folder "Trade-MFN Status," Blind memo, "Responses to USSR Claims about Jackson-Mills-Vanik Amendment." For an illumination of ideology and anti-Semitism as crucial determinants of Soviet Jewish (and Israeli) policy, see Ya'acov Ro'i, "The Problematics of the Soviet-Israeli Relationship," in *Soviet Foreign Policy, 1917–1991: A Retrospective*, ed. Gabriel Gorodetsky (London: Frank Cass, 1994): 146–157.

11. Soviet politburo meeting, 20 March 1973, in Morozov, Documents on Soviet Jewish Emigration, 172; NPP, HAK Office Files, Box 71, Folder "Gromyko 73," memcon Kissinger-Brezhnev-Dobrynin, 24 September 1973; NPP, HAK Office Files, Box 71, Folder "Gromyko 73," memo Kissinger for

Files, 28 September 1973; Dobrynin, *In Confidence*, 337. Moscow failed to utilize Dobrynin's acumen and prominence on the Washington scene in other contexts as well. See Steven M. Miner, "Soviet Ambassadors from Maiskii to Dobrynin," in *The Diplomats*, ed. Gordon Craig and Francis L. Loewenheim (Princeton: Princeton University Press, 1994), 623–625.

12. Philip Zelikow, "The Statesman in Winter: Kissinger on the Ford Years," *Foreign Affairs* 78:3 (May/June 1999): 127. See also Robert L. Beisner, "History and Henry Kissinger," *Diplomatic History* 14:4 (1990): 513; Robert D. Schulzinger, *Henry Kissinger: Doctor of Diplomacy* (New York: Columbia University Press, 1989), 239. Kissinger may be measured by another valid but perhaps narrower criterion: as a bureaucratic infighter. As Gaddis notes, he proved extraordinarily adept at hanging on to power in a harsh environment. John Lewis Gaddis, "Rescuing Choice from Circumstances: The Statecraft of Henry Kissinger," in *The Diplomats*, ed. Craig and Loewenheim, 564.

13. For the first conviction, see Henry Kissinger, *The Necessity for Choice* (New York: Doubleday, 1961), 357; Henry Kissinger, *A World Restored: Metternich, Castlereagh, and the Problems of Peace, 1812–1822* (Gloucester, Mass.: Smith, 1957), 317, 324. For the second, see ibid., 1, 322; Henry Kissinger, "The White Revolutionary: Reflections on Bismarck," *Daedalus* 97 (Summer 1968): 893. Political scientist Michael Smith, who detects this dilemma, finds historian Kissinger more arrogantly inclined toward the first part of the equation than I do. Smith, *Realist Thought from Weber to Kissinger* (Baton Rouge: Louisiana State University Press, 1986), 198.

14. Kissinger, *World Restored*, 317, 320–321, 325; Kissinger, "The White Revolutionary," 899, 910, 921.

15. See, for instance, his 1968 admonitions reprinted in Henry Kissinger, *American Foreign Policy*, 3rd edition (New York: Norton, 1977), 79.

16. "The Meaning of History: Reflections on Spengler, Toynbee and Kant," unpublished undergraduate thesis, 345–346, cited in Greg Russell's important article, "Kissinger's Philosophy of History and Kantian Ethics," *Diplomacy and Statecraft* 7:1 (March 1996): 117.

17. Kissinger, "The White Revolutionary," 898.

18. Ibid., 893.

19. A relatively early study of Kissinger that emphasizes this doctrine is Peter W. Dickson, *Kissinger and the Meaning of History* (New York: Cambridge University Press, 1978).

20. Kissinger, *American Foreign Policy*, 1977 edition, 11–12.

21. Kissinger, *A World Restored*, 326. My emphasis. For an oblique reference to this tension, see Robert S. Litwak, "Henry Kissinger's Ambiguous Legacy," *Diplomatic History* 18:3 (Summer 1994): 439.

22. Kissinger, *A World Restored*, 317; see also Kissinger, *American Foreign Policy*, 1977 edition., 48.

23. Kissinger, *American Foreign Policy*, 1974 edition, 47.

24. "The Process of Détente," Statement Delivered to the Senate Foreign Relations Committee, September 19, 1974, *American Foreign Policy*, 1977 edition, 145–146, 172.

25. Kissinger, "The White Revolutionary," 921.

26. Kissinger, *A World Restored*, 326.

27. See James A. Reichley, *Conservatives in an Age of Change: The Nixon and Ford Administrations* (Washington, D.C.: Brookings, 1981), 113.

28. Kissinger, *A World Restored*, 329.

29. Henry Kissinger, *The Troubled Partnership: A Reappraisal of the Atlantic Alliance* (New York: McGraw Hill, 1965), 64. See also Richard Weitz, "Henry Kissinger's Philosophy of International Relations," *Diplomacy and Statecraft* 2:1 (1991): 107.

30. Kissinger, *Diplomacy*, 752.

31. This assessment accords with Gil Loescher and John Scanlan, *Calculated Kindness: Refugees and America's Half-Open Door, 1945–Present* (New York: Free Press, 1986), 91, as well as with Minton Goldman, "United States Policy and Soviet Jewish Emigration from Nixon to Bush," in *Jews and Jewish Life in Russia and the Soviet Union*, ed. Ya'acov Ro'i (London: Frank Cass, 1995), 341.

32. Albert D. Chernin, "Making Soviet Jews an Issue: A History," in *A Second Exodus*, ed. Friedman and Chernin, esp. 29–32, 41, 45, 51.

33. Richard Melanson, *American Foreign Policy Since the Vietnam War: The Search for Consensus from Nixon to Clinton*, 2nd edition (Armonk, N.Y.: M. E. Sharpe, 1996), 43; Kissinger, *White House Years*, 65.

34. Orbach, *The American Movement*, 3; Chernin, "Making Soviet Jews an Issue," 58–59.

35. Melanson, *American Foreign Policy*, 43. See also Keith Nelson, "Nixon, Kissinger and the Domestic Side of Détente," in *Re-Viewing the Cold War: Domestic Factors and Foreign Policy in the East-West Confrontation*, ed. Morgan and Nelson (Westport, Conn.: Praeger, 2000), 129–130.

36. Goodman conversation with author, New York City, February 6, 2003.

37. NPP, NSC Country Files (Europe-USSR), Box 709, Folder II, Walsh to Kissinger, 26 May 1969; NPP, WHCF Subject Files, Box 71, Folder "10/1/69-11/30/69," Letter Melencamp to Rothman, 27 October 1969; Chernin, *The Second Exodus*, 51.

38. Library of Congress, Garment Papers, Box 26, Folder 6, memo Kissinger to Garment, 13 November 1969.

39. NPP, Nixon tapes, first chronological series, 501–12, Nixon-Kissinger conversation, 19 May 1971; NPP, Nixon tapes, first chronological series, 505–4, Nixon-Kissinger conversation, 26 May 1971.

40. Burr introduction to Kissinger Transcripts, 8.

41. NPP, WHCF:SMOF: Garment Alpha-Numerical files, Box 116, Folder "Jewish Matters 69–70 (1 of 3)," Kissinger to Garment, 27 September 1969; NPP, NSC Name Files, Box 815, Folder "Garment, Leonard," Kissinger to Haldeman, 12 January 1971.

42. Gerald S. Strober and Deborah H. Strober, *Nixon: An Oral History of His Presidency* (New York: HarperCollins, 1994), 60; NPP, WHCF, Subject Files, Colo. 158, Box 71, Folder "10/1/70-10/31/70," Garment to Kissinger and Haig, 21 October 1970; NPP, NSC Subject Files, Box 405, Folder "Jewish Defense League Jan. 71," "State Drafts on the Soviet Jewry Issue," Haig to Kissinger, n.d.; NPP, Nixon tapes, 501–12, Nixon-Kissinger conversation, 19 May 1971; NA, RG 59, Box 2740, Subject Numeric Files, Folder "Pol US-USSR 1/3/73, memo Matlock to Hillenbrand, 9 April 1972.

43. Dobrynin to Gromyko, 12 July 1969, *Cold War International History Bulletin* 3 (Fall 1993): 63–67 (with an introduction by James Hershberg).

44. NPP, WHCF, Subject Files, Box 71, Folder "12/1/70-12/31/71-12/31/71," Garment to Dwight Chapin, 28 December 1970; ISA, FM 4550/5, Israeli Consulate New York to FM, 29 December 1970; GFL, Robert T. Hartmann Papers, Box 100, Folder "Soviet Jews 1970–1972," UPI-144, 31 December 1970; NPP, Garment Papers, Box 117, Folder "Jewish Matters 1971 (2 of 2), memcon Bush-Jewish and Christian Leaders, 8 June 1971.

45. NA, Haldeman Diary (CD version), 29 December 1970; NPP, NSC Country Files-Europe, Box 714, Folder "USSR Volume VII," Elliot to Kissinger, 6 January 1971; NPP, WHCF Subject Files, Box 71, Folder "1/1/71–4/30/71," Mario Biaggi to Nixon, 4 January 1971; NCSJA, RG I-181, Box 30, Folder "State Department 1970–1976," Schacter to NCSJ membership, 6 August 1971.

46. Stern, *Water's Edge*, 47.

47. NA, Haldeman diary (CD version), 15 February 1972; NPP, NSC Subject Files, Box 341, Folder "HAK-President memcons 1971–," Nixon to Kissinger, 11 March 1972; NPP, Garment Papers, Box 119, Folder "Soviet Jewry 72 2 of 3," Garment to Hauser, 13 March 1972.

48. See Stanley Hoffmann, "Détente," in *The Making of America's Soviet Policy*, ed. Joseph S. Nye Jr., 246.

49. NCSJA, RG I-181, Box 30, Folder "Nixon Administration," NCSJ press release, 14 February 1972; NPP, Garment Papers, Box 119, Folder "Soviet Jewry '72 (3 of 4), Maass-Stein-Fisher statement, 25 April 1972; NPP, Kissinger telcons, Chronological File, Box 16, Folder 1, Kissinger-Garment telcon, 21 September 1972.

50. NA, Haldeman diary (CD version), 18 July 1970 and 1 February 1972; NPP, Nixon Handwriting, Box 8, Folder "November 1970," Gar-

ment to Nixon, 23 November 1970; ISA, FM, File 4607/7, Baruch to Bar, 7 January 1971. See also Destler, Gelb, and Lake, *Our Own Worst Enemy* (New York: Simon and Schuster, 1984), 22.

51. Stern, *Water's Edge*, 19; "The Doubt Is Growing," *Jewish Journal* editorial, 30 August 1972; Library of Congress, Garment Papers, Box 5, Folder 2, Garment to Haldeman, 15 September 1972; NPP, Garment Papers, Box 118, Folder "Soviet Jewry 1972" (1 of 4)," Stein to Nixon, blind date (September 1972?); NYPL, *The Politics of American Jews* collection, Richard Maass OH, 5 June 1974.

52. Bowker and Williams, *Superpower Détente*, 64.

53. Burr, *Kissinger Transcripts*, 366 fn.6.

54. NPP, NSC name files, Box 819, Folder "Senator Javits," Haig to Kissinger, 30 August 1972; NPP, NSC, presidential correspondence 1969–1974, Box 756, Folder "Israel-Prime Minister Golda Meir 1971–1972," Haig to Kissinger, 31 August 1972; NYPL, *The Politics of American Jews* collection, Schacter OH, 30 May 1974.

55. NPP, HAK Office Files, Box 71, Folder "Gromyko 1971–1972," memcon Kissinger-Gromyko, 2 October 1972; NYPL, *The Politics of American Jews* Collection, Maass OH, 5 June 1974; NPP, Kissinger telcons, Chronological File, Box 15, Folder 9, telcon Kissinger-Peterson, 7 September 1972.

56. Stern, *Water's Edge*, 47–48.

57. NPP, NSC Presidential/HAK memcons, Box 1026, Folder 17, memcon Kissinger-members of the Senate Foreign Relations Committee, 4 October 1972.

58. For a vivid description of the interview and its impact, see Isaacson, *Kissinger*, 457–479. For further illustrations of Kissinger's euphoric state of mind, see Jussi Hanhimäki, "Selling the 'Decent Interval': Kissinger, Triangular Diplomacy, and the End of the Vietnam War," *Diplomacy and Statecraft* 14:1 (March 2003), 159.

59. NPP, Kissinger telcons, Chronological File, Box 16, Folder 1, Kissinger-Peterson telcon, 7 September 1972, and Kissinger-Garment telcon, 6 September 1972. For the Nixon-Kissinger cultivation of the trade-Vietnam linkage, see, for instance, NPP, HAK Office Files, Box 71, Folder "Gromyko 1971–1972," Kissinger memo, 29 September 1971; NPP, NSC Subject Files, Box 341, Folder "HAK-President memcons 1971–," Nixon to Kissinger, 20 April 1972.

60. See NPP, HAK Office Files, Box 71, Folder "Gromyko 1971–72," Kissinger to Nixon, 1 October 1972.

61. NPP, HAK Office Files, Box 74, Folder "Moscow Summit 1972 1 of 2," Peterson to Kissinger, 8 September 1972; NA, Haldeman diary (CD version), 16 September 1972; NPP, Garment Papers, Box 119, Folder "Soviet Jewry 1972–73," Garment to Kissinger, 30 September 1972; NPP,

HAK Office Files, Box 74, Folder "Trip to Moscow Sept. 1972," memcon Kissinger-Brezhnev, 12 September 1972.

62. See NPP, HAK Office Files, Box 67, Folder "Map Room August 72–May 73 1 of 3," Sonnenfeldt to Kissinger, 15 December 1972; NPP, HAK Office Files, Box 68, Folder "Dobrynin-Kissinger May 73 – June 7, 1973," Brezhnev to Nixon, 13 May 1973; NPP, Kissinger to Nixon, HAK Office Files, Box 75, Folder "Meetings with Brezhnev," 14 June 1973; NPP, HAK Office Files, Box 71, Folder "Gromyko 1973," Sonnenfeldt to Kissinger, 21 September 1973, and Kissinger memo for files, 28 September 1973; NPP, Box 76, Folder "Sec. Kissinger's Pre-summit trip to Moscow, March 24–28," memcon Kissinger-Brezhnev, 25 March 1974. Nixon sounded the same wrong signal but changed course a little earlier. Compare NPP, HAK Office Files, Box 68, Folder "Dobrynin-Kissinger May 1973," Nixon to Brezhnev, 1 May 1973; NPP, HAK Office Files, Box 71, Folder "Gromyko 1973," memcon Nixon-Gromyko-Kissinger, 28 September 1973; NPP, HAK Office Files, Box 72, Folder "US-USSR Presidential exchanges 1974," memcon Gromyko-Nixon, 2 February 1974.

63. Brezhnev personally was a champion of East-West trade and invested much domestic political capital in the perceived economic benefits of détente. Jackson-Vanik dealt a blow to his position. This accentuated his progressive disappointment with the administration's mishandling of Jackson-Vanik. See NPP, HAK Office Files, Box 69, Folder "Dobrynin-Kissinger Vol. 20," Brezhnev to Nixon, 21 November 1973; memcon Kissinger-Brezhnev, 24 October 1974, in Burr, *Kissinger Transcripts*, esp. 330; Freedman, "Soviet Jewry and Soviet-American Relations," in *A Decisive Decade*, 45; FBIS Special Report: Pressures for Change in Soviet Foreign Economic Policy (Washington, D.C.: FBIS, April 5, 1974, report no. 306); Sonnenfeldt email message to author, 30 August 2002; Peter M. E. Volten, *Brezhnev's Peace Program* (Boulder, Colo.: Westview Press, 1982), 231, 238; Garthoff, *Détente and Confrontation*, 101–102.

64. See NPP, NSC Presidential/HAK memcons, Box 1027, Folder "memcons Apr.–Nov.1973," memcon Nixon-Senate Commerce Committee, 8 May 1973.

65. NPP, NSC-Presidential/HAK memcons, Box 1027, Folder "April-November memcons (4 of 5)," memcon Kissinger-Garment-Fisher, 19 July 1973.

66. See, for instance, NPP, Cabinet Room Nixon Tapes, tape 123/1, Nixon-Jewish leadership meeting, 19 April 1973; Stern, *Water's Edge*, 73–74; NCSJA, RG I-181, Box 5, Folder "Richard Maass," Richard Maass memo for record, 23 June 1973; William Mehlman, "A Case of Bad Faith," *Times of Israel*, 12 August 1974, 26–31.

67. See the references in the previous note and NCSJA, RG I-181, Box 5, Folder "Richard Maass," Maass to Fisher, 10 May 1973; NCSJA, RG I-181, Box 6, Folder "Goodman 1974," June Silver to Bergman, 25 January

1974; NYPL, Maass OH, *The Politics of American Jews* collection, 5 June 1974; NPP, Kissinger telcons, Chronological File, Box 25, Folder 9, Kissinger-Fisher telcon, 24 April 1974. Notably, even Fisher complained about the level of coordination with Nixon and Kissinger. Library of Congress, Garment Papers, Box 40, Folder 4, Fisher to Garment, 28 May 1973.

68. NYPL, *Soviet Jewry in America* series, Rager OH, 8 June 1990; Levanon, *"Nativ,"* 400–402.

69. Kissinger, *American Foreign Policy*, 1974 edition, 186.

70. Henry Kissinger, "The Nature of the National Dialogue on Foreign Policy," in *The Nixon-Kissinger Foreign Policy: Opportunities and Contradictions*, ed. Fred Warner Neal and Mary Kersey Harvey (Santa Barbara, Calif.: Center for the Study of Democratic Institutions, 1974) (volume 1 of four volumes edited from the proceedings of *Pacem in Terris III* conference, 8–11 October 1973), 6.

71. Ibid., 7–10. See also NPP, NSC Name Files, Box 815, Folder "Leonard Garment," Garment to Nixon, 18 April 1973.

72. See Neal, *The Nixon-Kissinger Foreign Policy*, 70–71, 148–149.

73. See, for instance, Ambassador Herman Elits's observations, in Friedman and Levantrosser, eds., *Cold War Patriot and Statesman*, 141–144.

74. Isaacson, *Kissinger*, 513–522. For references to the resupply debate and divergent accounts of Kissinger's role, consult ibid., 811 note 3; Strober and Strober, *Nixon: An Oral History*, 148–150; Kissinger, *Crisis*, 180.

75. NYPL, *The Politics of American Jews* collection, Maass OH, 5 June 1974; NYPL, *Soviet Jewry in America* series, Maass OH, 17 March 1989. Jackson's moves infuriated Kissinger. See Kissinger, *Crisis*, 202, 228.

76. See Kissinger, *Crisis*, 302–303. That the oil crisis turned Europe, Japan, and ARAMCO shareholders against Israel certainly disturbed Kissinger. NPP, WHSF:SMOF:Haig, Box 8, Folder "Kissinger," memo Haig to Kissinger, 13 October 1973; NPP, NSC Presidential/HAK memcons, Box 1027, Folder "memcons HAK Apr.–Nov. 73 1 of 5," memcon bipartisan leadership meeting, 27 November 1973.

77. Memcon Kissinger-Jewish intellectuals, 6 December 1973, reprinted in Zaki Shalom, "Kissinger and the American Jewish Leadership after the 1973 War," *Israel Studies* 7:1 (Spring 2002): 198–208; AJC, BGX collection, Folder "Soviet Trade," David Geller to Elmer Winter, 11 January 1974 ; NYPL, *Soviet Jewry in America* series, Eugene Gold OH, 10 January 1990. For Richard Maass's disenchantment with Kissinger following the October War, compare AJC, BGX, Box 25, Folder "Soviet Union 72–73," memo Maass to NCSJ members, 4 May 1973; NYPL, Maass OH, 5 June 1974, *The Politics of American Jews* series. The American Jewish Congress, a dissenting and minority voice in the gallery of American Jewish organizations, endorsed Kissinger and his Soviet Jewish policy throughout. See Arthur

Hertzberg, *A Jew in America: My Life and a People's Struggle for Identity* (San Francisco: Harper, 2002), 361–365, 378–379; AJC, BGX, Box 25, Folder "Soviet Union Trade," memo Philip Baum, "The Jackson Amendment-What Now?," 15 April 1973; NA, RG 59, Box 1114, Folder "FT US-USSR 1-1-73" memcon Goodman-Rashish, 10 October 1973; NYPL, *Soviet Jewry in America* collection, Philip Baum OH, 24 May 1989.

78. As historian and practitioner alike, Kissinger was quite oblivious to the "honest broker" asset. See Kissinger, "The White Revolutionary," 898; NPP, HAK Office Files, Box 69, Folder "Dobrynin-Kissinger Vol. 22," Memcon Kissinger-Gromyko, 15 April 1974; NA, RG 59, Records of HAK, Box 1, Folder "nodis memcons Sept.-Dec. 1973," memcon Kissinger-Morris Abram and Saul Linowitz, 8 February 1974.

79. Sonnenfeldt email message to author, 30 August 2002; NPP, Kissinger telcons, Dobrynin file, Box 28, Folder 2, Kissinger-Dobrynin telcon, 19 July 1973. According to Zubok, this policy was largely the product of the local bureaucracy that Brezhnev failed to restrain. Zubok, *Failed Empire*, 232.

80. Kissinger, *Years of Upheaval*, 988; Paula Stern, *Water's Edge*, 84–86; NA, RG 59, Records of Counsellor, Box 9, Folder "trade bill March–May 1974," Sonnenfeldt to Kissinger, 27 April 1974.

81. Kaufman, *Jackson*, 268–269; ISA, FM, 5370/2, Shomron to FM, 27 April 1973; NA, RG 59, Subject-Numeric Files, Box 1114, Folder "FT US-USSR 1/1/73," memcon Goodman-Meyer Rashish, 10 October 1973.

82. Kaufman, *Jackson*, 271; NA, RG 59, Records of Counsellor, Box 9, Folder "trade bill June–July 1974," Sonnenfeldt to Kissinger, 17 July 1974.

83. See Kissinger, *Years of Upheaval*, 993; NPP, Kissinger telcons, Chronological File, Box 25, Folder 4, telcon Kissinger-Jackson, 18 March 1974; NA, RG 59, Records of HAK, Box 9, Folder "nodismemcons July 74 Folder 3," memcon Kissinger-Allon, 31 July 1974.

84. Garthoff, *Détente and Confrontation*, 508.

85. Kissinger, *Years of Upheaval*, 985–998; Garthoff, *Détente and Confrontation*, 461; memcon Kissinger-Brezhnev, 24 October 1974, in William Burr, *The Kissinger Transcripts*, 341.

86. NPP, Kissinger telcons, Chronological File, Box 19, Folder 8, telcon Kissinger-Jackson, 17 April 1973.

87. NPP, Kissinger telcons, Chronological File, Box 22, Folder 3, Nixon-Kissinger telcon, 17 September 1973; NPP, Kissinger telcons, Chronological File, Box 22, Folder 6, Kissinger-Jackson telcon, 1 October 1973.

88. NPP, Kissinger telcons, Chronological File, Box 23, Folder 6, Kissinger-Haig telcon, 25 October 1973; NPP, Kissinger telcons, Chronological File, Box 23, Folder 7, Kissinger-Haig telcon, 26 October 1973.

89. NPP, NSC Name Files, Box 819, Folder "Senator Jackson," Cooper to Kissinger, 16 November 1973; NA, RG 59, Records of Counsellor, Box 9, Folder "trade bill March–May 1974," Sonnenfeldt to Kissinger, 2 March 1973. The citation is from the Cooper memo. Kissinger did discuss the issue with Jackson on a few occasions. See: NPP, WHSF:SMOF:Haig, Box 40, Folder "senior staff meetings Sept.–Dec. '73," senior staff meeting, 26 November 1973.

90. NA, RG 59, Records of HAK, Box 2, Folder "nodismemcons Jan–June 74 Folder 3," memcon Kissinger-Golda Meir, 15 January 1974; NA, RG 59, Records of Counsellor, Box 9, Folder "trade bill March-May 1974," Sonnenfeldt to Kissinger, 25 April 1974; NPP, Kissinger telcons, Chronological File, Box 26, Folder 6, telcon Kissinger-Max Fisher, 19 July 1974; NA, RG 59, Records of HAK, Box 9, Folder "nodismemcons August 1974," memcon Kissinger-Dinitz, 16 August 1974.

91. NA, RG 59, Records of Counsellor, Box 9, Folder "trade bill March-May 1974," Jenkins to HAK, 12 April 1974; NPP, Kissinger telcons, Chronological Files, Box 25, Folder 9, telcon Kissinger-Flanigan, 26 April 1974.

92. For proof of mutual respect during Nixon's first term, see: NPP, NSC Subject File, Box 341, Folder "HAK-Presidential memoranda 1969–1970," Nixon to Haldeman and Kissinger, 7 August 1969.

93. NA, RG 59, Records of Counsellor, Box 9, Folder "trade bill August 1974," Sonnenfeldt to Kissinger, 14 August 1974.

94. NA, RG 59, Records of HAK, Box 9, Folder "nodismemcons August 1974," memcon Kissinger-Sonnenfeldt, 7 August 1974.

95. NPP, Kissinger telcons, Chronological File, Box 19, Folder 9, Kissinger-Dobrynin telcon, 19 April 1973; NPP, Kissinger telcons, Dobrynin File, Box 28, Folder 3, Kissinger-Dobrynin telcon, 30 October 1973; NPP, Box 76, Folder "Sec. Kissinger's Pre-summit trip to Moscow, March 24–28," memcon Kissinger-Brezhnev, 25 March 1974.

96. NPP, NSC Presidential/HAK memcons, Box 1026, Folder 3, memcon Kissinger-Alkhimov, 5 March 1973; NPP, Kissinger telcons, Chronological File, Box 26, Folder 6, telcon Kissinger-Max Fisher, 19 July 1974.

97. Taking issue with Isaacson, Gaddis argues that Kissinger did not neglect the role of educator. Compare: Gaddis, "rescuing choice," 586; Isaacson, *Kissinger*, 242. In the policy sphere under question, Kissinger evolved from relative neglect to resolute effort. See NPP, Kissinger telcons, Chronological File, Box 20, Folder 2, telcon Kissinger-James Reston, 3 May 1973; NPP, Kissinger telcons, Chronological File, Box 21, Folder 4, telcon Kissinger-Marilyn Berger, 21 July 1973; NPP, NSC-Presidential/HAK memcons, Box 1027, Folder "April–November 1973 (3 of 5)," memcon Kissinger-Marcy, 14 September 1973.

98. "More Polls," *Near East Report* 18:4 (23 January 1974), 16; Eugene R. Wittkopf, *Faces of Internationalism: Public Opinion and American Foreign Policy* (Durham, N.C.: Duke University Press, 1990), 104; "Trade and Freedom," *New York Times* editorial, 18 September 1973.

99. See especially: George, "Domestic Constraints," in *Change in the International System*, ed. Holsti et al.; John Lewis Gaddis: "The Rise, Fall and Future of Détente," *Foreign Affairs* 62:2 (Winter 1983/1984), 365–367; Dan Caldwell, "U.S. Domestic Politics and the Demise of Détente," in *The Fall of Détente: Soviet-American Relations During the Carter Years*, ed. Odd Arne Westad (Oslo: Scandinavian University Press, 1997), 104; Nelson, "Nixon, Kissinger and the Domestic Side of Détente," in *Reviewing the Cold War*, ed. Morgan and Nelson.

100. Dana Ward, "Kissinger: a Psychohistory," in *Henry Kissinger: His Personality and Policies*, ed. Dan Caldwell (Durham, N.C.: Duke University Press, 1983), 27, 33; Isaacson, *Kissinger*, 31. For the affect of the Weimar years on Kissinger's basic political outlook, see Suri, *Henry Kissinger*, chapter 1.

101. Murray Freedman, "The Jewish Community Comes of Age," introduction to *A Second Exodus*, ed. Freedman and Chernin, 6–7; NYPL, *Soviet Jewry in America* collection, Eugene Gold OH, 1990.

102. Melanson, *American Foreign Policy since the Vietnam War*, esp. 82; NA, Stephen Ambrose's introduction to Haldeman Diary (CD version); NCSJA, RG I-181, Box 30, Folder "Nixon Administration," Stanley Lowell to Nixon, 23 June 1974.

103. For contemporaneous evidence, see: NPP, Nixon Handwriting, Box 6, Folder "June 1970," Garment to Nixon, 11 June 1970; NPP, HAK Office Files, Box 71, Folder "Gromyko 1973," memcon Kissinger-Gromyko, 24 September 1973; Memcon Kissinger-Sonnenfeldt-Hyland, 18 March 1974, in Burr, *Kissinger Transcripts*, 225–226. The "eclipse of the sun" quote is from the 24 September 1973 memcon. For the two phases in Kissinger's later reflections, compare Kissinger, *White House Years*, 1271–1273; Kissinger, *Years of Upheaval*, 235–246; Kissinger, *Diplomacy*, 731, 761; Kissinger, "Between the Old Left and the New Right," *Foreign Affairs* 78:3 (May/June 1999): 107.

104. Robert D. Schulzinger, "The Naive and Sentimental Diplomat: Henry Kissinger's Memoirs," *Diplomatic History* 4:3 (Summer 1980): 304.

105. Critical assessments of the Nixon-Kissinger modus operandi abound. For pertinent recent examples see Jean A. Garrison, *Games Advisors Play: Foreign Policy in the Nixon and Carter Administrations* (College Station: Texas A&M University Press, 1999); David Mayers, *The Ambassadors and American Soviet Policy* (New York: Oxford University Press, 1995), 221–227.

106. NPP, NSC, HAK Office Files, Box 67, Folder 4, memo Sonnenfeldt to Kissinger, 2 January 1973; NA, RG 59, Subject-Numeric Files, Box 1114, Folder "FT 4.4. US-USSR," Memo Wright, Stoessel and Armstrong to Rogers, 26 January 1973.

107. NPP, Kissinger telcons, Chronological File, Box 19, Folder 1, Kissinger-Shultz telcon, 2 March 1973; NPP, 12 March 1973, Kissinger telcons, Dobrynin file, Box 27, Folder 9, Kissinger-Dobrynin telcon, 12 March 1973.

108. Isaacson, *Kissinger*, 617–619; NCSJA, RG I-181, Box 6, Folder "Goodman 1974," memo Sheila Woods to Jerry Goodman, 27 December 1974.

109. Isaacson, *Kissinger*, 619; Dobrynin, *In Confidence*, 338.

110. Passed on 19 September 1974, this amendment certainly figured in Brezhnev's progressive disillusionment with Washington as it seriously hindered his plans for import-led growth in the Soviet Union. See Bowker and Williams, *Superpower Détente*, 196; Stern, *Water's Edge*, 208–209; NPP, HAK Office Files, Box 71, Folder "Gromyko 1974," memcon Gromyko-HAK-Dobrynin, 29 April 1974; NPP, HAK Office Files Countries-MidEast, Box 144, Folder 2, memo Joseph Sisco and Sonnenfeldt to Kissinger, 12 June 1974; memcon Kissinger-Sonnenfeldt-Hyland, 18 March 1974, in Burr, *Kissinger Transcripts*, 225. Predictably, American and Israeli supporters of Jackson-Vanik led the way in faulting the Stevenson amendment. See William Korey, "Jackson-Vanik and Soviet Jewry," *International Council of B'nai B'rith World Reports* (May 1983): 1–16; Statement by Javits, Ribicoff, Jackson, Vanik on East-West trade and freedom of emigration, 15 January 1975, appended to Dorothy Fosdick OH, NYPL, *Soviet Jewry in America* collection; Levanon, "*Nativ*," 403.

111. NPP, HAK Office Files, Box 74, Folder "Moscow Summit 1972 1 of 2," Peterson to Kissinger, 8 September 1972; NPP, NSC Name Files, Box 819, Folder "Senator Jackson," Charles Cooper to Kissinger, 16 November 1973; Jackson Papers, Accession No. 3560-28, Box 1, Folder 10, memo Richard Perle to Jackson re meeting with Eberle, 25 February 1974; GFL, Ron Nessen Files, Box 3, Folder "Press Secretary Briefings," Ron Nessen News Conference, 18 October 1974; Stern, *Water's Edge*, 208–209; I. M. Destler, "Congress," in *The Making of America's Soviet Policy*, ed. Nye, 48.

112. NPP, NSC, Box 718, Folder "USSR Vol. 20," Memo Sonnenfeldt to Kissinger, 29 March 1972; AJC, BGX, Box 25, Folder "Soviet Union Trade," Bookbinder note for record on meeting with Armitage, 21 March 1973; NA, RG 59, Subject-Numeric Files, Folder "FT 4.4. US-USSR," Memcon Fina-Spiegel, 2 January 1973.

113. Sonnenfeldt entries at note 62 in this chapter; NPP, HAK Office Files, Box 67, Folder "Map Room August 72–May 73 1 of 3," Sonnenfeldt

to Kissinger, 9 April 1973; NPP, HAK Office Files, Box 68, Folder "Map Room D 2 of 2," Sonnenfeldt to Kissinger, 15 June 1973; NPP, NSC Name Files, Box 819, Folder "Map Room D 2 of 2," Sonnenfeldt to Kissinger, 20 July 1973. Although resentful about this pattern, Sonnenfeldt has since defended Kissinger's Soviet Jewish emigration record. Strober and Strober, *Nixon: An Oral History*, 169; Sonnenfeldt email message to author, 30 August 2002.

114. NA, Haldeman diary, CD version, 25 November 1970; NPP, HAK Office Files, Box 73, Folder "1972 economic commission," Haig to Kissinger, 26 May 1972; NA, RG 59, Records of HAK, Box 3, Folder "nodis letters HAK 73–77," memcon Kissinger-Dayan-Dinitz, 7 December 1973; Melvin Small, *The Presidency of Richard Nixon* (Lawrence: University Press of Kansas, 1999), 53–55; Melanson, *American Foreign Policy*, 32–33.

115. Kissinger made this incisive remark in the comfortable company of conservative supporters. NPP, NSC Presidential/HAK memcons, Box 1026, Folder "HAK memcon-Group of Supporters," memcon Kissinger-conservative supporters, 5 January 1972.

116. Ronald W. Pruessen, "The Predicaments of Power," in *John Foster Dulles and the Diplomacy of the Cold War*, ed. Richard H. Immerman (Princeton, N.J.: Princeton University Press, 1990), 43. This section draws heavily on Pruessen's line of argument regarding Dulles. See also Pruessen, "From Good Breakfast to Bad Supper: John Foster Dulles between the Geneva Summit and the Geneva Foreign Ministers Conference," in *Cold War Respite: The Geneva Summit of 1955*, ed. Gunter Bischof and Saki Dokrill (Baton Rouge: Louisiana State University Press, 2000), 253–270.

117. Kissinger's Cambodian and Chilean policies amply demonstrate his tendency, even before 1972, to ignore in practice his own theoretical maxims about the recognition of limits and the need to stay in touch with domestic opinion. See Isaacson, *Kissinger*, 171–179; Peter Kornbluh, *The Pinochet File* (New York: New Press, 2003).

118. As noted in chapter 2, Morgenthau was inclined toward the Jackson position from the outset. His cleavage with Kissinger deepened following the October War. See Mollov, "Jewry's Prophetic Challenge"; ISA, FM, 4607/3, Blind memo, 20 February 1970; Leonard Gwertzman, "Analysis on Jews Disputed," *New York Times*, 10 November 1971; memcon Kissinger-Jewish intellectuals, 6 December 1973, note 77, p. 201. Kissinger did find encouraging realist support in George F. Kennan. NPP, Kissinger telcons, Chronological File, Box 22, Folder 3, Kissinger-Kennan telcon, 14 September 1973.

119. For evidence, see Kissinger-Deng Xiaoping memcon, 26 November 1974, in Burr, *Kissinger Transcripts*, 294–295; Charles G. Stefan, "The Drafting of the Helsinki Final Act: A Personal View of the CSCS's Geneva Phase (September 1973 until July 1975)," *SHAFR Newsletter* (June 2000).

Most scholars doubt that Kissinger's greater sensitivity represented any profound change of heart. See Hugh M. Arnold, "Henry Kissinger and Human Rights," *Human Rights Quarterly* 2:4 (October–December 1980): 51–71; David P. Forsythe, *Human Rights and World Politics* (Lincoln: University of Nebraska Press, 1989), chapter 3; Arjan Van Den Assem, "The Perseverance of Beliefs: The Reaction of Kissinger and Brzezinski to the End of the Cold War," *Acta Politica* 2 (2000): 169–194; Suri, *Kissinger*, 242–246. This view is corroborated by newly declassified evidence that shows that as late as October 1976, Kissinger gave full support to the Argentine military junta's "dirty war." See the National Security Archive's briefing book, http://www.nsarchive.org/NSAEBB/NSAEBB104/index.htm (accessed 15 February 2004).

120. Rubinstein, *Moscow's Third World Strategy*, 145; Robert H. Donaldson and Joseph L. Nogee, *Soviet Foreign Policy since World War II* (New York: Pergamon Press, 1981), 270; Golan, *Soviet Policies in the Middle East*, 85.

121. Zubok, *A Failed Empire*, 234.

122. Jackson-Vanik may thus be viewed as an ironic development, since it illustrates historian Hanhimäki's recent observation that Nixon and Kissinger's concerted engagement of the Soviet Union unexpectedly facilitated the ascendancy of "soft power" methods and issues. See Jussi M. Hanhimäki, "'Dr. Kissinger' or' Mr. Henry'? Kissingerology, Thirty Years and Counting," *Diplomatic History* 27:5 (November 2003): 655.

Chapter 4. Nixon's Final Months, the Legacy of the Period, and the Lessons of the Case

1. NA, RG 59, Records of HAK, Box 2, Folder memcons, nov.-dec. 73 f.2, Memcon Nixon-Golda et al., 1 November 1973.

2. Isaacson, *Kissinger*, 523. Employing Freedom of Information Act (FOIA) documents, Suri demonstrates persuasively that Nixon and Kissinger indeed resolved from the early hours of the war that neither side should be allowed a clear and decisive victory. See Suri, *Kissinger*, 258; Suri, "Kissinger, the American Dream," 733–734.

3. NPP, NSC Country Files-Middle East, Box 664, Folder Middle East War memos and misc. Oct. 6–Oct. 17, memo Kissinger to Nixon, 6 October 1973; NA, Folder Pol 7. US/Kissinger XR pol 27 Box 14, Kissinger-Dinitz memcon, 9 October 1973; ISA, RG 93, 4997/1, Dinitz notes for record, 26 October 1973; Quandt, *Decade of Decisions*, 215; nsarchive, documents 10, 83. As the editor of this collection William Burr notes in his introduction, Kissinger never acknowledged that he recommended against preemption.

4. Suri, *Kissinger*, 341–342, note 24; NA, RG 59, Folder Records of HAK 1973–1977, Box 2, Kissinger-Meir memcon, 3 November 1973; NPP, NSC HAK Office, Folder Dobrynin-Kiss Vol. 20/Box 69, Scowcroft to Nixon, 21 October 1973; nsarchive, documents 18, 46, 49, 51, 71, 72, 73, 82.

5. Itzhak Galnoor, "The Consequences of the Yom Kippur War: Transformations in the Israeli Political System," in *The Yom Kippur War: A Reconsideration*, ed. Bar-Siman-Tov and Haim Opaz, 165–180 (Hebrew); ISA, RG 43, 7059/7, Gazit to Dinitz, 26 November 1973.

6. ISA, RG 93, 4997/1, telcon Dinitz-Meir, 28 October 1973; memcon Kissinger-Fisher, *Israel Studies* 7:1 (2002): 213; NA, RG 59, Records of HAK, Box 7, Folder nodis memcons May 1974 f.4, Kissinger-Meir memcon, 4 May 1974.

7. Rabin, *Memoirs*, 186–190; Joseph Goldstein, *Rabin* (Tel Aviv: Shoken, 2006), 267 (Hebrew).

8. Kissinger-Jewish leadership memcon, 27 December 1973, reprinted in Zaki Shalom, "Kissinger and the American Jewish Leadership after the 1973 War," *Israel Studies* 7:1 (Spring 2002): 210.

9. Ibid., 201–203.

10. NPP, WHSF:SMOF:Haig, Box 8, Folder Kissinger Haig to Kissinger, 13 October 1973; NA, RG 59, Folder Records of HAK 1973–1977, Box 2, Kissinger-Meir memcon, 3 November 1973; NA, RG 59, Records of HAK, Box 8, Folder nodis memcons May 74 Folder 8, memcon Kiss-Rabin-Allon, 22 May 1974. See also Suri, *Kissinger*, 209.

11. NPP, HAK Office Files, Box 76, Folder Kissinger trip to Moscow, Tel Aviv and London, memcon Kissinger-Meir, 22 October 1973; NA, RG 59, Records of Kissinger, Box 1, Folder nodis memcons Sept.–Dec. 73, memcon Kissinger-Jewish leaders, 11 March 1974.

12. NA, RG 59, records of HAK, Box 22, Folder classified external memos December 74-April 1975 Folder 2, memcon Kiss-Rabin-Allon, 13 October 1974.

13. Ibid.; NA, RG 59, Records of HAK, Box 7, Folder nodis memcons May 1974 f.4, Kissinger-Meir memcon, 4 May 1974; NPP, Box 723, Folder USSR Vol.30, Moscow embtel 4360, Kissinger to Eagleburger and Dinitz, 26 March 1974; Isaacson, *Kissinger*, 570–571; nsarchive, documents 32A, 32B, 35, 81.

14. Quandt, *Decade of Decisions*, 220.

15. Stein, *Heroic Diplomacy*, 111–112; ISA, RG 43, 7059/8, Gazit to Dinitz, 3 December 1973.

16. Isaacson, *Kissinger*, 571.

17. NPP, HAK Office Files, Folder 1, Box 141, Kissinger to Nixon, n.d. (June 1974); NA, RG 59, Records of HAK, Box 2, Folder 7, LSE to HAK, 3 October 1975. Even Rabin, known to cultivate an image of self-

composure, conceded the affect of these emotional factors. See Rabin, *Memoirs*, 201–202.

18. Meir, *My Life*, 444. See an unpublished paper by Abraham Greenbaum, "The U.S. Airlift to Israel in 1973 Reconsidered,".11.

19. NPP, WHCF:SMOF:Garment Alpha-Numerical Files, Box 116, Folder Jewish Matters 69–70 (1 of 3), memo Kissinger to Garment, 27 September 1969. See also Suri, *Kissinger*, 128–129.

20. NA, RG 59, Records of HAK, Box 2, Folder memcons, nov.–dec. 73 f.2, Kissinger-Meir memcon, 1 November 1973.

21. ISA, RG 43, 7059/8, Gazit to Dinitz, 11 December 1973; NA, RG 59, Records of HAK, Box 6, Folder nodismemcons Jan–June 74, Kissinger-Dinitz-Shalev memcon, 9 January 1974; ISA, 4997/1, telcon Dinitz-Galili, 13 February 1974; NA, RG 59, Records of HAK, Box 10, Folder nodismemcons October '74, memcon Kissinger-Dinitz, 5 October 1974.

22. Especially Edward N. Luttwak and Walter Lacquer, "Kissinger and the Yom Kippur War," *Commentary* 58 (September 1974): 33–40; Matti Golan, *The Secret Conversations of Henry Kissinger: Step-by-Step Diplomacy in the Middle East* (New York: New York Times Book Co., 1976). The Israeli government tried to suppress Golan's book, which is based largely on anonymous Israeli sources. See also Greenbaum, "The Airlift Reconsidered," 12, note 26. By late 1975, Kissinger came under the direct fire of the American Jewish leadership for exerting pressure on Israel, a criticism that, according to his testimony, hurt him like no other. See Edward B. Glick, *The Triangular Connection: America, Israel and American Jews* (London: G. Allen and Unwin, 1982), 99. Conversely, Suri maintains Israeli leaders still trusted Kissinger's basic commitment to Israel. Suri, *Kissinger*, 267.

23. Dobrynin, *In Confidence*, 303–305.

24. Stein, *Heroic Diplomacy*, 163–165.

25. Quoted in Kissinger, *Years of Upheaval*, 1137.

26. NA, NSC HAK Office Files, Box 129, Folder 3, Nixon-Secretary Simon memcon, 9 July 1974.

27. ISA, RG 43, 7045/2, Dinitz to Meir, 13 August 1974; ISA, RG 43, 7031/5, 20 August 1974.

28. See Melvin I. Urofsky, *We Are One!* (Garden City, N.J.: Anchor Books, 1978), 370–372; Mark Garson, *The Neoconservative Vision: From the Cold War to Culture Wars* (Lanham: Madison Books, 1997).

29. See: Friedman, *The Neoconservative Revolution*, 207–211; McAlister, *Epic Encounters*, chapter 4.

30. NA, RG 59, Records of HAK, Box 20, Folder nodis memcons 1977 Folder 1, Winston Lord to Kissinger, 9 February 1976.

31. Quandt, *Decade of Decisions*, 270.

32. Ibid., 281.

33. See p. 12 in chapter 1 of the present volume.

34. For proponents of this school, see Shlomo Avineri, "Ideology and Israel's Foreign Policy," *Jerusalem Quarterly* 37 (1986), 10; Pinchas Eliav, "The Jewish Dimension in Israel's Foreign Relations," in *Ministry for Foreign Affairs*, ed. Yager et al., 911.

35. This section draws on the overview of the approaches presented by political scientist Gabriel Sheffer. See Sheffer's introduction in *U.S.-Israeli Relations at the Crossroads*, ed. Sheffer, 6. See also Peter L. Hahn, "Special Relationships," *Diplomatic History* 22:2 (1998): 263–272.

36. Bar-Siman-Tov, "A Special Relationship?," 231–262; Ben-Zvi, *The United States and Israel: The Limits of the Special Relationship*, 83.

37. See, for example, McAlister, *Epic Encounters*; Michael Benson, *Truman and the Founding of Israel* (Westport: Praeger, 1997).

38. John J. Mearsheimer and Stephen M. Walt, *The Israel Lobby and U.S. Foreign Policy* (New York: Farrar, Straus and Giroux, 2007). See also Cheryl Rubenberg, *Israel and the American National Interest: A Critical Examination* (Urbana: University of Illinois Press, 1986); and Tivnan, *The Lobby*.

39. Inbar, *Rabin and Israel's National Security*, 54–55; Rabin, *Memoirs*, 179.

40. ISA, FM 4159/10, Bitan to Herzog, 14 December 1969.

41. ISA, FM 4156/3, Ben Haim to Prime Minister's Office, 7 October 1969; CZA, S62/765, Gold, "Who Speaks for the Jews?," 4 May 1972.

42. Arthur Herzberg, *A Jew in America*, 302; CZA, S100/1071, Herzberg to Meir, 31 December 1969.

43. Urofsky, *We Are One!*, 390.

44. Ibid.; Novik, *The United States and Israel*, 67; NYPL, *The Politics of American Jews* collection, Rita Hauser interview, 22 August 1973, Ben Wattenberg interview, 11 August 1974, and Richard Maass interview, 5 June 1974.

45. See Jerold S. Aurbach, "Are We One? Menachem Begin and the Long Shadow of 1977," in *Envisioning Israel: The Changing Ideals and Images of American Jews*, ed. Alon Gal (Hebrew edition) (Sde-Boker: Ben Gurion Legacy Center, 1999), 290.

46. For discussion of this phenomenon, see Irving Janis, *Groupthink* (Boston: Houghton Mifflin, 1972).

47. Opinions on this crucial "what-if" question diverge sharply among Israeli practitioners. For the argument that Sadat was not truly willing to negotiate peace prior to 1973, see Mordechai Gazit, "Was the War Avoidable?," in *The Yom Kippur War*, ed. Bar-Siman-Tov and Opaz (Hebrew), 17–21; and Gazit, "Egypt and Israel—Was There a Peace Opportunity Missed in 1971?" For the argument that a more conciliatory

line would have made a difference, see Ya'acobi, "The Attempt," esp. 47, 55; Elizur, in *Ministry for Foreign Affairs*, 301; and Eban, *Autobiography*, 476; Bar-Joseph, "Last Chance."

48. ISA, RG 93, 4996/A2, Dinitz to Eagleburger, 30 September 1973; Kissinger, *Crisis*, 12–13; nsarchive, document 13.

49. ISA, RG 93, 7792/A8, Dinitz to Kidron, 18 July 1973; ISA, FM 5294/12, Leef to Israeli Military Intelligence, 8 August 1973; nsarchive, document 36A.

50. See p. 56 in chapter 3.

51. See Nancy B. Tucker, "Taiwan Expendable? Nixon and Kissinger Go to China," *The Journal of American History* 92:1 (June 2005): 109–135; William Burr, *The Kissinger Transcripts*, 407–408.

52. See, for instance, Kissinger's introduction to Friedman and Levantrosser, eds., *Cold War Patriot and Statesman*; Kissinger, *Diplomacy*, 711. Some scholars second Kissinger's argument. See Gaddis, "Rescuing Choice from Circumstance," 586.

53. NPP, NSC Presidential/HAK memcons, Box 1026, Folder "HAK memcon-Group of Supporters," memcon Kissinger-conservative supporters, 5 January 1972.

54. NA, Haldeman diary (CD version), 15 February 1972; NPP, NSC Subject Files, Box 341, Folder "HAK-President memcons 1971–," Nixon to Kissinger, 11 March 1972.

55. See, for instance, Nixon's remarks at Huntington, West Virginia, 26 October 1972, The American Presidency Project website, www.presidency.ucsb.edu/ws/index.php?pid=3656 (accessed 7 January 2006).

56. George, "Domestic Constraints," esp. 295.

57. Hanhimäki, *Flawed Architect*, 304.

58. Garthoff, *Détente and Confrontation*, 333.

59. Alexander George, "Political Crises," in *The Making of America's Soviet Policy*, ed. Nye, 140–142.

60. NA, Haldeman diary entry, CD version, 12 June 1972.

61. NPP, Kissinger telcons, Box 13, Folder 9, Nixon-Kissinger telcon, 9 April 1972. The Soviets actually tried to discourage the Vietnamese attack. See Ilya Gaiduk, *The Soviet Union and the Vietnam War* (Chicago: Ivan R. Dee, 1996), 231–233.

62. NPP, NSC Subject Files, Box 341, Folder "HAK-President memcons 1971-Memo Nixon to Kissinger and Haig, 20 April 1972.

63. NPP, Kissinger telcons, Box 14, Folder 2, Nixon-Kissinger telcon, 6 May 1972.

64. For somewhat parallel interpretations, see Nelson, "Nixon, Kissinger, and the Domestic Side of Détente," in *Re-viewing the Cold War*, ed. Nelson and Morgan, 137–139; Kissinger, "Between the Old Left and the New Right," 107.

65. See, for instance, Nina Tannenwald, "Ideas and Explanation: Advancing the Theoretical Agenda," *Journal of Cold War Studies* 7:2 (Spring 2005): 13–42; Neta C. Crawford, "The Passion of World Politics: Propositions on Emotion and Emotional Relationships," *International Security* 24:4 (Spring 2000): 116–156; M. H. Hunt, *Ideology and American Foreign Policy* (New Haven,: Yale University Press, 1987); Frank Costigliola, "Like Animals or Worse: Narratives of Culture and Emotion by U.S. and British POWs and Airmen Behind Soviet Lines, 1944–1945," *Diplomatic History* 28:5 (November 2004): 749–780.

66. Suri, *Power and Protest*, 213.

67. This notion draws on Judith Goldstein and Robert O. Keohane, eds, *Ideas and Foreign Policy: Beliefs, Institutions, and Political Change* (Ithaca and London: Cornell University Press, 1993).

68. For Nixon's self-perception, see Greenberg, *Nixon's Shadow*, 280; NPP, Nixon Handwriting, Box 16, Folder "January 1972," Colson to Nixon, 19 January 1972.

69. ADST Oral History Collection, Peter Rodman OH, 22 May 1994; NPP, NSC Presidential/HAK memcons, Box 1026, Folder "HAK memcon-group of supporters," Kissinger-conservative supporters (memcon), 5 January 1972.

Bibliography

Manuscript Collections

Nixon Presidential Project Materials (NPP), College Park, Maryland
    NSC-Country Files (USSR, Israel)
    NSC-Presidential-HAK memcons
    NSC-Presidential Correspondence
    NSC-Institutional Files
    NSC-Saunders Files
    NSC-Kissinger Office Files
    Nixon Handwriting
    Nixon Personal Files
    Kissinger Telcons Series
    Nixon Tapes
National Archives II, College Park, Maryland
    Record Group 59, Rogers Office Files
    Record Group 59, Helmut Sonnenfeldt Files
    H. R. Haldeman Diary (CD version)
Library of Congress, Washington, D.C.
    Leonard Garment Papers
Gerald Ford Library, Ann Arbor
University of Washington, Seattle
    Henry Jackson Papers
American Jewish Committee Records, New York City
National Conference on Soviet Jewry Records, New York City
The National Security Archive, George Washington University, Washington, D.C., "The October War and U.S. Policy," *Electronic Briefing Book 98*
Israel State Archive, Jerusalem
Records of the Prime Minister's Office (Record Group 43)
Knesset Security and Foreign Affairs Committee Records (Record Group 60)
Simcha Dinitz Papers (Record Groups 72 and 93).

Golda Meir Papers (Record Group 106)
    Records of the Foreign Ministry (Record Group 130.20)
Central Zionist Archive, Jerusalem
    Jewish Agency Records
    Nahum Goldmann Papers
    Soviet Jewish Organizations Records
Labor Party Archive, Beit Berl, Israel
Records of the Counselor

Oral History Collections, Interviews

Association for Diplomatic Studies and Training (ADST) Oral History
    Collection
Avineri, Shlomo (20 September 2005, Jerusalem)
Dinstein, Yoram (14 August 2003, Tel Aviv)
Eran, Amos (24 October 2002, by phone)
Goodman, Jerry (6 February 2003, New York City)
New York Public Library, DOROT section, *Soviet Jewry in America* Oral
    History Series
New York Public Library, DOROT section, *The Politics of American Jews*
    Oral History Series
Rosenne, Meir (23 January 2006, Jerusalem)
Sonnenfeldt, Helmut (email message to author, 30 August 2002)
Strober, Gerald S., and Deborah H. Strober. *Nixon: An Oral History of
    His Presidency*. New York: HarperCollins, 1994.

Public Records: Published

FRUS 1964–1968, Volume 18, *Arab-Israeli Dispute*, 1964–1967.
Khanin, Zeev, and Boris Morozov, eds. *Traitors to Mother Russia: Jewish
    Emigration through Soviet Eyes*. Tel Aviv: Tel Aviv University Press,
    2005 (Hebrew).
Knesset Minutes, 1969–1975 (Hebrew)
Morozov, Boris, ed. *Documents on Soviet Jewish Emigration*. Portland:
    Frank Cass, 1999.
The Nixon Presidential Press Conferences. New York: Coleman, 1978.

Other Works Cited

Adamsky, Dima P. "Zero Hour for Bears: Inquiring into the Soviet Deci-
    sion to Intervene in the Egyptian-Israeli War of Attrition, 1969–1970."
    Cold War History 6:1 (February 2006): 113–136.

Adamsky, Dima P. "How American and Israeli Intelligence Failed to Estimate the Soviet Intervention in the War of Attrition." In *The Cold War and the Middle East: Regional Conflict and the Superpowers,* ed. Nigel Ashton. London and New York: Routledge, 2007. 113–135.

Arnold, Hugh M. "Henry Kissinger and Human Rights." *Human Rights Quarterly* 2:4 (October–December 1980): 51–71.

Aurbach, Jerold S., "Are We One? Menachem Begin and the Long Shadow of 1977." In *Envisioning Israel: The Changing Ideals and Images of North American Jews,* ed. Alon Gal. Sde-Boker: Ben Gurion Legacy Center, 1999 (Hebrew edition). 288–303.

Avineri, Shlomo. "Ideology and Israel's Foreign Policy." *Jerusalem Quarterly* 10 (1986): 133–144.

Bar-Joseph, Uri. *The Watchman Fell Asleep.* Lod: Zmora-Bitan, 2001 (Hebrew).

Bar-Joseph, Uri. "Last Chance to Avoid War: Sadat's Peace Initiative of February 1973 and Its Failure." *Journal of Contemporary History* 41:3 (July 2006): 545–556.

Bar-On, Mordechai. "50 Years of Israeli-American Relations." In *Ministry for Foreign Affairs: The First Fifty Years,* ed. Moshe Yager et al. (Hebrew). 265–285.

Bar-Siman-Tov, Yaacov. "A Special Relationship?" *Diplomatic History* 22:2 (Spring 1998): 231–262.

Bar-Siman-Tov, Yaacov. *The Israeli-Egyptian War of Attrition, 1969–1970.* New York: Columbia University Press, 1980.

Benson, Michael. *Truman and the Founding of Israel.* Westport, Conn: Praeger, 1997.

Ben-Zvi, Abraham. *The United States and Israel: The Limits of the Special Relationship.* New York: Columbia University Press, 1993.

Bialer, Uri. *Between East and West: Israel's Foreign Policy Orientation 1948–1956.* Cambridge: Cambridge University Press, 1990.

Bialer, Uri. "Top Hat, Tuxedo and Cannons: Israeli Foreign Policy from 1948 to 1956 as a Field of Study." *Israel Studies* 7:1 (2002): 1–80.

Boaz, Arie. *Unseen yet Always Present: The Life Story of Shaul Avigur.* Tel Aviv: Ministry of Defense, 2001 (Hebrew).

Bowker, Mike, and Phil Williams. *Superpower Détente: A Reappraisal.* London: Sage, 1988.

Bundy, William. *A Tangled Web: The Making of Foreign Policy in the Nixon Presidency.* New York: Hill and Wang, 1998.

Burr, William. *The Kissinger Transcripts.* New York: The New Press, 1998.

Buwalda, Petrus. *They Did Not Dwell Alone: Soviet Jewish Emigration from the Soviet Union, 1967–1990.* Washington, D.C.: Woodrow Wilson Center Press, 1997.

Caldwell, Dan. "U.S. Domestic Politics and the Demise of Détente." In *The Fall of Détente: Soviet-American Relations During the Carter Years,* ed. Odd Arne Westad. Oslo: Scandinavian University Press, 1997. 95–117.

Chernin, Albert D. "Making Soviet Jews an Issue: A History." In *A Second Exodus: The American Movement to Free Soviet Jews,* ed. Murray Freedman and Alfred D. Chernin. Hanover, N.H., and London: Brandeis University Press, 1999. 15–69.

Cohen, Avner, and William Burr. "Israel Crosses the Threshold." *The Bulletin of the Atomic Scientists* 62:3 (2006): 22–30.

Costigliola, Frank. "Like Animals or Worse: Narratives of Culture and Emotion by U.S. and British POWs and Airmen Behind Soviet Lines, 1944–1945." *Diplomatic History* 28:5 (November 2004): 749–780.

Crawford, Neta C. "The Passion of World Politics: Propositions on Emotion and Emotional Relationships." *International Security* 24:4 (Spring 2000): 116–156.

Dawisha, Adeed. "Egypt." In *The Cold War and the Middle East,* ed. Yezid Sayigh and Avi Shlaim. Oxford: Clarendon Press, 1997. 27–47.

Destler, I. M., Leslie Gelb and Anthony Lake. *Our Own Worst Enemy.* New York: Simon and Schuster, 1984.

Destler, I. M. "Congress." In *The Making of America's Soviet Policy,* ed. Joseph Nye Jr. New Haven: Yale University Press, 1984. 37–62.

Diagle, Claire. "The Russians Are Going: Sadat, Nixon and the Soviet Presence in Egypt, 1970–1971." *Middle East Review of International Affairs* 8:1 (2004): 1–15.

Dickson, Peter W. *Kissinger and the Meaning of History.* New York: Cambridge, 1978.

Dinitz, Simcha. "The American-Israeli Dialogue during the War." In *The Yom Kippur War,* ed. Yaacov Bar-Siman-Tov and Haim Opaz. Jerusalem: Davis Institute,1999 (Hebrew). 153–164.

Dobrynin, Anatoly. *In Confidence: Moscow's Ambassador to Six Cold War Presidents.* Seattle: University of Washington Press, 2001.

Donaldson, Robert H., and Joseph L. Nogee. *Soviet Foreign Policy since World War II.* New York: Pergamon Press, 1981.

Eban, Abba. *Abba Eban: An Autobiography.* New York: Random House, 1977.

Elazar, Daniel J. *Community and Polity: The Organizational Dynamics of American Jewry,* 2nd edition. Philadelphia: Jewish Publication of America, 1995.

Eliav, Pinchas. "The Jewish Dimension in Israel's Foreign Relations." In *Ministry for Foreign Affairs,* ed. Moshe Yager et al.(Hebrew). 909–915.

Forsythe, David P. *Human Rights and World Politics.* Lincoln: University of Nebraska Press, 1989.

Freedman, Robert O. *Soviet Policy Toward the Middle East since 1970.* New York: Praeger, 1975.

Freedman, Robert O. ed. *Soviet Jewry in the Decisive Decade.* Durham, N.C.: Duke University Press, 1984.

Freidman, Leon, and William F. Levantrosser, eds. *Cold War Patriot and Statesman: Richard M. Nixon.* Westport, Conn.: Greenwood Press, 1993.

Friedman, Murray. *The Neoconservative Revolution: Jewish Intellectuals and the Shaping of Public Policy.* Cambridge: Cambridge University Press, 2005.

Gaddis, John Lewis. "Rescuing Choice from Circumstances: The Statecraft of Henry Kissinger." In *The Diplomats,* ed. Gordon Craig and Francis L. Loewenheim. Princeton: Princeton University Press, 1994. 564–592.

Gaddis, John Lewis. "The Rise, Fall and Future of Détente." *Foreign Affairs* 62:2 (Winter 1983/84): 354–377.

Gaiduk, Ilya. *The Soviet Union and the Vietnam War.* Chicago: Ivan R. Dee, 1996.

Galnoor, Itzhak. "The Consequences of the Yom Kippur War: Transformations in the Israeli Political System." In *The Yom Kippur War,* ed. Yaacov Bar-Siman-Tov and Haim Opaz. Jerusalem: 1999 (Hebrew). 165–180.

Garment, Leonard. *Crazy Rhythm: My Journey from Brooklyn, Jazz and Wall Street to Nixon's White House.* New York: Times Books, 1997.

Garrison, Jean A. *Games Advisors Play: Foreign Policy in the Nixon and Carter Administrations.* College Station.: Texas A&M University Press, 1999.

Garson, Mark. *The Neoconservative Vision: From the Cold War to Culture Wars.* Lanham: Madison Books, 1997.

Garthoff, Raymond. *Détente and Confrontation: American-Soviet Relations from Nixon to Reagan.* Washington, D.C.: Brookings, 1994.

Gazit, Mordechai. "Egypt and Israel—Was There a Peace Opportunity Missed in 1971?" *Journal of Contemporary History* 32:1 (1997): 97–115.

Gazit, Mordechai. "The Role of the Foreign Ministry and the Foreign Service." In *Ministry for Foreign Affairs,* ed. Moshe Yager et al. (Hebrew). 1085–1091.

Gazit, Mordechai. "Was the War Avoidable?" In *The Yom Kippur War,* ed. Yaacov Bar-Siman-Tov and Haim Opaz. Jerusalem: 1999.(Hebrew). 9–21.

George, Alexander L. "Domestic Constraints on Regime Change in U.S. Foreign Policy: The Need for Policy Legitimacy." In *Change in the International System,* ed. O. R. Holsti, R. M. Siverson, A. L. George. Boulder, Colo.: Westview Press, 1980.

George, Alexander L. "Political Crises." In *The Making of America's Soviet Policy*, ed. Joseph Nye Jr. New Haven: Yale University Press, 1984. 129–157.

Gilboa, Eitan. *American Public Opinion Towards Israel and the Arab-Israeli Conflict*. Lexington, Mass.: Lexington Books, 1987.

Ginor, Isabella. "Under the Yellow Arab Helmet Gleamed Blue Russian Eyes: Operation KAVKAZ and the War of Attrition, 1969–1970." *Cold War History* 3:1 (2002): 127–156.

Glad, Betty, and Michael Link. "President Nixon's Inner Circle of Advisors." *Presidential Studies Quarterly* 26:1 (1996): 13–40.

Glick, Edward B. *The Triangular Connection: America, Israel and American Jews*. London: G. Allen and Unwin, 1982.

Golan, Galia. *Soviet Policies in the Middle East from World War Two to Gorbachev*. Cambridge: Cambridge University Press, 1990.

Golan, Matti. *The Secret Conversations of Henry Kissinger: Step-by-Step Diplomacy in the Middle East*. New York: The New York Times Book Co., 1976.

Golden, Peter. *Quiet Diplomat: A Biography of Max M. Fisher*. New York: Cornwall Books, 1992.

Goldman, Minton F. "United States Policy and Soviet Jewish Emigration from Nixon to Bush." In *Jews and Jewish Life in Russia and the Soviet Union*, ed. Ya'acov Ro'i. London: Frank Cass, 1995. 338–364.

Goldstein, Joseph. *Rabin*. Tel Aviv: Shoken, 2006. (Hebrew).

Goldstein, Judith, and Robert O. Keohane, eds. *Ideas and Foreign Policy: Beliefs, Institutions, and Political Change*. Ithaca and London: Cornell University Press, 1993.

Gottschalk, Alfred. "Perspectives." In *The Yom Kippur War: Israel and the Jewish People*, ed. Moshe Davis. New York: Ayer Co., 1974. 36–48.

Greenbaum, Abraham. "The U.S. Airlift to Israel in 1973 Reconsidered" (unpublished paper).

Greenberg, David. *Nixon's Shadow: History of an Image*. New York: Norton, 2003.

Hacohen, Debra. *Immigrants in Turmoil: The Great Wave of Immigration to Israel and Its Absorption, 1948–1953*. Jerusalem: Yad Ben-Zvi, 1994 (Hebrew).

Hagel, Peter, and Pauline Peretz. "States and Transnational Actors: Who's Influencing Whom? A Case Study in Jewish Diaspora Politics During the Cold War." *European Journal of International Relations* 11:4 (2005): 467–493.

Hahn, Peter L. "Special Relationships." *Diplomatic History* 22:2 (1998): 263–272.

Hanhimäki, Jussi M. "'Dr. Kissinger' or 'Mr. Henry'? Kissingerology, Thirty Years and Counting." *Diplomatic History* 27:5 (November 2003): 637–676.

Hanhimäki, Jussi. "Selling the 'Decent Interval': Kissinger, Triangular Diplomacy, and the End of the Vietnam War." *Diplomacy and Statecraft* 14:1 (March 2003): 159–194.

Hanhimäki, Jussi. *The Flawed Architect: Henry Kissinger and American Foreign Policy.* Oxford: Oxford University Press, 2004.

Hertzberg, Arthur. *A Jew in America: My Life and a People's Struggle for Identity.* San Francisco: Harper, 2002.

Hoff, Joan. *Nixon Reconsidered.* New York: Basic Books, 1994.

Hoffmann, Stanley. "Détente." In *The Making of America's Soviet Policy,* ed. Joseph S. Nye Jr. New Haven: Yale University Press, 1984. 231–269.

Hunt, Michael H. *Ideology and American Foreign Policy.* New Haven, Conn.: Yale University Press, 1987.

Inbar, Efraim. "Jews, Jewishness and Israel's Foreign Policy." *Jewish Political Studies Review* 2:3–4 (Fall 1990): 165–183.

Inbar, Efraim. *Rabin and Israel's National Security.* Washington, D.C.: Woodrow Wilson Center Press, 1999.

Isaacson, Walter. *Kissinger: A Biography.* New York: Touchstone, 1992.

Janis, Irving. *Groupthink.* Boston: Houghton Mifflin, 1972.

Johnson, Robert D. *Lyndon Johnson and Israel: The Secret Presidential Recordings.* Tel Aviv: S. Daniel Abraham Center for International and Regional Studies, 2008.

Karsh, Ephraim. "Israel." In *The Cold War and the Middle East,* ed. Yezid Sayigh and Avi Shlaim. Oxford: Clarendon Press, 1997.

Kaufman, Robert G. *Henry Jackson: A Life in Politics.* Seattle: University of Washington Press, 2000.

Kennen, I. L. *Israel's Defense Line: Her Friends and Foes in Washington.* Buffalo, N.Y.: Prometheus Books, 1981.

Kimball, Jeffrey. "Peace with Honor: Richard Nixon and the Diplomacy of Threat and Symbolism." In *Shadow on the White House: Presidents and the Vietnam War, 1945–1975,* ed. David L. Anderson. Lawrence: University Press of Kansas, 1993.

Kissinger, Henry. *American Foreign Policy,* 3rd edition. New York: Norton, 1977.

Kissinger, Henry. *Diplomacy.* New York: Touchstone, 1994.

Kissinger, Henry. "The Nature of the National Dialogue on Foreign Policy." In *The Nixon-Kissinger Foreign Policy: Opportunities and Contradictions,* ed. Fred Warner Neal and Mary Kersey Harvey. Santa Barbara, Calif.: Center for the Study of Democratic Institutions, 1974.

Kissinger, Henry. *The Necessity for Choice.* New York: Doubleday, 1961.

Kissinger, Henry. *The Troubled Partnership: A Reappraisal of the Atlantic Alliance.* New York: McGraw Hill, 1965.

Kissinger, Henry. "The White Revolutionary: Reflections on Bismarck." *Daedalus* 97 (Summer 1968): 888–924.

Kissinger, Henry. *White House Years.* Boston: Little, Brown, 1979.

Kissinger, Henry. *A World Restored: Metternich, Castlereagh, and the Problems of Peace, 1812–1822.* Gloucester, Mass.: Smith, 1957.

Kissinger, Henry. *Years of Upheaval.* Boston: Little, Brown, 1982.

Klieman, Aharon. *Statecraft in the Dark.* Boulder. Colo.: Westview Press, 1988.

Klinghoffer, Judith A. *Vietnam, Jews and the Middle East: Unintended Consequences.* New York: St. Martin's Press, 1999.

Kochavi, Noam. "Idealpolitik in Disguise: Israel, Jewish Emigration from the Soviet Union and the Nixon Administration, 1969–1974: Culture, Media and U.S. Interests in the Middle East since 1945, 1974." *International History Review* 29:3 (September 2007): 550–572.

Korey, William. "Jackson-Vanik and Soviet Jewry." *The Washington Quarterly* 7:1 (1984): 116–128.

Korn, David A. *Stalemate: The War of Attrition and Great Power Diplomacy in the Middle East, 1967–1970.* Boulder, Colo.: Westview Press, 1992.

Kornbluh, Peter. *The Pinochet File.* New York: New Press, 2003.

Lazarowitz, Arlene. "Different Approaches to a Regional Search for Balance: The Johnson Administration, the State Department, and the Middle East, 1964–1967." *Diplomatic History* 32:1 (2008): 25–54.

Lazin, Fred A. *The Struggle for Soviet Jewish Emigration in American Politics: Israel versus the American Jewish Establishment.* Lanham: Lexington Books, 2005.

Lenczkowski, George. *American Presidents and the Middle East.* London and Durham: Duke University Press, 1990.

Levanon, Nehemia. "Israel's Role in the Campaign." In *A Second Exodus: The American Movement to Free Soviet Jews,* ed. M. Freedman and Alfred D. Chernin. Hanover, N.H., and London: Brandeis University Press, 1999.

Levanon, Nehemia. *"Nativ" Was the Code Name.* Tel Aviv: Am Oved, 1995 (Hebrew).

Liebman, Charles. *Pressure without Sanctions.* Rutherford: Fairleigh Dickinson University Press, 1977.

Little, Douglas. *American Orientalism: The United States and the Middle East since 1945.* Chapel Hill: University of North Carolina Press, 2002.

Litwak, Robert S. "Henry Kissinger's Ambiguous Legacy." *Diplomatic History* 18:3 (Summer 1994): 437–445.

Loescher, Gil, and John Scanlan. *Calculated Kindness: Refugees and America's Half-Open Door, 1945–Present.* New York: Free Press, 1986.

Luttwak, Edward N., and Walter Lacquer. "Kissinger and the Yom Kippur War." *Commentary* 58 (September 1974): 33–40.

Martin, G. *A Matter of Priorities: Labor Zionism and the Plight of Soviet Jewry, 1917–1996.* Jerusalem: Diamond Books, 1996.

Mayers, David. *The Ambassadors and American Soviet Policy.* New York: Oxford University Press, 1995.

McAlister, Melanie. *Epic Encounters: Culture, Media and the U.S. Interests in the Middle East since 1945*. Berkeley: University of California Press, 2005.

Mearsheimer, John J., and Stephen M. Walt. *The Israel Lobby and U.S. Foreign Policy*. New York: Farrar, Straus and Giroux, 2007.

Meir, Golda. *My Life*. Jerusalem: Steimatsky, 1975.

Melanson, Richard. *American Foreign Policy since the Vietnam War: The Search for Consensus from Nixon to Clinton*, 2nd edition. Armonk, N.Y.: M. E. Sharpe, 1996.

Miner, Steven M. "Soviet Ambassadors from Maiskii to Dobrynin." In *The Diplomats*, ed. Gordon Craig and Francis L. Loewenheim. Princeton: Princeton University Press, 1994.

Mollov, Benjamin M. "Jewry's Prophetic Challenge to Soviet and Other Totalitarian Regimes According to Hans J. Morgenthau." *Journal of Church and State* 39:3 (Summer 1997): 561–575.

Morgan, William D., and Charles S. Kennedy, eds. *American Diplomats: The Foreign Service at Work*. New York: iUniverse, 2004.

Morgenthau, Hans J. "Henry Kissinger, Secretary of State: An Evaluation." *Encounter* [Great Britain] 43:5 (1974): 57–61.

Namir, Mordechai. *Israeli Mission to Moscow*. Tel Aviv: Am Oved, 1971 (Hebrew).

Nelson, Keith. "Nixon, Kissinger and the Domestic Side of Détente." In *Re-viewing the Cold War: Domestic Factors and Foreign Policy in the East-West Confrontation*, ed. Morgan and Nelson. Westport, Conn.: Praeger, 2000.

Nixon, Richard. *In the Arena: A Memoir of Victory, Defeat and Renewal*. New York: Simon and Schuster, 1990.

Nixon, Richard. *No More Vietnams*. New York: Arbor House, 1985.

Nixon, Richard. *RN: The Memoirs of Richard Nixon*. New York: Grosset and Dunlap, 1978.

Novick, Peter. *The Holocaust in American Life*. Boston: Houghton Mifflin, 1999.

Novik, Nimrod. *The United States and Israel: Domestic Determinants of a Changing U.S. Commitment*. Boulder, Colo.: Westview Press, 1986.

Ofer, Dalia. "The Aliya, the Diaspora and the Yishuv." *Cathedra* 43 (March 1987): 69–90 (Hebrew).

Ofer, Dalia. "Immigration and *Aliya*: New Aspects of Jewish Policy." *Cathedra* 75 (April 1995): 142–173 (Hebrew).

Orbach, William. *The American Movement to Aid Soviet Jews*. Amherst: University of Massachusetts Press, 1979.

Organsky, A. F. K. *The $36 Billion Bargain: Strategy and Politics in U.S. Assistance to Israel*. New York: Columbia University Press, 1990.

Parker, Richard B. *The Politics of Miscalculation in the Middle East*. Bloomington: Indiana University Press, 1993.

Parmet, Herbert. *Richard Nixon and His America*. Boston: Little, Brown, 1990.

Peretz, Pauline. "The Action of Nativ's Emissaries in the United States: A Trigger for the American Movement to Aid Soviet Jews, 1958–1974." *Bulletin du Centre de Recherché Français de Jérusalem* 14 (Spring 2004): 112–128.

Peretz, Pauline. *Le Combat pour les Juifs Soviétiques: Washington—Moscou—Jérusalem 1953–1989*. Paris: Armand Colin, 2006.

Pickar, Avi. "The Beginning of Selective Immigration in the 1950s." *Iyunim Bitkumat Israel* 9 (1999): 338–394.

Pinkus, Benjamin. "Israel's Activity on Behalf of Soviet Jews." In *Organizing Rescue: Jewish National Solidarity in the Modern Period*, ed. S. Ilan Troen and Benjamin Pinkus. London: Frank Cass, 1991. 373–402.

Prados, John, ed. *The White House Tapes: Eavesdropping on the President*. New York: The New Press, 2003.

Pruessen, Ronald W. "From Good Breakfast to Bad Supper: John Foster Dulles Between the Geneva Summit and the Geneva Foreign Ministers Conference." In *Cold War Respite: The Geneva Summit of 1955*, ed. Gunter Bischof and Saki Dokrill. Baton Rouge: Louisiana State University Press, 2000. 253–270.

Pruessen, Ronald W. "The Predicaments of Power." In *John Foster Dulles and the Diplomacy of the Cold War*, ed. Richard H. Immerman. Princeton: Princeton University Press, 1990. 23–45.

Quandt, William B. *Decade of Decisions: American Policy toward the Arab-Israeli Conflict, 1967–1976*. Berkeley: University of California Press, 1977.

Rabin, Yitzhak. *The Rabin Memoirs*. Boston: Little, Brown, 1979.

Rafael, Gideon. *Destination Peace: Three Decades of Israeli Foreign Policy*. Jerusalem: Idanim, 1981 (Hebrew version).

Reichley, James A. *Conservatives in an Age of Change: The Nixon and Ford Administrations*. Washington, D.C.: Brookings, 1981.

Richter, James G. "Perpetuating the Cold War: Domestic Sources of International Patterns of Behavior." *Political Science Quarterly* 107:2 (Summer 1992): 271–301.

Ro'i, Ya'acov. "The Problematics of the Soviet-Israeli Relationship." In *Soviet Foreign Policy, 1917–1991: A Retrospective*, ed. Gabriel Gorodetsky. London: Frank Cass, 1994.

Ro'i, Ya'acov. Introduction to *Traitors to Mother Russia: Jewish Emigration through Soviet Eyes*, ed. Zeev Khanin and Boris Morozov. Tel Aviv: Tel Aviv University Press, 2005 (Hebrew).

Rubenberg, Cheryl. *Israel and the American National Interest: A Critical Examination*. Urbana: University of Illinois Press, 1986.

Russell, Gregory. "Kissinger's Philosophy of History and Kantian Ethics." *Diplomacy and Statecraft* 7:1 (March 1996): 97–124.

Sadat, Anwar. *In Search of Identity.* London: Collins, 1978.

Safire William. *Before the Fall: An Inside View of the Pre-Watergate White House.* Garden City, N.Y.: Doubleday, 1975.

Sarvanskaya, Svetlana. "Unintended Consequencies: Soviet Interests, Expectations and Reactions to the Helsinki Final Act." In *Helsinki 1975 and the Transformation of Europe,* ed. Oliver Bange and Gottfried Niedhart. Oxford: Berakahn Books, 2008. 175–190.

Schulzinger, Robert D. "The Naive and Sentimental Diplomat: Henry Kissinger's Memoirs." *Diplomatic History* 4:3 (Summer 1980): 304–315.

Schulzinger, Robert D. *Henry Kissinger: Doctor of Diplomacy.* New York: Columbia University Press, 1989.

Shalom, Zaki. "Kissinger and the American Jewish Leadership after the 1973 War." *Israel Studies* 7:1 (Spring 2002): 198–217.

Shapira, Anita. *Yigal Allon: Spring of His Life.* Tel Aviv: Hakibutz Hameuchad, 2004 (Hebrew).

Sheffer, Gabriel, ed. *U.S.-Israeli Relations at the Crossroads.* London: Frank Cass, 1997.

Shifter, Richard. "The Impact of the United States on Soviet Emigration Policy." In *Russian Jews on Three Continents: Migration and Resettlement,* ed. Ya'acov Ro'i et al. London: Frank Cass, 1997. 87–112.

Small, Melvin. "Containing Domestic Enemies: Richard M. Nixon and the War at Home." In *Shadow on the White House,* ed. David L. Anderson. Lawrence: University Press of Kansas, 1993.

Small, Melvin. *The Presidency of Richard Nixon.* Lawrence: University Press of Kansas, 1999.

Smith, Michael. *Realist Thought from Weber to Kissinger.* Baton Rouge: Louisiana State University Press, 1986.

Stefan, Charles G. "The Drafting of the Helsinki Final Act: A Personal View of the CSCS's Geneva Phase (September 1973 until July 1975)." *SHAFR Newsletter* (June 2000): 1–10.

Stein, Janice, and Richard N. Lebow. *We All Lost the Cold War.* Princeton: Princeton University Press, 1994.

Stein, Kenneth. *Heroic Diplomacy: Sadat, Kissinger, Carter, Begin and the Quest for Arab-Israeli Peace.* New York: Routledge, 1999.

Stern, Paula. *Water's Edge: Domestic Politics and the Making of American Foreign Policy.* Westport, Conn: Greenwood, 1979.

Suri, Jeremi. *Henry Kissinger and the American Century.* Cambridge: Harvard University Press, 2007.

Suri, Jeremi. "Henry Kissinger, the American Dream, and the Jewish Immigrant Experience." *Diplomatic History* 32:5 (November 2008): 719–747.

Tannenwald, Nina. "Ideas and Explanation: Advancing the Theoretical Agenda." *Journal of Cold War Studies* 7:2 (Spring 2005): 13–42.

Thomas, Daniel C. "Human Rights Ideas, the Demise of Communism, and the End of the Cold War." *Journal of Cold War Studies* 7:2 (Spring 2005): 110–141.

Tivnan, Edward. *The Lobby: Jewish Political Power and American Foreign Policy.* New York: Simon and Schuster, 1987.

Tucker, Nancy B. "Taiwan Expendable? Nixon and Kissinger Go to China." *The Journal of American History* 92:1 (2005): 109–135.

Twersky, Isadore. "Survival, Normalcy, Modernity." In *Zionism in Transition,* ed. M. Davis. New York: Herzl Press, 1980. 347–366.

Urofsky, Melvin I. *We Are One!* Garden City, N.J.: Anchor Books, 1978.

Van Den Assem, Arjan. "The Perseverance of Beliefs: The Reaction of Kissinger and Brzezinski to the End of the Cold War." *Acta Politica* 2 (2000): 169–194.

Volten, Peter M. E. *Brezhnev's Peace Program.* Boulder, Colo.: Westview Press, 1982.

Ward, Dana. "Kissinger: A Psychohistory." In *Henry Kissinger: His Personality and Policies,* ed. Dan Caldwell. Durham, N.C.: Duke University Press, 1983. 3–63.

Weitz, Richard. "Henry Kissinger's Philosophy of International Relations." *Diplomacy and Statecraft* 2:1 (1991): 103–29.

Westad, Odd Arne. *The Global Cold War: Third World Interventions and the Making of Our Times.* Cambridge: Cambridge University Press, 2005.

Wittkopf, Eugene R. *Faces of Internationalism: Public Opinion and American Foreign Policy.* Durham, N.C.: Duke University Press, 1990.

Yaacobi, Gad. "The Attempt to Reach an Interim Agreement with Egypt in 1971–1972 and Its Lessons." In *The October War: A Reassessment,* ed. Yaacov Bar-Siman-Tov and Haim Opaz. Jerusalem: Davis Institute, 1999. (Hebrew).

Yager, Moshe et al., eds. *Ministry for Foreign Affairs: The First Fifty Years.* Jerusalem: Keter, 2002 (Hebrew).

Yaqub, Salim. "The Politics of Stalemate: The Nixon Administration and the Arab-Israeli Conflict, 1969–1973." In *The Cold War and the Middle East: Regional Conflict and the Superpowers,* ed. Nigel Ashton. London and New York: Routledge, 2007. 35–58.

Zelikow, Philip. "The Statesman in Winter: Kissinger on the Ford Years." *Foreign Affairs* 78:3 (May/June 1999): 123–128.

Zubok, Vladislav. *A Failed Empire: The Soviet Union in the Cold War from Stalin to Gorbachev.* Chapel Hill: University of North Carolina Press, 2007.

Zubok, Vladislav M. "The Soviet Union and Détente in the 1970s." *Cold War History* 8:4 (November 2008): 427–447.

INDEX

Allon, Yigal, 26, 33, 35, 41, 69, 102n89
American Israel Public Affairs Committee, 74
American Jewish community: coordinated campaign with Israel to tilt American policy in Israel's favor, 74; "creative duplicity" of Nixon in dealings with, 11; criticism of Kissinger for exerting pressure on Israel, 121n22; fear of anger of for Rogers Plan, 11; Nixon's regard for, 4, 9, 11; passivity during Holocaust, 43; presidential decisions based on feelings about, 11; pressure to assist in Soviet Jewish emigration, 34; resentment in unwarranted Israeli intrusion in American domestic affairs, 75; and Soviet exit tax, 36; and Soviet Jewish emigration policy, 32; support for Jackson-Vanik amendment, 38; suspicion of Nixon by, 14
American Jewish Conference on Soviet Jewry, 34
American Jewish Congress, 114n77
American-Soviet General Principals agreement, 1
American-Soviet Summit (1972), 19, 55–57
Arab-Israeli conflict, 3, 50; convergence of American and Israeli perspectives on, 26; fueled by superpower rivalry, 25; Nixon's ambivalence in, 4, 18; possible superpower settlement of, 68;

presidential instructions on, 7; protests against Israeli military supplies in, 11; Soviet Union and, 91n122
Argov, Shlomo, 14
Avineri, Shlomo, 45, 106n137

Barbour, Wohlworth, 12, 16, 22, 89n98
Ben-Gurion, David, 23, 29, 30
Biblical Prophecy conference (1971), 23
Black September 1970, 4, 18, 74
Brezhnev, Leonid, 43, 68; difficulty in attaining MFN status, 38; disappointment in administration mishandling of Jackson-Vanik amendment, 112n63, 117n110; favors East-West trade, 112n63; against opposition to détente in Soviet Union, 6; and perceived economic benefits of détente, 112n63; view on exit tax, 33, 35; warnings to United States on probability of Yom Kippur War, 6, 26, 27

Cambodia, 12
Carter, Jimmy, 73
Central Intelligence Agency, 53
Clawson, Ken, 23
Conference of Major Jewish Organizations, 40
Conference of Presidents of Major American Jewish Organizations, 34